A VERY SHORT WAR

A VERY SHORT WAR

The *Mayaguez* and the Battle of Koh Tang

BY JOHN F. GUILMARTIN, JR.

Foreword by John Keegan

Texas A&M University Press
College Station

The paper used in this book meets the minimum requirements
of the American National Standard for Permanence
of Paper for Printed Library Materials, Z39.48–1984.
Binding materials have been chosen for durability.

Library of Congress Cataloging-in-Publication Data

Guilmartin, John Francis.
    A very short war : the SS Mayaguez and the Battle of Koh Tang / by
John F. Guilmartin, Jr.—1st ed.
        p.   cm. — Texas A&M University military history ; 46)
    Includes bibliographical references and index.
    ISBN 0-89096-665-6 (alk. paper)
    1. Mayagüez incident, 1975. 2. Mayagüez (Ship)   I. Title.
II. Series: Texas A & M University military history ; 46.
E865.G85   1995
959.704'34—dc20   95-17325
                                                                            CIP

*To the marines and airmen who gave their lives
12–15 May 1975*

Contents

Illustrations

FIGURES

MAPS

Foreword

I HAVE LONG BEEN AN ADMIRER of John Guilmartin and his work, which was brought to my attention in the most casual of ways. Bumping into my friend Christopher Duffy in the library of the Royal Military Academy Sandhurst one day in 1977 or thereabouts, I heard him say, "This chap Guilmartin is awfully good." Renaissance history was not then an interest of mine, largely because I knew little about it, but I greatly respected Christopher Duffy's scholarly opinion, all the more because it was rarely expressed and he was sparing with praise. I soon laid hands on *Gunpowder and Galleys* and saw what Christopher meant.

I continue to regard that slim book—both an account and an analysis of the struggle between Christian Europe and Ottoman Turkey for control of the Mediterranean in the sixteenth century—as among the two or three very best works of military history I have ever read. It has many qualities. It is written with admirable clarity—I would call it "accessible" had academe not perversely made that adjective a veiled insult. It is based on very wide reading in a number of languages, one of them, Turkish, not commonly known by Westerners. It is a model of how sources should be used; for it extracts the pith rather than overloading the reader with material merely to demonstrate the author's industry. Its apparatus, similarly, is exact but economical. It makes extensive use of theory and concept, but does not torture material to fit fashionable modes of thought. It is brilliantly original, both in subject matter and in the way the unfamiliar is made comprehensible. Above all, like every outstanding monograph, it uses particular events to illuminate large problems and to connect phenomena widely separated in space and time. To take but one example, John Guilmartin's keen understanding of the technology and use of the composite bow, one of the most deadly weapons ever conceived by a warrior people, allows him to show how the routine of shepherd life on the steppe in the centuries of Turkic nomadism translated into mastery of close-range inland sea warfare—until gunpowder destroyed the irreplaceable crews of galley archers.

In his new book, a study of a tiny action fought at the tail end of the Vietnam War, Guilmartin uses analysis of local combat to illuminate another key military technology, not that of weapons but of communication. Information has always been a key commodity of successful command in war, and of successful performance by those closer to the heat of action than the commander usually is. Information moves upwards and downwards: upwards from those nearest to the enemy, downwards from the commander in the form of orders framed in the light of what he learns from the bottom. The smaller the action, the clearer the flow in both directions. That, at any rate traditionally, has always been the case. Small, short battles made for quick, clear-cut decisions.

Now, Guilmartin suggests, tradition no longer holds. As battles got bigger and longer—at their worst during the First World War—information clogged in both directions. Those at the front could not communicate with the rear; the rear—which was the command center—framed orders on partial and out-of-date information. "Real time" progressively receded as battles increased in scale. The solution, soldiers concluded, was to amplify means of rapid communication, and that solution, founded on the appearance of the tactical radio in the late 1930s, did indeed achieve great success in the Second World War.

If something is good, people want more of it. One of the most striking developments in warfare since the appearance of the tactical radio has been its refinement and multiplication. More and more participants have radios which net into wider and wider systems; satellite technology so ramifies the mechanism that a head of state may follow small-unit action on a minute-by-minute basis; he may also—and this is really Guilmartin's moral—directly intervene, with highly undesirable effect. Worse, his may not be the only intervention; there can be others at the intermediate level, with the result that the formidable capacity of a modern communications network is forced to devote itself to explaining confusions and contradictions thus produced, so that the miracle of radio results in the nightmare of crossed wires and Chinese whispers.

It is not only in the military world that the communication superhighway is proving to be more of a curse than a blessing. So it is, too, in the international money market which, in its effort to protect players against bad decisions made through information overload, has equipped computerized trading systems with "stop loss" mechanisms that actually precipitate and then exaggerate currency fluctuations. The semicrash of 1987 was the product not of human judgment about the relative worth of money but of machines obediently instituting their masters' prejudgments of what would be good for them.

As far as we know, no power has been foolish enough to introduce the equivalent of "stop loss" mechanisms into the computerized systems that control nuclear launch mechanisms—though it was an option considered by some of the brainboxes in strategic think tanks at the high tide of the nuclear theology business in the 1960s. The business of politicians, it has been said, is to tell officials what the public will not stand, and all politicians in nuclear-capable states have thus far made it clear to defense planners that extinction by computer is not a policy for which their electorates will vote. Professor Guilmartin's message, though it concerns matters less fraught than nuclear life-and-death, has a similar import. He is telling decision makers within the military command system that there can be too many fingers in the pie, that hands-off is usually better than hands-on and that there is no substitute for trusting a capable commander who is on the spot. The *Mayaguez* incident of May 1975 precipitated only a short and small war; it might have been shorter and smaller still, Professor Guilmartin persuades us, had the top brass not thought they knew better than the men on the ground.

John Keegan
Kilmington Manor
Warminster, Wiltshire
United Kingdom

Preface

AT THE MOST BASIC LEVEL, this book is an attempt by a soldier to understand and explain what happened—or what might have happened—in a brief but intense clash of arms in which his unit, the 40th ARRS (Aerospace Rescue and Recovery Squadron), was involved: the SS *Mayaguez* incident and the battle of Koh Tang. At the time of the events in question I was not only a professional soldier—an air force major and H-53 helicopter pilot assigned to an air rescue squadron at Nakhon Phanom, Thailand—but a historian specializing in military and naval history. That combination of circumstances and training gave me access to information and insights to which the military historian is rarely privy. But that same combination inevitably colored the way in which I approached my subject, so a few words of explanation are in order.

I was only peripherally involved in the *Mayaguez*–Koh Tang affair, but I had served in the preceding months with many of the individuals mentioned in the narrative, notably in the Phnom Penh and Saigon evacuations. In the process, I had formed professional judgments concerning their characters and abilities. I lost friends in the crashes of two Nakhon Phanom—based special operations H-53s: one in January and the other on May 13. I was hardly a detached and dispassionate observer of the events that followed the seizure of the *Mayaguez*.

Above and beyond my military and personal interests in the *Mayaguez*–Koh Tang operation were academic ones. Though my primary research specialty was sixteenth-century Europe, I was particularly concerned with the motivational and psychological aspects of warfare, regardless of era. These factors played a significant role in the events of 12–15 May 1975, as indeed they did in the Phnom Penh and Saigon evacuations. When I arrived in Thailand in January of that year, I had no intention of doing serious research on the Vietnam War. The events of the ensuing spring changed my mind.

United States forces avoided disaster in the *Mayaguez*–Koh Tang operation by the narrowest of margins: such a close brush with disaster can be a powerful stimulus to the analytic processes. Even before the smoke cleared, I was automatically trying to find out what had gone wrong and why. I knew that I was in a peculiarly advantageous position to do so. My motivation in the first instance was primarily military: concern for the state training and readiness of our armed forces and loyalty to my comrades-in-arms. My scholarly training and impulses quickly came into play, but because they did so in a context that was powerfully shaped by my military experience, some explanation is in order.

I received my training as a historian at Princeton University in 1967–70. My studies there focused on the sixteenth-century struggle between the Spanish Habsburgs and Ottoman Turks for control of the Mediterranean. Most of my published work has been in the early modern period with an emphasis on operational and technological issues. This focus was shaped by my undergraduate education at the U.S. Air Force Academy, from which I graduated in 1962. Before attending graduate school, I served as a helicopter pilot in Southeast Asia during 1965–66, where I was assigned to Detachment 5, 38th Air Rescue Squadron, based at Udorn, Thailand. Det. 5 was the first permanently constituted long-range combat aircrew recovery helicopter unit ever and was the lineal antecedent of the 40th Aerospace Rescue and Recovery Squadron described below. Our aircraft was the HH-3E (the first *H* is for rescue and the second for helicopter), direct ancestor of the HH-53Cs that I flew in 1975.

After a faculty tour teaching history at the Air Force Academy, I returned to the Rescue Service in the spring of 1974 and reported to the 40th Aerospace Rescue and Recovery Squadron at Nakhon Phanom in January 1975. (The Air Rescue Service had hitched its wagon to NASA and the Apollo Program's star, hence *space* and *recovery* in the title.) Perhaps prompted by an overdose of military history, I arrived with three premonitions: that the year 1975 would be a bad one for the United States and our friends in Southeast Asia, that the climax would come in April, and that my squadron and I would be up to our collective necks in it. My premonition was right on the mark: Cambodia and South Vietnam fell in April, and our sister H-53 unit, the 21st Special Operations Squadron, and we were involved in Operation Eagle Pull and Operation Frequent Wind, the evacuation of Phnom Penh on 12 April and of Saigon on 29–30 April, respectively. I flew in both operations, in the latter operating from the attack carrier USS *Midway.*

My premonition did not encompass the *Mayaguez*–Koh Tang affair. In retrospect, it could not have, for this occurrence represented one of those occasions in war where small events, whether arising serendipitously or prompted by human emotion and desperation, can produce disproportionately large events.

Both the 40th and 21st were young squadrons with respect to officer seniority; as a relatively junior major, therefore, I was the 40th's senior line pilot. But I was new to the H-53 and acquired the time needed for upgrade to instructor pilot only after the Saigon evacuation. In the interim I specialized in maintenance check flights; that is, test flights following maintenance. This is a much less routine procedure in helicopters than in fixed-wing aircraft and was even less so with air force versions of the H-53, for reasons that are addressed in detail in Appendix B. Suffice it to say at this point that helicopters are extremely complex machines, as difficult to maintain as to fly. Before Eagle Pull and Frequent Wind, I had been responsible for performing the check flights on the last 40th aircraft brought into commission before deployment—one flight control rigging check done at night before Frequent Wind was particularly memorable—and had flown each of the aircraft in question in the ensuing operation. When the *Mayaguez* crisis broke, I assumed the same function. My crew and I helped the night shift, augmented by the phased inspection dock crew, get two HH-53s in commission before the maneuver was over. One of the two, Jolly Green 44, played a decisive role. I missed Koh Tang by one aircraft.

I was thus close enough to the operation to have a feel for it. At the same time, I was sufficiently removed to approach it with a degree of personal detachment. At that point, I had never considered writing about the Southeast Asian conflict as a historian. I had, however, some sense of the historical significance of the events through which my comrades and I were living and kept a journal with that in mind. The journal was to prove invaluable when I set out to unravel the operational complexities of the *Mayaguez*–Koh Tang affair.

Although the war in Southeast Asia was not part of my academic research and writing agenda, I did not let that prevent me from studying and reflecting on it. As a soldier and historian, I was convinced that military history should transcend narrow periodization and that military history and the theory of war were opposite sides of the same coin. I further believed that there were more or less universal aspects to the experience of combat and that personal experience could provide the historian with valuable insights into understanding its nature, a view anything but popular among academic historians during the late 1960s and early '70s. I was also convinced—another position unpopular in academia—that the individual and group dynamics of combat were a valid, indeed essential, focal point for the study of warfare. It would be nice to report that I was out in front on the issue, but I wasn't: aside from conversations with like-minded academics and historically sensitive fellow officers, I did nothing to give my beliefs wider circulation. Not until the publication of John Keegan's magnificent *The Face of Battle* in 1976 did military history focusing on the human dynamics of combat gain a measure of acceptance in academic circles. I believe my study provides strong support for the validity of Keegan's thesis. Form your own judgment.

My interest in the human dynamics of combat was reactivated by the Saigon evacuation. Beginning in my undergraduate days, I had read extensively from the work of Brig. Gen. S. L. A. Marshall, World War II army historian and pioneer of the use of immediate postaction interviews to sort out what *really* happened in the chaos of combat.[1] Marshall, along with sociologists Edward Shils and Morris Janowitz, was also responsible for introducing the concept of small-unit cohesion into the vocabulary of military history.[2] While teaching at the Air Force Academy in 1970–73, I had become a believer in the value of Marshall's postaction interview technique. I applied it to myself shortly after recovery aboard *Midway,* committing my impressions of the evacuation to my journal while they were fresh in my mind. Returning to the journal a week or so later, I was struck by the extent to which my memory had smoothed the jagged edges off of my discordant impressions of the moment, imposing order on chaos—and I take pride in the fact that I was using the term *chaos* to describe the reality of combat long before the appearance of chaos mathematics. It was almost like reading someone else's account. That is not to say that the initial impressions recorded in my journal were objectively "correct" or that my later, cleaned-up notion of what had happened was inaccurate. Quite the contrary. In talking things over with my crew and our wingmen, comparing recollections and resolving inconsistencies and discrepancies as best we could—a close approximation of Marshall's methods—I had acquired a far more accurate picture of what had actually happened.

But I had forgotten the subjective feel of the experience. My understanding of the way my crew and I had dealt with the chaos about us, an essential ingredient to our survival, had suffered accordingly. My notes scribbled immediately after the fact enabled me to recapture important elements of the experience that I would otherwise have lost. I have tried not to forget.

In our essential responses and reactions to the circumstances we faced, my crew and I were no different from other Frequent Wind helicopter crews. Like our marine, air force, and navy brothers, we were well trained and well disciplined as individuals and as a crew. We had applied that training and discipline to accomplish the mission while preserving our aircraft and ourselves. But to me, as a historian and a soldier, the question was *how,* and the experience had given me a new slant. It was evident that many decisions that had seemed, after the smoothing-off process in the memory had run its course, to be systematically thought-out products of a single mind were, in fact, products of a series of swift, instinctive collective judgments made by several crew members working in concert. Decisions had emerged from a series of modifications, reinforcements, and vetoes that made little individual imprint on the conscious mind and were quickly forgotten. I came away from the experience with two lessons: first, my understanding of the way in which a well-trained helicopter crew—and by extension any well-trained, closely knit crew operating complex machinery—functions under the stress of combat had changed materially. Second, and more important to the purpose at hand, I had become keenly aware of just how perishable the memory of combat is. It was not just, or even primarily, a matter of losing detail. The quality of the experience is ephemeral.

The above recollections were still fresh in my mind when the *Mayaguez*–Koh Tang operation took place, and I talked and listened to as many participants as I could as soon afterward as possible. But in contrast to the comparatively leisurely hours aboard *Midway* after Frequent Wind, our schedules were hectic and opportunities were few. Fatigue was also a limiting factor. We had been hard on the go for months, and the *Mayaguez* crisis came as the culmination of what seemed like—and was—an incredibly intense experience. Thus my interviews, if they can be so dignified, were fragmentary and informal. At best, they were scribbled down on the spot in my journal, a small loose-leaf notebook that I carried in the leg pocket of my flight suit. More often, they were committed to memory until I had time to write—hours, and in some cases days, later.

Much of what I was told had to be evaluated with skepticism. Those with whom I spoke were aware of my historical interest in what they said, and much of what I was told might have compromised—and indeed might still compromise—them professionally. For all that, so far as I can judge none of my informants was other than forthright in his responses. If there was a central tendency, it was frank openness in venting frustration and bitterness with no pretense at "objectivity," combined with a painstaking effort to be factually accurate.

I did not intend to rely on word of mouth in isolation. My archival instincts kicked in, and I assembled such unclassified documentation relating to the operation as I could lay hands on, much of it transient material that would shortly disappear. At that point, I had no long-range plan. Instead I was driven by the simple awareness that whatever I did not preserve would be permanently lost.

My concern with the *Mayaguez*–Koh Tang affair lay dormant through my retirement from the air force in 1983 and an adjunct appointment at Rice University in Houston, Texas, teaching military history and directing the Space Shuttle History Project under a Rice-NASA contract. Then, in 1986, I was offered a one-year appointment to the U.S. Naval War College as a Secretary of the Navy Research Fellow. The offer to teach at Newport, Rhode Island, came just after I had accepted a permanent position at Ohio State, where my work was to focus on early modern Europe. Ohio State granted me a year's leave of absence, and I accepted. It struck me that my stay at Newport would provide an opportunity, probably the last for many years, to return to my notes and documentation from 1975. It was the first serious thought that I had given to undertaking a discrete study of the *Mayaguez* affair.

My lecturing and teaching duties at Newport forced me to address contemporary defense issues in a more comprehensive and systematic way than I had done previously. At the same time, interaction with staff, faculty colleagues, and students in the serious yet extraordinarily open and free-wheeling intellectual atmosphere of the place forced me to rethink my ideas on the theory of war. In the process, I was struck by the extent to which certain prevalent, and in my view erroneous, notions and assumptions concerning war had become imbedded in our national consciousness. Chief among these is what I term assumed proportionality of cause and effect: the implicit assumption that large and powerful results can come only from large and powerful causes and that small impulses, considered individually, have a negligible effect on the overall process. This assumption is closely linked to the belief that trends in human affairs generally drive toward some central tendency and that deviations from this central tendency can be understood and described by continuous linear curves and bell-shaped statistical distributions. I was later to learn that my colleague-to-be at Ohio State, Alan Beyerchen, was reaching the same conclusion in a more rigorous and systematic manner.

The assumed proportionality of cause and effect is more prevalent in the worlds of politics, business, and journalism than in the military profession. Indeed, military professionals implicitly reject this notion when addressing operational and tactical problems. Witness, for example, the painstaking attention given to detail in training, planning, and execution. But even military professionals tend to adopt the same assumption when addressing problems of strategy and policy. Probably because civilian officials responsible for such decisions at the national level often have little in-depth knowledge of technical and tactical military considerations, the tendency is to treat these factors as "black boxes" that can be dealt with in isolation.

In military affairs, the presumed proportionality of cause and effect is thus manifested in a tendency to assume that weapons systems capabilities and tactics can be decoupled from policy and strategy considerations. If military action is deemed desirable from the policy standpoint—politically advisable and operationally feasible—downstream linkages between policy and strategy on the one hand and operations and tactics on the other need not be considered.

My conviction that cause and effect in war are not necessarily related to one another in any linear fashion developed into a two-part hypothesis. First, as a general proposition, the relationship between cause and effect cannot be described or modeled, even approximately, as continuous curves and bell-shaped statistical distributions. Second, tactical and technological factors play potentially major roles in determining the relationship between cause and effect at every level. Developing this hypothesis was one thing. Demonstrating it was another, particularly if the demonstration was to be credible to actual soldiers, sailors, and airmen for whom the study of history and the theory of war are means to a practical end and not an end in themselves.

While at Newport, I realized that the *Mayaguez*–Koh Tang operation provided a manageable test of my ideas concerning the proportionality of cause and effect. Since cause and effect clearly *are* proportional at times, or at least appear so after the fact, there was no need to prove a general case. To make my point I needed only to clearly document a case, preferably a recent one involving U.S. forces, where cause and effect were *not* proportional. In such a case, seemingly minor tactical events and unanticipated human and technological perturbations would produce, or threaten to produce, major changes in outcome with respect to strategic or policy goals. The *Mayaguez*–Koh Tang affair was made to order for that purpose. A complementary motivating factor was my long-standing curiosity about the ways in which individuals, crews, and organizations react to the stress of combat. This curiosity was stimulated by the possession of a database that enabled me to study these factors with a much finer grain than is normally possible.

There was a final motivating factor behind my decision to undertake this study. It seemed appropriate that the actions of the American fighting men who put their lives on the line in the *Mayaguez* crisis in response to the lawful orders of their commander in chief deserved to be remembered by something more than the final roll of names inscribed in the black granite of the Vietnam War Memorial on the Washington Mall. When I began my study I sensed that far more praise than blame would attach itself to their efforts. To my gratification, but not to my surprise, that turned out to be the case.

Acknowledgments

THIS BOOK COULD NEVER have been written without the help of a host of individuals, not all of whom are named below for reasons of space and discretion. In addition to counsel and information, which in many cases I could have obtained in no other way, they provided the critical increment of motivation on a number of occasions just when it was most needed. Although I can never fully discharge my debt to them, I trust that the pages that follow will serve as partial payment.

More than I can say here, I am indebted to those air force participants in the battle of Koh Tang who freely discussed with me, often with brutal candor, their parts in the operation in the chaotic hours, days, and months immediately afterward, while impressions were still fresh in their minds. I owe a similar debt of gratitude to several marine participants and near-participants.

The core of my research was done in 1986–87 while I was a Secretary of the Navy Research Fellow at the U.S. Naval War College, Newport, Rhode Island. I am indebted to the head of the Strategy Department, Dr. Alvin Bernstein, for sponsoring my stay at Newport and to him and my colleagues in SECNAV Research and the Strategy Department for their suggestions, encouragement, and support. Drs. Alberto Coll, Eliot Cohen, Steve Rosen, and David Rosenberg and Col. Stanley Pratt, USMC, were particularly helpful. I am especially grateful to Bert Coll for pointing me to Christopher Jon Lamb's Georgetown dissertation, *Belief Systems and Decision Making in the Mayaguez Crisis*, since published by the University of Florida Press (1989). I owe a special debt of gratitude to my teaching partner Stan Pratt, a first-rate intellectual and a dedicated military professional, for enriching my appreciation of what it means to be a marine. The president of the college, Rear Admiral Jack Baldwin, and his chief of staff, Capt. Bob Watts, USN, offered encouragement and insights into naval surface operations. Capt. J. Michael Rodgers, USN, captain of USS *Henry B. Wilson* in the Koh Tang operation, shared with me his recollections and gave generously of his time in elucidating destroyer functions and the peculiarities of naval terminology. His insights and his assistance in helping me to contact other key participants were invaluable.

My research at Newport was aided immeasurably by the SECNAV Research secretaries, Barbara Atkins and Paula Hanson. I owe them a special debt of gratitude for keeping the administrative aspects of my existence under control, holding at bay the minions of finance, travel, security, and all the rest. By serving as extensions of my persona—and by bringing their delightful senses of humor into play on appropriate (and frequently unexpected) occasions—they enhanced my productivity enormously. I am indebted as well to the personnel of the USAF Historical Research Center, Maxwell AFB, Alabama (AFHRC), particularly Marvin L. Fisher and Patsy Robertson, archivists par excellence. Their declassification efforts and freely offered help in guiding me through the center's holdings made the most of my time and led me to important sources that I would otherwise have missed. Capt. George W. Cully, USAF, chief of the AFHRC's Inquiries Division, later helped to fill several unexpected gaps in my research with commendable speed.

I am obligated to Dr. Richard Kohn, then chief of air force history, Headquarters USAF, for prompting me to start writing by inviting me to contribute an article to a special issue of *Revue de l'Histoire Militaire Francaise* on civil-military relations that he was editing. I suggested an analysis of the *Mayaguez*–Koh Tang affair as a case study of direct interaction between the highest and lowest levels of command, and he agreed. In the end, Dick decided not to use my piece—a bit too much blood and thunder?—and did me a favor in so doing. I am indebted to Fred Rainbow, then editor-in-chief of *Naval Institute Proceedings*, for encouraging me to turn my article into a monograph.

I owe thanks to Lt. Jeffrey P. Tilbury and QMC Dalton H. Carter, USN, of the Naval ROTC Detachment at Ohio State University, for a quick course in the uses of *The Nautical Almanac* and for computing the 15 May 1975 tides at Koh Tang. Admiral Baldwin reviewed the manuscript in an earlier form as did Rear Adm. W. J. Holland, Jr., USN (Ret.). I am indebted to them both for their encouragement and criticism. I am obligated to Karl Volkmer of Vancouver, British Columbia, for his careful and critical reading of successive chapter drafts. Lt. Col. Vern Sheffield, USAF, my wingman in the Saigon evacuation and one of the finest pilots with whom I have been privileged to fly, reviewed the penultimate draft. His professional and editorial integrity, his operational savvy, and his first-hand knowledge of the way in which the battle of Koh Tang was planned and fought from U Tapao provided a check on my analysis that I could have found nowhere else.

I am obligated to Lt. Col. James H. Davis, USMC (Ret.), and to Sgt. Maj. Lester A. McNemar, USMC, commander and gunnery sergeant, respectively, of Golf Company, 2nd Battalion, Ninth Marines, which bore the brunt of battle on Koh Tang. They informed me of the marine side of the operation in a clinical, unsparing, and thoroughly professional manner. I am particularly indebted to Colonel Davis and his wife, Sue, for their warm hospitality during my visit to their home in Virginia in September 1991. At that time Jim and I visited the Vietnam War Memorial to review the names of our fallen comrades at the bottom of the last, tragic panel. It was there that this book began to assume its final shape, written for the men whose names we reviewed that Saturday morning.

I am also obligated to Chief Master Sgt. Wayne Fisk, USAF (Ret.), pararescueman extraordinaire and the last man off the island, for reviewing my account of the final extraction one more time. I am indebted to Special Agent Richard Keith, FBI, Golf Company's executive officer and 2/9's acting operations officer during the Koh Tang fight, whom I located through Colonel Davis's good offices just as the manuscript was going to press. He shared with me his recollections of the engagement on short notice and was speedy and thorough in reviewing relevant portions of the narrative for accuracy and completeness. I am also indebted to Vern Sheffield and Robert Gradle for providing me copies of air force photographs of the Koh Tang action.

Finally, I am indebted to Dr. Earl H. Tilford of the U.S. Army War College, Carlisle Barracks, Pennsylvania, who served as the principal reader of my manuscript for the Texas A&M University Press, for his thoroughness and incisive editorial suggestions.

The analysis and conclusions in the pages that follow are my own and bear the sponsorship and approval of no institution or organization. Those to whom I am indebted for assistance, not all of them cited above, deserve much of the credit for whatever success I have enjoyed in elucidating the *Mayaguez* incident and the battle of Koh Tang. The responsibility for error and oversight is mine and mine alone.

A VERY SHORT WAR

Introduction

BETWEEN A QUARTER PAST TWO in the afternoon of Monday 12 May 1975 and a quarter past eight the following Thursday evening, local time, in the Gulf of Thailand, air, naval, and ground forces of the United States of America engaged in a brief, vicious struggle with the armed forces of the Khymer Rouge of Cambodia. Although the scale of the action was small, the stakes were not. Prospects for a serious setback for the United States were present at the beginning. For reasons that changed as events unfolded, those prospects remained to the end.

The clash was initiated by the seizure of an American merchant ship, the SS *Mayaguez*, off the Cambodian coast. The factors that prompted President Gerald Ford to order U.S. military forces into combat revolved around the policy implications of permitting a hostile government to seize an American flag vessel with impunity and hold its crew captive. During the crisis, the ship and crew were recovered within three days, erasing the initial cause of hostilities. But before this transpired, military measures undertaken in pursuit of President Ford's policy goals and the Khymer Rouge response to these measures had taken on a life of their own, introducing entirely new issues and problems into the scenario. Those issues and problems demanded solutions that had little to do with the original objectives.

These difficulties were dealt with quickly and, as it turned out, effectively; for exactly that reason they attracted little public attention. In addition, the origins of the problems and issues at stake were largely operational in nature. Consequently, they could not be understood—or in some cases even perceived—without a comprehensive grasp of tactical considerations, and the action was extraordinarily complex tactically. Much of the risk run by U.S. forces originated in technical factors that were beyond the knowledge of the American news media and general public. These included differences in U.S. Air Force and Marine Corps staff procedures, the capabilities and limitations of radio telecommunications systems, the ability of jet fighters to accurately attack ground targets in close proximity to friendly forces, procedures controlling the collection and analysis of intelligence and its distribution, and the performance and flight characteristics of the helicopters that took the marines to their objectives. Factors such as these set the tactical parameters of the battle, shaping and reshaping opportunity and danger from beginning to end. Without taking such considerations into account, the *Mayaguez* affair looks like a straightforward exercise in the application of overwhelming force, a series of basic screw-ups, or both. It wasn't that simple, and therein lies the tale.

Less than four days elapsed between the seizure of the *Mayaguez* and the final disengagement of U.S. forces, and the speed with which events developed gave America little time to react. Most important, the commitment of U.S. ground forces to combat, by law and tradition an important threshold of controversy and debate, ended before public opinion could react and before political opposition to the president's actions could solidify. The *Mayaguez* affair briefly dominated headlines and television news coverage, with supporters of the Ford administration proclaiming victory and critics protesting that excessive force was used. Keenly conscious of recent American humiliations in Vietnam, Ford frequently referred to the *Mayaguez* in campaign speeches while running for president against the Democratic nominee, Governor Jimmy Carter, the following summer and fall. Congressional critics of the administration called for and got a General Accounting Office (GAO) investigation of the operation. They secured early release of the findings in a manner calculated to embarrass the president and enhance Carter's candidacy.[1]

But the GAO report was only mildly critical. It generated little media attention and produced no public outcry, dashing the hopes of those who had pressed for its early release. Left with no reason to pursue the matter further, they dropped it. But Ford failed in his bid for election. The American public and press are not prone to dwell on the successes of presidents who have been voted out of office, and other issues seized America's attention. The information required to undertake even a tentative operational and tactical analysis did not begin to appear in the public domain until a year and a half later, with the appearance of a series of articles in the *U.S. Naval Institute Proceedings*.[2] In the interim, those few who were privy to the requisite knowledge were inhibited from participating in the brief public debate over the *Mayaguez* crisis by security restrictions. Within the bowels of the Pentagon—or so I infer, for the principals were exceedingly close-mouthed—there was a short, bitter spate of interservice finger-pointing and soul-searching. A faint echo of the debate found its way into the last volume of the official Marine Corps history of the Vietnam War in the form of critical remarks about air force helicopter tactics by Adm. George P. Steele, commander of the Seventh Fleet, during the events under consideration. In fact, serious errors were made within the military command structure, but no service had a monopoly on them, and there was plenty of embarrassment to go around. The net result was silence, which is unfortunate because there was a great deal to be learned from these operations.

By the time security restrictions were lifted public interest had waned, and the military actions undertaken in response to President Ford's decisions in May 1975 never became a matter of public debate. Save among serious students of war and policy, who have been well served by Christopher Jon Lamb's fine study, *Belief Systems and Decision Making in the* Mayaguez *Crisis*, which treats decision making at the highest levels of the Ford administration, the affair quickly faded from our collective consciousness. To the extent that it was remembered at all, it was as an incident or a crisis. A good case can be made for either definition, but to those involved at the ship's company, battalion, and squadron level, that wasn't the way it looked at the time. It was a small war.

CHAPTER 1

Prelude: Eagle Pull
and Frequent Wind

AS APRIL GAVE WAY to May in the spring of 1975, America's war in
Southeast Asia seemed finally at an end. Few would have debated the
point, and the dominant sentiment in the United States was surely relief. It was a sentiment that U.S. military personnel who took part in
Operation Frequent Wind, the evacuation of Saigon on 29–30 April,
could share. They had few illusions about the magnitude of the tragedy
they had witnessed. But shame for America's abandonment of South
Vietnam—a feeling difficult to avoid aboard refugee-choked ships and
at air bases where fleeing VNAF (Republic of Vietnam Air Force) aircraft
had discharged their human cargoes—was balanced by pride in a tough
job well done. That same sense of relief was no doubt shared by American soldiers who had participated in the final stage of Operation Eagle
Pull, the evacuation of the Cambodian capital of Phnom Penh on 12
April, barely two weeks before.

Both Eagle Pull and Frequent Wind involved major commitments of
forces (the code names stood for the plans as well as the operations, and
both meanings apply here). Both were executed quickly on a more or
less ad hoc basis. Both thus inflicted more than the usual quota of wear
and tear on the forces involved. To compound the problem, the two
operations occurred in quick succession; they did so, moreover, at a
time when a military takeover in Laos by the Communist Pathet Lao
seemed a real possibility, as indeed it was. The threat to the U.S. Embassy in Vientiane was a matter of serious concern for American commanders in the Pacific,[1] not to mention the helicopter crews who would
have had to evacuate the place under fire. There was no time between

Eagle Pull and Frequent Wind for rest and refit, and the crisis to which the two evacuations were prelude came close behind: the SS *Mayaguez* was seized by forces of the Cambodian Communist regime a month to the day, and very nearly to the hour, after the last Eagle Pull sortie landed.

Nor was the impact of Eagle Pull and Frequent Wind confined to operational forces. Enormous strides had been made in electronic communications in the years following the withdrawal of U.S. combat forces from Vietnam. Specifically, the use of communications satellites and airborne platforms to relay voice telecommunications over global distances had become routine. The result was a dramatic improvement in the ability of higher headquarters to communicate with one another and with forces in the field. But the changes had been implemented during a period in which U.S. forces were not at war. Little thought had been given to their operational implications, as became evident when the new capabilities were used in crisis situations. In both Eagle Pull and Frequent Wind, President Ford, the White House staff, and the National Military Command Center (NMCC) in the Pentagon were able to communicate with U.S. troops in Southeast Asia with unprecedented speed and clarity. During the final hours of the American presence in Vietnam, President Ford and Secretary of State Henry Kissinger were able to talk directly by telephone with the U.S. Embassy in Saigon. The unprecedented quality of long-range electronic communications played a vital, arguably a decisive, role in Frequent Wind. In the process it shaped expectations at the highest levels of command concerning the functioning of command and control relationships.

If we view the *Mayaguez* affair as a chess problem, the Phnom Penh and Saigon evacuations put the pieces on the board. But the chess analogy, though accurate, falls short, for the impact of the two evacuations was not only physical. To be sure, Eagle Pull and Frequent Wind determined the geographic disposition of forces, strength returns, and figures on aircraft in commission. More subtly, they imposed deferred maintenance and fatigue. Of at least equal importance, the two evacuations exerted an indirect influence on the unquantifiable but vitally important determinants of combat effectiveness: morale, motivation, reciprocal bonds of trust and confidence between troops and leaders, and attitudes toward collateral units and other services. It speaks well for the forces involved that the net effect of Eagle Pull and Frequent Wind on those intangibles was—or so is my judgment—overwhelmingly positive. That judgment, of course, is unprovable in any rigorous mathematical sense. I offer the narrative that follows as evidence.

It would be difficult to imagine two operations that resembled one another more closely in concept yet differed more in execution. Both entailed the evacuation of a capital city about to fall to Communist forces. In both cases, the evacuees were a mixture of U.S. citizens, local nationals who had supported America in a long and bitter conflict and were therefore at risk, and friendly foreign nationals. Both were anticipated by contingency plans. Both were to be implemented on orders from the ambassador. Both were delayed until Communist victory was imminent. In the end, both depended on military helicopters.

Eagle Pull was a model operation. The early success of the Khymer Rouge dry season offensive, launched on New Year's Eve 1974, provided the trigger.[2] Ambassador John Gunther Dean directed the preparation of prioritized lists of evacuees. As the situation worsened in February and March, he collapsed the regional advisory and intelligence structure, bringing affected Americans and Cambodians to Phnom Penh for evacuation by air. By the end of March, Americans were concentrated in the capital, and the embassy staff had been reduced to a minimum. This was in anticipation of Eagle Pull contingency plans, which envisioned three options: Option I, using scheduled airlines and civilian charter flights from Phnom Penh's Pochentong Airport; Option II, a fixed-wing military airlift; and Option III, a helicopter evacuation in the event that Pochentong was closed to fixed-wing traffic.[3] Insertion of a marine ground security force (GSF) to maintain order around the helicopter landing zones (LZs) was integral to Option III.

Operational control would be exercised by USSAG (United States Support Activities Group). This was the vestigial remnant of MACV (Military Assistance Command Vietnam), relocated from Saigon to Nakhon Phanom RTAFB (Royal Thai Air Force Base)[4] after the 25 January 1973 Paris Accords and commanded by an air force general instead of an army one. Housed in facilities originally built for Task Force Alpha, established during Rolling Thunder to monitor the so-called McNamara Line of sensors dropped across the Ho Chi Minh Trail, USSAG was a part of, yet apart from, the rest of the base at Nakhon Phanom. Commanding USSAG was air force Lt. Gen. John J. Burns, a veteran World War II fighter pilot with eighty combat missions over North Vietnam in F-4s as a Thailand-based deputy wing commander for operations and vice wing commander during 1967–68.[5] Burns also commanded the Seventh Air Force, the operational headquarters for tactical air force units in Thailand. Upon implementation, Burns, commanding both USSAG and the Seventh Air Force, would report to the commander in chief, Pacific, Adm. Noel Gayler, in Hawaii. Naval forces and air operations over water would fall under the command of Rear Adm. George P. Steele, commander of the Seventh Fleet, acting in support of Burns and responsive to his guidance.

The Seventh Air Force fell administratively under the commander in chief of Pacific Air Forces (PACAF), Gen. Louis L. Wilson, Jr., with headquarters in the Philippines. Thailand-based air force tactical forces fell administratively under the Thirteenth Air Force, based at Clark Air Base, the Philippines. These forces were subordinate to PACAF and would come under Burns's command upon implementation. Similarly, the Seventh Fleet fell under the commander in chief, Pacific Fleet, Adm. Maurice F. Weisner and would become responsive to Burns upon implementation. Thus, although Wilson and Weisner were outside the Eagle Pull chain of command, they commanded the forces involved up to the point of execution and controlled their logistic support. The same basic relationships applied during the *Mayaguez* affair.

Eagle Pull dated from the spring of 1973, when Phnom Penh had nearly fallen to the Khymer Rouge only to be saved at the eleventh hour by American air power. The evacuation plan had been progressively refined in response to changing circumstances.[6] Many adjustments were made to the plan, but fleet deployment schedules were juggled to maximize the availability of marine heavy helicopter assets, or H-53s, during the dry campaigning season, which generally runs from mid-October to mid-May.[7] In addition, two air force H-53 squadrons based at Nakhon Phanom, the 40th ARRS (Aerospace Rescue and Recovery Squadron) and 21st SOS (Special Operations Squadron), were left in place as an emergency evacuation force as U.S. troops withdrew from Indochina. The 21st flew CH-53s, the basic cargo version of the H-53 equipped for special operations, while the 40th was equipped with HH-53s, modified for the combat rescue mission. The two squadrons were to play a central role in the *Mayaguez* affair.

Option III of Eagle Pull evolved to encompass five alternative scenarios that addressed differences in warning time and numbers of evacuees.[8] All but one involved marine H-53s operating from carriers in the Gulf of Thailand. This offered the advantage of having the ground security force (GSF) of marine infantry inserted and extracted by helicopter crews trained in assault operations and accustomed to working with the troops they transported. If there was insufficient time to deploy a naval task force into the Gulf of Thailand, the GSF was to deploy from Okinawa to Ubon Royal Thai Air Force Base by USAF Military Airlift Command (MAC) C-141 transports for insertion by air force H-53s deployed south from Nakhon Phanom. A variant of this scenario was played out a month later.

The decision to retain two air force H-53 squadrons in Thailand meant that from fifteen to twenty combat-capable, long-range helicopters were immediately available in the theater. That same decision directly affected the experience, outlook, and training of the two squadrons. The reasons are worth brief consideration. The air force personnel

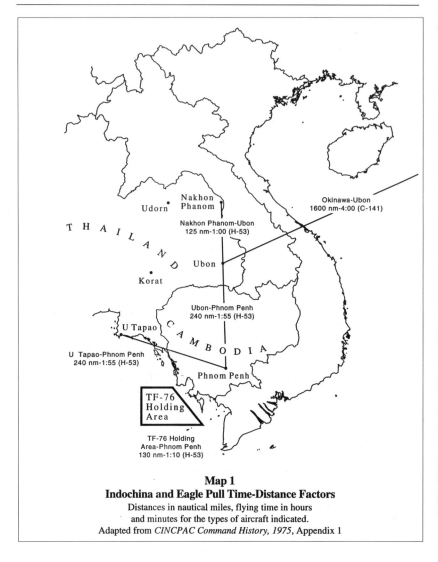

Map 1
Indochina and Eagle Pull Time-Distance Factors
Distances in nautical miles, flying time in hours
and minutes for the types of aircraft indicated.
Adapted from *CINCPAC Command History, 1975*, Appendix 1

system resisted transferring individuals from one type of aircraft to another: the H-53 force was small, and the two squadrons comprised a significant fraction of that force.[9] As the presence of the U.S. Air Force in Southeast Asia diminished, the number of H-53 pilots and flight mechanics assigned there remained constant, placing a strain on the H-53 community. At the same time, squadron-level pilot experience declined as combat veterans retired, left the service, or transferred to staff assignments and fixed-wing flying duties. As our military backed out of Southeast Asia, service in Thailand was no longer on the professional fast track. Nakhon Phanom was considered a backwater, and few officers with enough seniority to influence their assignments volunteered to serve there. As a result, the overwhelming majority of the pilots assigned to the 40th and 21st were junior company-grade officers. The median rank of those who flew in the *Mayaguez* operation was first lieutenant, and the average was only marginally higher.[10] With a handful of exceptions, what combat experience they had when the *Mayaguez* crisis broke was gained in Eagle Pull and Frequent Wind.[11] But while experience was low, commitment was high, and they accepted the vicissitudes of a one-year tour at Nakhon Phanom with good humor. The young pilots who flew H-53s in the *Mayaguez* affair were serious about their business, well-trained, and eager.

Conversely, enlisted aircrew experience in the two units was high. Flight mechanics were all fully qualified; a substantial proportion were serving a second Southeast Asia tour, and S.Sgt. Bobby Bounds was on his fifth.[12] Rescue aircrews also included pararescuemen, parachute-trained and medically trained combat rescue specialists, called PJs for the symbol entered in the aircraft forms to record a parachute jump. A bare majority of the 40th's PJs were young two- and three-stripers on their first or second assignment. The rest, however, were staff sergeants and above, almost all with combat experience. Most of the senior PJs, perhaps a third of the section, had experienced two or more Southeast Asia tours; three was not uncommon, and T.Sgt. Wayne Fisk, a veteran of the November 1970 Son Tay raid, was, like Bounds, on his fifth.[13]

Measured by the parameters established by air force standardization and training directives, the aircrews were extremely competent. To cite two examples, standards of aircraft systems knowledge were very high, an important consideration with a machine as complex as the H-53. So were standards of instrument flying. Using formal readiness criteria, both squadrons were mission capable,[14] but the statistics concealed weaknesses. When combat ended in 1973, air force safety consciousness began to encroach progressively on tactical flying training, and by 1975 such training was restricted to stereotyped simulations of insertions and extractions by individual aircraft.[15] In the case of the 40th, this included training with Korat-based A-7 fighter-bombers designated for the RESCORT (rescue escort) role, but this instruction was not required and was conducted only sporadically. In practice it amounted to little more than orientation for the fighter pilots.

During the mid-1960s, instructor pilots at the Rescue Combat Crew Training School had developed maneuvers that minimized exposure to hostile fire during pickups by using the g forces developed in a tight turn to slow the aircraft. Called tactical approaches, these maneuvers were equally well suited to combat rescues and special operations insertions and extractions. By 1966–67, tactical approaches were a standard part of the repertoire of the American Air Force combat helicopter pilot. Typically initiated at treetop level, these maneuvers required rapid changes of altitude and airspeed. Transient bank angles of 90° were not unusual, and an H-53 could decelerate from 120 knots to a hover in fifteen seconds or less.[16] Safety personnel and senior officers viewed tactical approaches with suspicion. Hard maneuvering close to the ground cut against the grain, and there was a sneaking suspicion that tactical approaches were fun (they were!). Not surprisingly, training in tactical approaches was progressively curtailed. By the spring of 1975, regulations prohibited turning approaches lower than 500 feet above the ground. The great majority of the pilots assigned to the 21st and 40th, then, had received only a sketchy orientation in tactical approaches during their initial H-53 training. The regulations also said that you could do anything you needed to do to survive in combat, but combat is no place to try out a demanding maneuver for the first time.

Nor were tactical approaches the only training deficiency. There was also little or no training in formation flying. In fact, except for aerial refueling, rescue crews were explicitly prohibited from flying in formation—except in combat, a curious exception. Special operations pilots were allowed to practice formation flying, and rescue pilots kept their basic stick and rudder skills sharp with aerial refueling, but the problem went beyond piloting skills. The younger pilots had received their primary flight instruction in the army-run undergraduate helicopter pilot training program and had not been trained in air force formation procedures.

After February 1975 there was no gunnery range in Thailand where the helicopters' machine guns could be fired, and training with live ammunition had been infrequent before that.[17] As events were to confirm, effective gunnery was being compromised by a lack of practice. The machine guns were mechanically complex, Gatling-type six-barreled 7.62-mm miniguns driven by their own electric motors. Accuracy was not an issue: the minigun puts out a stream of tracers that the gunner can aim instinctively like water from a hose. With a rate of fire of two thousand rounds per minute, the weapon was highly effective against "soft" targets. From the gunner's standpoint, the main benefits of regular training were quickness in engaging targets and reduced ammunition consumption. But miniguns were prone to jam unless gunners and maintenance workers were practiced in dealing with their quirks. In the absence of live firing, maintenance skills atrophied, and the weapons were in fact unreliable.[18]

The two squadrons differed with regard to maintenance. The 40th had organic squadron maintenance; that is, the personnel and facilities needed to maintain the 40th's helicopters were under the control of the squadron commander. In contrast, the 21st's helicopters were maintained by the consolidated maintenance squadron of the 56th SOW (Special Operations Wing), which controlled the base. The 21st's helicopters were only a fraction of its responsibilities. Other duties included maintaining a squadron of forty OV-10 twin turboprop forward air control (FAC) aircraft, a detachment of two T-39 jet executive transports,[19] a squadron of EC-47 electronic surveillance aircraft in the process of decommissioning, and, until it was dispatched to Saigon on 25 April to take President Thieu of South Vietnam into exile, a reciprocating-engined C-118 transport.[20]

These divided responsibilities did not help H-53 maintenance. An example makes the point: the H-53's avionics and hydraulic systems were notoriously finicky. While those on the 21st's helicopters were maintained by specialists who worked on other aircraft as well, the 40th's were maintained exclusively by H-53 specialists. In addition, the 56th SOW was reducing personnel strength in anticipation of base closure within a year,[21] which caused shortfalls and turbulence in manpower. By contrast, the 40th was high on the Rescue Service's list of priorities, and maintenance was fully manned. The advantages of fewer layers of bureaucracy and more manpower were apparent. By general consent the 40th squadron's maintenance was exceedingly good, indeed so good that the 40th was suspected of falsifying its in-commission rate.[22] Experienced helicopter maintenance personnel of my acquaintance considered wing-level maintenance less satisfactory than organic squadron maintenance. This was particularly so with the H-53, which was notoriously difficult to maintain, and in fact the 40th's in-commission rates were higher.[23] But although intense rivalry existed between the two helicopter squadrons and also between the 40th and 56th, cooperation between their respective maintenance crews was close and effective when they deployed from the home station.[24] It is sufficient to note that they met the extraordinary challenges that confronted them in the spring of 1975.

A final point concerning the H-53 must be made. The air force H-53 fleet was small, fewer than fifty aircraft, but of that number at least two had been lost for unknown reasons under circumstances that suggested mechanical failure. The only survivors were two PJs thrown from the open ramp as their aircraft went out of control. Analysis of the two crashes and of a third, nonfatal accident pointed to a flaw in the flight control system.[25] Information about the accidents had been briefed to all crew members, and the circumstances surrounding them were general knowledge. The fatal air force mishaps differed from those suffered by other H-53 users, notably the navy and marines, in that there was no evidence of enemy action, adverse weather, or aircrew error.[26] The air force H-53 safety record was otherwise excellent, but the two unexplained losses left a gnawing doubt. Then, on 24 January 1975, an H-53 assigned to the 21st squadron crashed near Nakhon Phanom while on a maintenance check flight, killing all four aboard. The accident investigation was inconclusive but implicated the primary flight control servos, the hydraulic pistons that transfer flight control inputs to the main rotor blades.[27]

Returning to the unfolding strategic scenario, evacuation operations from Phnom Penh's Pochentong Airport proceeded in an orderly manner: first, by scheduled commercial airline; then, as the Khymer Rouge net tightened, by military airlift; and finally, to forestall adverse congressional reaction should a crew be lost to enemy fire, by civilian contract flights.[28] Shortly after his appointment as commander of USSAG and the Seventh Air Force in October 1974, Lieutenant General Burns ordered Eagle Pull updated. This was accomplished with full cooperation from Ambassador Dean and the marines.[29] There were gaps in preparation—joint training with marine and air force helicopter crews was sketchy and was undertaken only at the last minute[30]—but these had no adverse effect.

As the situation became critical, Admiral Gayler, working closely with Burns and Dean, ordered forces deployed in accordance with Eagle Pull contingency plans. When the day came to act, elements of TF (Task Force)-76, the amphibious component of the Seventh Fleet, were standing by in the Gulf of Thailand. These included the assault carrier *Okinawa* and the attack carrier *Hancock*, pressed into duty as a helicopter carrier, carrying some twelve CH-53As each of marine helicopter squadrons HMH-462 and HMH-463. A smaller force of 21st SOS and 40th ARRS H-53s was on alert at Ubon RTAFB. Landing zones (LZs) in Phnom Penh had been designated and marked, but in light of the small number of evacuees remaining, only one, LZ Hotel, would be needed.

On 28 March a pair of Airborne Battlefield Command and Control Center (ABCCC, pronounced "A B triple C") EC-130 aircraft of the 7th Airborne Command and Control Squadron, using the radio call sign "Cricket," had deployed to U Tapao from Clark Air Base in the Philippines with two battle staffs.[31] The Cricket battle staffs were to control aircraft flow and provide command coordination for the evacuation. A small marine command and control group had been quietly flown into Phnom Penh on 3 April, the day before Option I was implemented.[32] A four-man Air Force Combat Control team, ground combat-trained air traffic controllers with a full array of radios and signal gear to regulate the flow of helicopters into the LZs, had been deployed to Thailand from Clark and was standing by at Ubon. Most important, Ambassador Dean ordered fixed-wing evacuation operations at Pochentong terminated on 10 April.[33] His reasons were sound: fixed-wing planes could bring out far more evacuees in a given time than helicopters, but they required unobstructed runways for landings and takeoffs and were highly vulnerable while taxiing and loading. Communist rocket and artillery fire and the possibility of disorder among the civilian populace posed risks for a fixed-wing evacuation that the ambassador deemed unacceptable.

That same day Dean advised Admiral Gayler and Lieutenant General Burns that Eagle Pull would take place two days later.[34] The helicopters began lifting off at precisely seven o'clock on the morning of the twelfth. At ten minutes before nine, local time, a pair of 40th ARRS HH-53s from Ubon landed on LZ Hotel to disembark the combat control team. Four minutes later the first HMH-462 helicopter landed to disgorge GSF marines, quickly loaded up with evacuees, and departed for *Okinawa*.[35] An armada of Thailand-based air force fighter-bombers and side-firing AC-130 gunships orbited overhead to suppress Communist fire if needed. Cricket controllers monitored airborne traffic and provided a communications link with the USSAG/Seventh Air Force command post. The city had been gridded off into sectors of one kilometer square and assigned to OV-10 forward air control aircraft. The pilots monitored their areas for threatening activities, ready to call in suppressive fire through Cricket. While authorizing whatever level of force was necessary, the rules of engagement called for utmost restraint to minimize civilian casualties.

Earlier that morning Ambassador Dean had summoned acting Cambodian president Saukham Khoy and Prime Minister Long Bouret to the embassy, where he offered evacuation to them and other officials along with their families.[36] The prime minister declined, and Dean spent his final moments in the embassy pleading with him by telephone to release additional Cambodians deemed particularly at risk. Refused, Dean ordered the American flag lowered from the embassy staff, watched grim-faced as it was folded, and boarded a car for LZ Hotel. Within minutes, he was aboard a marine H-53 headed for safety. As the last load of evacuees departed at 1030, Cricket called in HMH-463's twelve H-53s to extract the ground security force. At ten minutes before eleven o'clock, Communist 107-mm rockets began exploding near the LZ.[37] Eight minutes later, they were followed by 82-mm mortar rounds, but the last load of GSF marines had lifted off a minute earlier. At a quarter past eleven, two 40th ARRS HH-53s landed to take the Command and Control Group and combat controllers back to Ubon. They cleared the LZ within minutes, and Eagle Pull was over. The helicopters had taken out 287 evacuees plus the 360-man GSF without incident.[38] There were no American casualties, and no U.S. firepower had been expended.

If Eagle Pull was a model, by-the-numbers operation, Frequent Wind was anything but. The problem was partly one of scale, for the number of potential evacuees was immensely larger. More critically, the fall of Saigon caught U.S. forces off-guard in a way that the fall of Phnom Penh had not. Few American observers had anticipated South Vietnam's military collapse in 1975, and planning for Frequent Wind did not begin until the winter of 1974–75.[39] Like Eagle Pull, Frequent Wind envisioned evacuation options that could be implemented in series or parallel, depending on political, strategic, and operational circumstances. Option I called for evacuation by civilian airlift from Saigon's Tan Son Nhut Airport and other airports in South Vietnam as required without direct military involvement. Option II involved evacuation by military airlift. Option III required evacuation by sealift from the port of Saigon. Option IV consisted of evacuation by helicopter to U.S. Navy ships standing by off the coast. Finally, Option V involved a mass movement by road to Vung Tau for evacuation by ship. As with Eagle Pull, the authority for execution and the responsibility for planning on the ground resided with the ambassador, and it was at this point that the two operations diverged.

The U.S. ambassador to South Vietnam was the Honorable Graham Martin, an able diplomat with a distinguished record and a longstanding personal commitment to the American cause in Southeast Asia. A forceful personality with courtly manners and an icy reserve, he was acutely conscious of his senior ambassadorial rank and the prerogatives that went with it. Hard-working to an extreme, Martin was capable of fierce loyalty to subordinates but demanded unswerving obedience in return. Autocratic in style, he did not take challenges to his views lightly.[40] From June 1973 when he assumed his post, Martin fought hard for the public support and congressional funding that South Vietnam needed to survive. For reasons readily understandable in light of the political realities he faced, Martin sought to put the best face on the political and military situation and insisted that his subordinates do likewise.[41] But what began as a strategy for dealing with Congress and the news media came to dominate the embassy's perception of reality.

By the spring of 1975, the ambassador was surrounded by an inner circle that accepted and fed his predispositions. As South Vietnam's military disintegrated under the hammer blows of the People's Army of Vietnam, the embassy clung to business as usual. In fairness to Martin, he was not alone in his slowness to appreciate how critical the situation was. Not until the withdrawal of South Vietnamese forces from the Central Highlands in panic-stricken rout after the fall of Ban Me Thuot on 18 March did the notion that South Vietnam might collapse before the onset of the wet monsoon begin to gain widespread acceptance in U.S. diplomatic and military circles.[42]

Planning for Frequent Wind was thus hamstrung by a paradoxical dual perspective that prevailed in the embassy. On the one hand, the prospect of swift and total military collapse seemed too awful to accept; on the other, the horrors of the disorder and chaos in the streets of Saigon that would surely attend military collapse—or an evacuation—seemed all too real. Nor was the latter fear illusory: the terrible scenes that attended the fall of Da Nang at the end of March were a clear and menacing portent.[43] The result was inaction. Bolstered by hopes for a negotiated settlement, Ambassador Martin resisted efforts to make visible preparations for evacuation, believing that they might cause panic. The magnitude of the problem and the lack of urgency interacted with almost human perversity.

In the evacuation, preparations for Option IV within Saigon depended on the initiative of a handful of individuals who played roles all out of proportion to their junior ranks and modest numbers. Prominent among these were officers of the Defense Attaché Office (DAO), organized as the Special Planning Group by the senior attaché and chief of the office, Maj. Gen. Homer Smith, U.S. Army. Their efforts, resisted by much of the embassy staff, included establishment of a central point for collection, processing, and extraction of evacuees in the old MACV headquarters at Tan Son Nhut, now termed the DAO Compound, code-named Alamo; identifying and preparing rooftop LZs for Air America helicopters to shuttle refugees to the DAO Compound; and drafting plans to transport evacuees from billets throughout the city to the compound by bus convoy.[44] Small but timely efforts were to produce disproportionately large results. One such effort bears mention: during the winter, Attaché Office communications officers had the foresight to order a satellite terminal, at the time a novelty. The terminal became operational on 30 March, the day after Da Nang fell.[45] From that point, the embassy enjoyed direct telephone contact with Washington.

The onrush of events afforded no respite. By the end of March, the exodus of refugees from the northern provinces by sea and the press of Vietnamese trying to leave the country by air had grown to unmanageable proportions. On 1 April the embassy set up an evacuation control center in the Tan Son Nhut compound to coordinate refugee movement; it quickly spun off an evacuation processing center to handle departures by air.[46] This amounted to de facto implementation of Option I. In support of Option III, an LST (landing ship tank) and three large barges were obtained and moored at the Newport docks along with two tugs, leased and kept in readiness to pull them to safety.

Like Option I, Option II was initiated de facto. This came in the unlikely form of Operation Babylift, a humanitarian airlift of orphaned infants to the United States. The Attaché Office took advantage of Babylift to thin out the ranks of nonessential personnel by assigning female embassy staffers as escorts for the infants and in early April obtained approval to use military aircraft that otherwise would have departed empty.[47] This was a useful start, but tragedy intervened when a C-5A committed to Babylift crashed near Saigon on 4 April.

At this point, the DAO military staff was carrying much of the burden of refugee processing. The embassy, meanwhile, was adhering strictly to the terms of the 1973 Geneva Accords, which limited to fifty the number of U.S. military personnel in South Vietnam. When the Military Airlift Command dispatched a team to Saigon to investigate the C-5 crash, the Attaché Office staff was charged with supporting the team. This was a major effort, which involved organizing transportation for search parties and hauling wreckage to Tan Son Nhut. All this stretched the embassy's small military staff to the limit. Refugee processing slowed, and preparations for Option IV ground to a halt.[48] At the same time, observance of the full bureaucratic niceties of U.S. and South Vietnamese emigration and immigration law held the flow of refugees through Tan Son Nhut to a trickle. The main sticking point was the requirement for all departing citizens to have full papers regardless of age. Nor was the U.S. Embassy's adherence to peacetime emigration procedures the only example of business as usual. In the wake of the C-5 crash, the Military Airlift Command reinstated rules requiring a seat and seat belt for every passenger when combat loading—removing seats and having evacuees sit on the floor—would have allowed far more people to be moved.

There were minor victories: Attaché Office personnel smuggled evacuees particularly at risk but without proper documentation past the watchful eyes of emigration police.[49] Military attachés secured State Department approval for a limited number of clandestine "black flights" to take intelligence operatives, their families, and others deemed particularly at risk to safety; these began departing from the Air America terminal at Tan Son Nhut on 17 April.[50] But despite the availability of an essentially unlimited airlift—the accident investigation team shuttled back and forth to Bangkok daily to ensure adherence to the limit of fifty military personnel in the country—only some five thousand evacuees departed from Tan Son Nhut between 1 and 19 April.[51]

Bureaucratic strictures were relaxed only after the South Vietnamese Army had fought and lost its last battle, at Xuan Loc on the approaches to Saigon, on 9–20 April. The logjam was broken by a pointed suggestion made to Ambassador Martin during a 19 April meeting with Admiral Gayler and Lieutenant General Burns that emigration procedures be streamlined to permit sponsors to certify minor dependents with a simple voucher.[52] Martin agreed, and the flow of refugees increased dramatically, rising briefly to a peak of seventy-five hundred per day. But it was too little and too late: the impressive effort served only to show what might have been.

Meanwhile, preparations outside Vietnam proceeded independently. Admiral Gayler ordered TF-76 with the 9th Marine Amphibious Brigade, a composite helicopter-infantry force under Brig. Gen. Richard E. Carey, USMC, embarked, to concentrate off Vung Tau. Elements were in place by 10 April, and Carey, an experienced helicopter aviator, flew into Saigon for a reconnaissance with key subordinates and staff on the twelfth, the day Eagle Pull was executed.[53] A platoon of marines was put in to provide security for Alamo, the Tan Son Nhut Compound.

Against these measures stood the embassy's reluctance to act and the general sense of complacency that prevailed among many Americans in Saigon. On 13 April, Major General Smith's deputy, Brig. Gen. Richard Baughn, USAF, convened a marine—Defense Attaché Office meeting to assess the situation and evaluate evacuation plans. Using military channels to bypass ambassadorial censorship, Baughn transmitted the consensus of the meeting in a message to Admiral Gayler, which unequivocally laid out the grim realities of the situation.[54] Martin fired Baughn on the spot and ordered him out of the country.[55] On the fourteenth, Major General Smith was reduced to the ludicrous expedient of canceling the military Post Exchange and Commissary privileges of civilian contract government employees to induce them to leave the country voluntarily.[56]

In the meantime, Eagle Pull was executed. TF-76 withdrew to Subic Bay in the Philippines for badly needed upkeep on 15 April. It arrived around midday on the seventeenth, only to be alerted for redeployment the following afternoon. TF-76 was on station and prepared for action by 20 April; included were *Okinawa* and *Hancock*, with HMH-462 and HMH-463 embarked. In the interim, the 9th Marine Amphibious Brigade had reorganized. Carey's command now included three infantry battalions of Regimental Landing Team 4 and HMM-165 equipped with CH-46s. These were smaller than the CH-53s with a nominal capacity of seventeen troops as opposed to thirty-eight but were a significant addition to the force's capability.[57]

To augment the marine helicopters, the navy had earlier approached the USSAG/Seventh Air Force staff with a proposal to operate air force H-53s from navy flight decks. Lieutenant General Burns concurred, and the attack carrier *Midway* was reconfigured for the purpose. Senior air force staffs viewed the proposal as a challenge to aircrew flying skill, de facto evidence that no helicopter pilots were present or consulted when the navy proposal was evaluated. No doubt inspired by memories of the 18 April 1942 Tokyo raid mounted by army B-25s launched from the carrier *Hornet*—or, more likely, by the movie *Thirty Seconds over Tokyo*, which dramatized the raid in the best World War II Hollywood tradition—higher headquarters at one point suggested painting the outline of a carrier deck on the runways at Nakhon Phanom. The idea was for the H-53 crews to practice carrier landings and takeoffs—as if painting lines on familiar runways would have made hovering any different!

In fact, the problem had nothing to do with flying skills. Granted, a heaving deck at night and in foul weather will give any helicopter pilot fits, but hovering is hovering and approaches to a carrier deck in weather good enough for a mass evacuation would pose no problems for air force crews. The real issue was deck-handling: who was in charge, when, and under what circumstances. Operating big helicopters in close proximity to one another at distances calculated to give an air force safety officer heart failure was not a simple matter. The navy took effective action to deal with the problem, flying in two experienced navy H-53 pilots to serve as liaison officers.

The transfer operation went smoothly. On 20 April *Midway* took on board ten H-53s from the 21st SOS and 40th ARRS flown out from U Tapao. Painted on the flight deck were H-53 pads positioned to provide six feet of rotor-to-rotor clearance in lieu of the navy/marine standard of two feet.[58] Carey now had available no less than forty-four H-53s and twenty-seven H-46s, of which he planned to launch forty and twenty-four, respectively.[59]

Option IV was ready, but still Ambassador Martin delayed, driven by hopes for a negotiated political settlement that would make a helicopter evacuation unnecessary. At the same time he was anxious to get as many Vietnamese to safety as possible: having belatedly come to support an all-out fixed-wing airlift, he continued to advocate it long after enemy action rendered it questionable. On 27 April, Communist rockets struck Saigon for the first time since 1973. Only four 122-mm rockets were fired, but the message was clear:[60] C-141 flights into Tan Son Nhut were terminated. The South Vietnamese Air Force began evacuating to bases in Thailand on the twenty-eighth, and that morning defecting South Vietnamese pilots flying captured AT-37 light attack aircraft attacked Tan Son Nhut. The flow of C-130s into Tan Son Nhut was interrupted, only to be resumed after dark; two made it in at about eight o'clock that evening, departing with 360 refugees. Martin requested no less than sixty C-130 sorties for the twenty-ninth. At this point, the armed forces of South Vietnam were utterly incapable of defending Saigon from the Communist columns that stood poised on the outskirts of the city.

The first three C-130s landed shortly before midnight. Two were loading and a third was taxiing into the loading area when a barrage of North Vietnamese rockets struck Tan Son Nhut. One of the transport planes was hit in the wing and set afire. As it began to burn, the crew and passengers scrambled into another, and the pilots of the remaining two took off. On climb-out, the crews were treated to a fiery display of descending rockets and rising tracers. The fixed-wing airlift was history. As dawn broke, the remaining South Vietnamese aircraft took off from every available runway and taxiway, littering the field with jettisoned ordnance and fuel tanks. At seven o'clock, the U.S. Air Force colonel supervising airlift operations at Tan Son Nhut informed General Smith that the runways were unusable. Acting on his own authority, Smith ordered the final preparation of Alamo's LZs.

Ambassador Martin temporized, pleading for the resumption of fixed-wing operations. During this crucial interval the unprecedented speed and clarity of communications between Saigon, Washington, and intermediate headquarters set the tempo of operations. At about seven-thirty Saigon time, President Ford convened a meeting of the National Security Council, in which Secretary of State Henry Kissinger argued for continuing the fixed-wing airlift. However, Secretary of Defense James Schlesinger and air force General George Brown, acting chairman of the Joint Chiefs, argued that Option IV was overdue.[61] Meanwhile, Martin drove to Tan Son Nhut by limousine to personally inspect the situation, arriving about nine that morning. While he was there he called the White House from Smith's office, but to no avail. About ten-thirty Smith, despairing of getting a decision from Martin, called Gayler to tell him that fixed-wing operations were out of the question. Gayler agreed to press the Joint Chiefs of Staff (JCS) to order Option IV. Before the JCS could act Martin relented, apparently in conversation with President Ford and—according to Alamo rumor—only in response to a direct presidential order.[62] However that may be, Ambassador Martin ordered Option IV at 1048, and the order to execute was transmitted at 1051 Saigon time.[63] It reached the helicopter crews at eleven o'clock.[64] Anticipating Martin's belated decision, General Smith had issued orders on his own authority at ten minutes after eight to begin moving evacuees to Tan Son Nhut by bus and Air America helicopter.[65] The evacuation was on.

As Air America Hueys lifted off and buses began to roll, the last vestiges of order vanished from the streets of Saigon, and Communist forces began to infiltrate the city. The plan called for the assembly to begin before dawn, when the streets were empty. As it happened, the bus convoys were mobbed. One was broken up by dissident South Vietnamese military elements and abandoned; others were diverted to the embassy compound, served only by two constricted helicopter pads and never intended as a mass evacuation point. Planned routes could not be followed, and many evacuees were left behind. Remarkably, with Marine Corps guards and loads of sixty to seventy per bus instead of forty as planned, the convoys continued to move, delivering some twenty-five hundred evacuees to the Tan Son Nhut Compound.[66] Air America's performance was equally remarkable. Four Hueys were stolen, and artillery fire forced abandonment of the Tan Son Nhut ramp and refueling facility at nine-thirty, but the remaining twenty helicopters lifted over one thousand evacuees to safety from rooftop pads.[67]

The delayed decision cost Carey's force much more than the time between first light and receipt of the implementation order. The marine plan had envisioned insertion of the ground security force into Tan Son Nhut at first light, timed to coincide with the arrival of the first bus convoys. Only a handful of evacuees—no more than three hundred—were to come out of the embassy proper, and for that the small rooftop pad was sufficient. Reality departed sharply from this scenario. The ground security force marines and H-53s were not on the same ships, and marine CH-53C/Ds, without external fuel tanks, lacked the fuel capacity to take off, load their troops, and make a round trip into Saigon. In consequence, two hours were required for "cross-decking," to match marines with helicopters and top off fuel. This should have been accomplished before dawn, and in fact the crews were standing by in their cockpits at four o'clock. As it was, ground security force insertion and refugee extraction did not begin until three in the afternoon, with less than five hours of daylight remaining.[68]

General Carey arrived at Tan Son Nhut by marine UH-1E shortly after two in the afternoon.[69] From that point, operations there went remarkably smoothly, despite endemic confusion, enemy action, and adverse weather. A 57-mm antiaircraft battery to the east of the incoming helicopters opened fire, only to be put out of action by a flight of anti-radiation Iron Hand F-4s at about three o'clock.[70] Three SA-2 surface-to-air missile batteries were within range and radiating but never fired.[71] Carey was forced to invoke the threat of an air strike to make South Vietnamese Army guards let the final bus convoy enter Tan Son Nhut at a quarter to six in the evening.[72]

Serious in daylight, the problem of midair collision posed by the sheer volume of helicopter traffic became acute after dark. Smoke, haze, and scattered clouds obscured visibility, and a thunderstorm blew up to the northwest. To make matters worse, the helicopters were taking sporadic fire from shoulder-fired, heat-seeking SA-7 missiles. Some of the crews extinguished their anticollision beacons and navigation lights to avoid giving their positions away.[73] In the darkness, near midair collisions between helicopters, some of them running fully blacked out, were common. At about seven-thirty, a power failure in the compound left the LZs illuminated only by dim emergency lighting. The marine team controlling the helicopter flow from atop the Alamo Compound roof was dependent on a single VHF/FM radio (a portable, relatively short-range radio; see Appendix A), which cut out intermittently.[74] Nevertheless, by eleven o'clock Alamo was cleared of evacuees. The marines prepared the buildings and satellite terminal for demolition. At fifteen minutes before midnight fuses were lit, and the last ground security force extraction sortie lifted off. The compound was left in ruins, and direct communications between Saigon and Washington were broken.[75]

Meanwhile, things had not gone smoothly at the U.S. Embassy. Diverted bus convoys and Air America Hueys short on fuel had deposited evacuees there, and miscellaneous Americans, Vietnamese, and third-country nationals had forced their way onto the grounds.[76] Around 1500 Carey was informed by telephone that there were two thousand evacuees in the embassy and a frantic mob was beating at the gates. He sent in marines to maintain order and diverted CH-46s to the rooftop and H-53s to the parking lot LZ.[77] But evacuees continued arriving. Military personnel had promised evacuation to numbers of Vietnamese, notably the Embassy Fire Brigade, which provided fire protection for the parking lot LZ. As a result, the number of evacuees remained constant—or so it seemed—regardless of how many were taken out. This created the impression that Ambassador Martin had created a bottomless pit: that evacuees would continue coming out as long as helicopters kept going in.[78] In fact, control was established by evening, and the crowd surrounding the embassy dissipated, but Carey had no communications with the embassy and was unaware of the true situation.[79] About midnight the TF-76 commander, Rear Adm. Richard Whitmire, ordered helicopter operations halted out of concern for aircrew fatigue. On learning of the order, Carey went into a cold rage, immediately countermanded it, and flew to Whitmire's flagship. There he obtained ex post facto approval for his action in a heated face-to-face confrontation with the admiral.[80]

Ambassador Martin's insistence that he remain behind until all evacuees had departed reinforced the impression that the evacuation would become an endless commitment unless drastic measures were taken. That impression was shared by the White House,[81] an unfortunate by-product of superb communications. The result was a presidential order that the ambassador be removed from the embassy, by force if necessary, and that a strict limit be placed on the number of additional sorties. The order was relayed by Cricket[82] to the pilot of a marine CH-46 and thence to the rooftop pad by a flight mechanic screaming above turbine whine and rotor noise: the helicopter would remain in place until the ambassador was aboard. Additional sorties would be provided only to bring out the remaining marines and embassy staff. At two minutes before five o'clock in the morning on 30 April, the helicopter lifted off with Martin on board. The last U.S. Marines retreated to the rooftop, sealing off doors behind them. A helicopter returned for them after daylight, and by eight o'clock they, too, were gone.[83] Some 420 Vietnamese and South Korean diplomats were left behind in the embassy courtyard.[84] The bottomless pit had not, in fact, existed. Six more H-53 sorties would have finished the job, but those who knew were unable to communicate with those who could have provided them.

Meanwhile, as Saigon dissolved into chaos, Option III came belatedly to life. The landing ship tank departed the Newport docks at three in the afternoon followed by the three chartered tugs with barges in tow, loaded well below capacity.[85] As midnight approached, the guided missile destroyer USS *Henry B. Wilson,* closest to shore of combatant surface vessels, tracked the final progress of the little armada toward the South China Sea by radar. As the barges neared the open sea small-arms fire erupted from the shore, and armed evacuees aboard the barges replied in kind. Tracers arced through the dead black of the tropical night. A tug captain panicked and parted his tow. On *Wilson's* radar screen, the "blip" formed by tug and barge split in half. To *Wilson's* skipper, Comdr. Mike Rodgers, and his bridge crew what had happened was obvious. Rodgers moved to protect the evacuees. When attempts to raise the tug by radio failed, *Wilson* closed in on the tug, illuminated it with searchlights, and leveled her 5-inch guns. Rodgers's message to the tug's captain, conveyed by loud hailer, was simple: "Reattach your tow, or I'll blow you out of the water." Within seconds, the tug's third mate came up on the appropriate radio frequency and agreed to reattach the tow.[86]

Some 7,800 evacuees were brought out by helicopter, including 1,373 Americans. It was a remarkable achievement, but few of the 6,500 or so non-Americans evacuated—principally but not exclusively Vietnamese—would have been high on any rationally prioritized list. Worse, many of those most at risk had been left behind.[87] Still, operational disaster had been avoided. A midair collision between refugee-filled helicopters, a vertigo-induced crash, or a reluctance to engage the enemy at the critical moment could have produced catastrophe, indeed almost surely would have. That no such thing happened is eloquent testimony to the aviators, air bosses (the officers, all aviators, in charge of navy carrier flight deck operations), deck crews, controllers, and, last but not least, the ground security force marines on the ground. Option IV, with some help from Option III and *Henry B. Wilson,* had narrowly averted even worse tragedy than that which transpired. That margin was provided by competent tactical leadership—Carey stands out—and exceptional airmanship.[88]

The conclusion of Frequent Wind returns us to the chess analogy. The Saigon evacuation left pieces scattered across the board with reckless abandon from Okinawa to Thailand; from the Philippines to the Gulf of Siam, the South China Sea, and beyond. Those pieces left on the board so disposed that they would become involved in the vicious little war that would shortly erupt were put in place by events and causes whose astonishing variety was matched only by the capriciousness with which they operated.

Cricket aircraft returned to their home station at Clark Air Base. *Coral Sea,* under Rear Adm. R. T. Coogan, commander of TF-73, headed for Australia to celebrate the anniversary of the battle for which she was named. Fought on 3–8 May 1942, it was the first major U.S. naval victory of World War II. On Okinawa, the marines of Battalion Landing Team 2/9, a unit that had played no part in Frequent Wind beyond providing replacement personnel, went about their business of squad-, platoon-, and company-level training. December, January, and February had found 2/9 in the personnel rotation cycle. Most of its veteran members had been replaced by young marines with little operational experience, and the unit was occupied with the business of re-forming itself into a fully combat-ready battalion.[89] *Okinawa* and HMH-462 returned to port in the Philippines for repairs and a well-deserved rest. *Hancock* left for Hawaii to return HMH-463 to its home station. The frigate *Harold E. Holt* took up a station south-southwest of the Philippines to intercept and render assistance to the first of the boat people as they made their way from Communist South Vietnam. Mike Rodgers thought his crew's efforts merited a liberty call, so when TF-76 dispersed, *Wilson* sailed for Kahosiung, Taiwan. *Midway* proceeded to Sattahip, the port of Bangkok, to take on board a load of former VNAF A-37 and F-5 fighters for transport to the United States. The Jolly Greens launched for Nakhon Phanom before *Midway* dropped anchor. The 21st crews stayed behind to sling-load the F-5s and A-37s aboard the carrier until a spate of broken slings and dropped aircraft prompted cancellation of the operation, and they departed for Nakhon Phanom.

CHAPTER 2

The Incident

ABOUT A QUARTER PAST TWO in the afternoon of 12 May 1975, Burton Coombes, third mate of the container ship SS *Mayaguez*, cruising off the Cambodian coast en route from Hong Kong to Sattahip, Thailand, sighted a gunboat headed his way. Steaming at 12.5 knots, the *Mayaguez* had just altered course 5° to port to clear the Poulo Wai archipelago, a tiny cluster of islands some fifty nautical miles off the Cambodian coast. Minutes later, the gunboat ran in parallel close along-side, fired a rocket past the bow, and opened up with machine guns. Third Mate Dave English ordered the radio operator to transmit an SOS in Morse code on standard maritime distress frequencies. He then broadcast an emergency message in the clear on HF (high frequency) voice radio (a long-range radio; see Appendix A). The ship's position was 09°48′ N, 102°53′ E, about seven nautical miles southeast of Poulo Wai. Within minutes, a boarding party from the gunboat had taken control of the ship for the Khymer Rouge government of Cambodia. It was 1421 hours local time in the Gulf of Siam. In Washington, D.C., it was 0321.[1]

The SOS was picked up by John Neal of the Delta Exploration Company in Djakarta, Java, who passed the message on to the U.S. Embassy there.[2] Within two hours the embassy had relayed information of the ship's seizure to Washington.[3] The news quickly worked its way up the chain of command. At twenty to eight in the morning eastern daylight time, President Gerald Ford was notified by Lt. Gen. Brent Scowcroft, USAF, deputy assistant for National Security Affairs, and by David Peterson, the CIA representative responsible for his daily intelligence briefing.[4] Secretary of State and national security adviser Henry Kissinger was informed of events in the Gulf of Siam at about the same time. He immediately called the president. Just over six hours had elapsed since the *Mayaguez* transmitted her SOS.

At about nine-thirty that morning, Ford consulted briefly with Kissinger and Scowcroft and called a meeting of the National Security Council (NSC), which convened at 1205.[5] A small inner circle of key actors coalesced around the president: Kissinger, Scowcroft, and Secretary of Defense James R. Schlesinger. Kissinger and Scowcroft were working out of the White House with the president, and Schlesinger was in the Pentagon.[6] This group was to exercise effective power at the top until the crisis was resolved.[7] Following the NSC meeting, the White House issued a press release declaring the seizure an act of piracy, holding the Cambodian Khymer Rouge government responsible, and suggesting that the United States might retaliate militarily if the vessel and her crew were not promptly released.[8]

Thus were set in motion forces that precipitated a short, significant chapter in the history of the United States. In the seventy-eight hours following the *Mayaguez's* SOS, U.S. Air Force aircraft bombed, strafed, and sank Khymer patrol boats in the Gulf of Siam. U.S. Marines invaded Cambodian territory, establishing a beachhead on a small island in the Gulf of Siam called Koh Tang,[9] then disengaged after a vicious fourteen-hour fight with Khymer Rouge forces. Other marines recaptured the ship, boarding from a U.S. Navy frigate in the first such action taken by marines since the early nineteenth century.[10] Carrier-based navy aircraft bombed targets on the Cambodian mainland in a sharp display of retaliation. American Air Force helicopters transported the marine invasion force to and from Koh Tang, and air force firepower supported them while there. The Khymer Rouge, for reasons that remain unclear, released the crew of the *Mayaguez* in midaction, sending them out from Kompong Som in a captured Thai fishing boat from which they were taken aboard a U.S. destroyer. That this successfully concluded the operation as defined by the original U.S. policy objectives was of absolutely no benefit to the hard-pressed marines on Koh Tang. The battle on the island continued with unabated ferocity for another eight hours, and the final crisis was not passed until the marines were extricated.

The U.S. force committed to combat was relatively small. It consisted of elements of a navy patrol wing, three air force tactical fighter wings and a special operations wing with two attached air rescue squadrons, elements of a battalion and a company of marines, an attack carrier with her embarked air wing supported by a guided missile destroyer, and a frigate. An army U-21 twin turboprop light transport was used for ad hoc reconnaissance of the island, while four army interpreters and two air force personnel trained in explosive ordnance disposal were as-

signed to accompany the marines. A volunteer crew of six Military Sealift Command volunteers got the *Mayaguez* underway after recapture.
Units committed to direct combat support included air force KC-135
tankers of the Strategic Air Command (SAC) for aerial refueling; various
air force communications relay and intelligence gathering aircraft, notably SAC U-2s and PACAF Airborne Battlefield Command, Control, and
Communications (ABCCC) EC-130s; the navy supply ship USS *Vega*;
and air force air traffic control, hospital, and ordnance personnel at U
Tapao Royal Thai Navy Base. Air Force Security Police volunteers assigned to the special operations wing were deployed for use as a boarding party to recapture the *Mayaguez* only to be recalled. These forces
were opposed by a dozen or so Khymer patrol boats and an understrength battalion of *Khmer Kraham*, the Khymer Rouge infantry.

By the standards of the Vietnam War, the results of the episode
seemed modest. A U.S. merchant vessel and crew were seized, briefly
held, and recovered; a Khymer naval base and oil storage facility was
bombed; eight or ten Khymer Rouge patrol boats were sunk; perhaps a
hundred Cambodians were killed or wounded, most of them military;
four American helicopters were shot down and destroyed; fifteen U.S.
servicemen were killed in action, with three missing and fifty wounded;
and an additional helicopter was lost in a related accident with twenty-
three on board killed.[11] American use of Thai bases made Thailand an
unwitting participant in the crisis. The introduction of U.S. Marines
into Thailand without prior consultation produced a sharp diplomatic
protest from the Kukrit Pramoj government, although this does not
seem to have been a major factor in the later Thai decision to order U.S.
forces out of Thailand.

But the *Mayaguez* affair has an interest and importance all out of
proportion to the modest scale of forces engaged and the tally of losses.
The symbolic significance of the affair as the last American military
act of the Vietnam War is underlined by the final names carved in the
black granite of the Vietnam War Memorial. More substantively, our
brief engagement with the Khymer Rouge came at the dawn of a new
era in American overseas commitments. As the *Mayaguez* incident
marked the final American military disengagement from Vietnam, it
came in the wake of Watergate politically. The *Mayaguez* crisis provided
the first real test of a new set of assumptions about the proper use of
presidential powers to make war, painfully worked out in the waning
days of American military involvement in Vietnam. Perhaps most important, it showed that American soldiers, sailors, and airmen could
and would fight in the wake of a humiliating defeat in Vietnam. This
was a point whose implications were more clearly understood and bet-

ter appreciated by America's friends and allies in Asia and its potential enemies than by most Americans.

Of particular concern here, the *Mayaguez* affair also marked the dawn of an era of enormous change in the technological and operational character of war. The period of American withdrawal from Vietnam was signified by the deployment of whole new categories of military technology that at the time of the *Mayaguez* incident had not been used except in experimental quantities. Examples include precision-guided antitank munitions, active homing antiship missiles, and truly mobile surface-to-air missile systems. But the advent of actual world-wide communications, offering national leaders the possibility of immediate control of military forces on a global basis, was surely among the most important. This capability to issue operational orders over global distances was fully exploited for the first time by an American president just two weeks before, in the Saigon evacuation. The *Mayaguez* crisis was to subject this capability and those who used it to an even more demanding test.

Just what was being tested deserves amplification, for the issues in question are still relevant. Geosynchronous communications satellites and computerized systems for encrypting and decoding messages in near real time have combined with sophisticated overhead relay platforms to give American commanders in chief an unprecedented immediacy and clarity of communications with their military forces in the field. This capability, coupled with sophisticated methods of technical intelligence gathering and analysis, promises to make possible the precise management of military force under tight control from the top. The ubiquitous popularity within the defense community of such acronyms as C^2 (C squared, for Command and Control) and C^3I (C cubed I, for Command, Control, Communications, and Intelligence) hints at the expectations raised by this revolution in information gathering and transmission technology. In fact, sober analysis suggests that this communications revolution will create as many problems as it solves until we have fully come to grips with its operational and tactical implications. The reasons are straightforward: in war, new technological capabilities are more easily appreciated than their operational implications. Indeed, technological cynics—or perhaps operational realists—have propounded a law of instantaneous degradation of operational capability that applies to the introduction of any new gadget.[12] The lessons of the *Mayaguez* affair are particularly pungent in this regard.

In part because of the communications considerations outlined above, study of the events of 12–15 May 1975 brings larger philosophical issues into focus. In keeping with the small scale of forces involved, military operations surrounding the *Mayaguez* affair were generally considered to have entailed only modest strategic risks for the United States. This widespread perception has endured despite surprisingly candid admissions by senior military officials and the observation of more perceptive analysts that the American forces were fortunate to get off with relatively light losses. Jon Christopher Lamb makes the point strongly in his excellent study *Belief Systems and Decision Making in the* Mayaguez *Crisis*.[13] In fact, close analysis of the *Mayaguez* action suggests that on several occasions American forces approached the brink of disaster, only to be pulled back by factors that had little to do with the stated purposes of the operation. More often than not, the key decisions that averted disaster were made in spite of, not because of, sophisticated command, control, and communications systems. The following account pays particular attention to the tactical impact of communications at every level, and much of what emerges runs counter to conventional wisdom.

It is arguable that the age of enormous change in the technological and operational character of war that began during the final stages of the Vietnam War came of age in the Persian Gulf War of 2 August 1990–1 March 1991. Certainly, Operations Desert Shield and Desert Storm saw the mass deployment and use of all the kinds of weaponry mentioned above and more, plus something entirely new: stealth aircraft and low-observable, precision-guided cruise missiles able to passively defeat radar-controlled defensive systems. Moreover, the dismemberment of Iraqi military power by air, followed by the remarkably swift defeat of Iraqi ground forces south of the Euphrates River by U.S. and coalition ground forces, demonstrated that all of these categories of weaponry could be made to work together in combat as an orchestrated whole. This would seem to offer powerful validation for the U.S. approach to command, control, and communications, at least under the circumstances. The optimist might conclude that critical analysis of the *Mayaguez* affair addresses problems to which solutions have been found, and there is perhaps an element of truth in that. If Desert Storm demonstrated anything, it was that our military leadership had taken to heart many of the lessons of the Vietnam War—of which Koh Tang was the final battle—and profited thereby. The realist, however, is obliged to note the enormous differences between the two cases. Not least among them is the fact that in Desert Shield/Desert Storm we had time to deploy and prepare according to our own schedule.

That, of course, was not a given, for Saddam Hussein might have sent his tanks into Saudi Arabia in August, or at any later time of his choosing, as indeed he did in the battle of Kafji, and our leaders and military forces had to plan accordingly. A fairer comparison, then, would be between our response to the seizure of the *Mayaguez* and what we might have done had the forces of Baath Socialist Iraq continued to drive south in the late summer of 1990. But how we planned to respond to such a contingency will remain an imponderable until the relevant documents have been declassified and the key actors released from the constraints of security restrictions. How we *would* have responded to such a circumstance will remain an imponderable forever.

More recently, the loss of some fourteen U.S. Army Rangers and special operations helicopter crew members in Mogadishu, Somalia, on 3 October 1993 in a miscarried raid against supporters of warlord Muhammad Aidid graphically demonstrated that major embarrassments can result from the commitment of relatively small forces.

For these reasons, if for no other, study of the *Mayaguez–Koh Tang* affair retains its relevance. It is relevant, too, for a narrower and more immediate reason, yet one no less valid: a number of key American leaders in Desert Shield/Desert Storm held senior executive branch appointments during the *Mayaguez* affair. These included most notably President George Bush, then de facto ambassador to Communist China as head of the American liaison office in Peking; and Lt. Gen. Brent Scowcroft, deputy assistant for National Security Affairs to President Ford in the first case and national security adviser to President Bush in the second. At the time of writing, these individuals had generally refrained from active participation in the public debate over the policies of the Democratic administration, but they will no doubt be heard from in the months and years to come. The account that follows establishes at least a partial operational benchmark based on past actions against which to evaluate their predictions and judgments.

I have made no attempt to track them down, but other military officers and executive branch appointees involved in Desert Shield/Desert Storm were no doubt involved in the *Mayaguez* affair and the battle of Koh Tang. This is likely also true of a handful of senior noncommissioned officers. I have no doubt that they, at least, learned from the events of May 1975, and it would be interesting to know how they applied their lessons. Though peripheral to the central purposes of this study, the same point also applies to prominent news media figures, to members of Congress, and to their staffs. Comparison of their actions and utterances in the two cases should be instructive, and this study will provide greater resources with which to do so.

CHAPTER 3

Strategy and Setting

OPERATIONAL RISK and the uncertainties from which risk flows are invariably present in war, a point on which all serious theorists and practitioners concur. There is general agreement, moreover, that such risk and uncertainty are directly linked to strategic factors. Reflective and experienced soldiers have understood this empirically since time immemorial. But the perception is difficult to put in words, is not readily appreciated except through personal experience, and is easily forgotten in time of peace. The classic formulation is that of the nineteenth-century German philosopher of war Carl von Clausewitz in his concept of friction, defined as all those factors that prevent orders from being carried out as intended and that distinguish real war from war on paper.[1]

It would seem axiomatic that improved communications (limited here to the transmission of information) should reduce the effects of friction. It would logically follow that those effects could be minimized, and in principle eliminated, by the kind of near-perfect communications made routine by the technological developments outlined in the preceding chapter. In fact, the historical record suggests otherwise: that the problem of friction is solvable by straightforward technological solutions only up to a point. The relationships between quantity and quality of communications on the one hand and their effectiveness in achieving a desired result on the other are exceedingly complex. It would seem intuitively obvious that the ability to transmit greater quantities of information more clearly in a given amount of time should increase the chances of success. Reflection, however, indicates that this is not necessarily so, if for no other reason than because information saturation can overload analytical and decision-making processes.

Although he lacked knowledge of single-sideband radios or communications satellites, Clausewitz clearly understood that attempts to reduce the effects of friction by improved information transmission alone are apt to backfire and that improving the quantity and quality of communications is a double-edged sword. In Clausewitz's day, improved communications meant rigid insistence on high standards of speed and precision in transmitting and obeying orders. His words on the subject, penned over a century and a half ago, are prescient: "Iron will-power can overcome this friction; it pulverizes every obstacle, but of course it wears down the machine as well."[2] The *Mayaguez* affair was to reaffirm the validity and relevance of his insight with bitter eloquence.

A few additional remarks about the nature of war are necessary before we proceed. First, uncertainty and unpredictability are among war's salient characteristics. Second, although some sources of uncertainty can be quantified and analyzed mathematically to predict their impact and thus reduce risk, many cannot. In general, quantitative methods of analysis have great utility in logistics (which Clausewitz perceptively termed the statistical element of strategy)[3] and in planning the movement of forces out of contact with the enemy. The reduction of risk by carefully calculating logistical requirements and wastage rates is an indispensable part of the art and craft of war. The value of such techniques diminishes sharply, however, when applied to problems that encompass the actions of a thinking, reacting enemy. Examples include calculations of kill probability (P_k) and JMEM (Joint Munitions Effectiveness Manual) data predicting the ordnance expenditure required to achieve desired levels of destruction on given targets. Although such techniques produce useful planning data and lay out the physical parameters of weapons effectiveness, they cannot predict the outcome of an engagement. Such tools can, if used properly, help to delineate the outer limits of feasibility—an important consideration—but they can do no more than that.

Once opposing forces come into contact, history clearly demonstrates the importance of intangible and unquantifiable variables such as leadership, discipline, training, unit cohesion, and esprit de corps in determining the outcome. Because they are impossible to quantify or evaluate with precision, these intangibles are prime sources of risk; they are also prime sources of combat effectiveness. These factors were to play a major role in the *Mayaguez* affair.

Before we turn to the engagement of 12–15 May 1975, we need to address a final theoretical issue: how strategic, operational, and tactical risk and uncertainty relate to one another. Risk is generally recognized as a tactical and operational phenomenon. It is also widely acknowledged that uncertainty, which is to say unpredictability, is a prime source of risk. There is, however, no consensus on the nature of the relationship between operational and tactical uncertainty and strategic risk. Although they recognized the importance of such quantifiable factors as numerical superiority, soldiers, scholars, and statesmen of an earlier day accepted uncertainty and unpredictability as inherent characteristics of war, and they were prepared to account for these characteristics up the operational spectrum from tactics to grand strategy. The frequently cited aphorism about a kingdom being lost for the want of a horseshoe nail makes the point. It was accepted as a given that a seemingly trivial incident might determine the outcome of a battle; that is, that cause and effect were not necessarily proportional. Moreover, it was generally believed that the outcome of a battle might determine the outcome of a war. The prevalence of this view of war is attested to by the former popularity of books based on lists of decisive battles, implicitly embracing the assumption that individual battles were at least potentially decisive.[4]

But the advent of industrialized mass warfare in the nineteenth century combined with the rational proclivities of the twentieth to shift the critical attention of military analysts and historians from the subjective and unpredictable to the quantifiable and probable. The wide acceptance of Lanchester's Laws, operations analysis, cost benefit effectiveness analysis, and the perceived value of statistically based decision-making processes are symptoms of a mind-set that emphasizes broad, underlying social, economic, and political factors. From this perspective, individual tactical decisions are considered unlikely to have much impact on the final strategic outcome. The implicit assumption seems to be that the brilliance and incompetence of such individual decisions will cancel out strategically and that in the end, numbers will tell. Granted, some military institutions are more capable tactically than others, but such competence takes effect in the aggregate. The notion that cause and effect are generally proportional in war and that the whole is equal to the sum of the parts—in short, that war is a linear phenomenon—became entrenched and has demonstrated remarkable staying power.[5]

In truth, there is no evidence that the basic nature of war has changed, although technological advances, in particular, influence the degree to which it is susceptible to quantitative analysis—which is to say predictable—at any given time and place. There are times when numbers are all-important—World War I—and where quantitative analysis could predict much about probable outcomes and can tell us a great deal about the reasons why after the fact. There are times when numbers count for almost nothing, and their effect is overridden by such intangibles as morale, cohesion, and leadership. The campaigns of Alexander the Great and the Arab conquests of the seventh and eighth centuries A.D. are examples that come readily to mind. There are also times when the tangible and intangible seem to be in rough balance: the Norman conquest of England and the battle of the Atlantic in World War II are examples. But in every case, the ability of leaders to perceive risk and uncertainty, to understand their sources and the nature of their influence, and to anticipate and control their effects has played a major role. This has been true strategically at the national level, operationally at the theater level, and tactically on the battlefield. If this is true of each level in isolation—as it plainly is—then I would argue that it is even more so when these factors are combined, for uncertainty and risk are always potentially cumulative in their impact. Risk and uncertainty, in other words, not only have the ability to add cumulatively to one another's effects but to multiply them in potentially catastrophic fashion.[6] In other words, war is at heart a nonlinear phenomenon: one in which cause and effect are not necessarily proportional and in which the whole, far from being the sum of the parts, is the product of interactions among them.[7]

It follows that tactical misassessments and errors of judgment have the capacity to generate and amplify operational and strategic mistakes, multiplying their impact in an escalating fashion.[8] The implications of long-range electronic communications are enormous in this context, for they make it possible to operate tactically, operationally, and strategically all at the same time. The potential benefits of this ability are readily apparent, but the evils are no less real and far less commonly appreciated. The *Mayaguez* affair places powerful evidence on both sides of the ledger.

POLICY AND STRATEGY

Here we turn from theory to the *Mayaguez* conflict proper, beginning with an assessment of goals and objectives. To be of more than narrowly technical relevance, operational analysis must consider strategic objectives and policy goals. It must also take into account the reality that policy and strategy are reactive and interactive. Each assumes relevance and leads to success or failure within a context established partly by the other and partly by the enemy. Any competent operational analysis or plan must therefore begin with policy and strategy considerations and must also address enemy intentions and capabilities.

At the time of the *Mayaguez's* seizure, little was known of Khymer Rouge motives in the affair. Little more can be said now. As Marxist-Leninist revolutionaries, the new rulers of Cambodia no doubt welcomed an opportunity to embarrass the United States. But having captured Phnom Penh less than a month before, they were surely preoccupied with consolidating their power. It is therefore unlikely that the leaders were willing to go to any great trouble or run any great risk to do so. It is apparent in retrospect that the roots of armed conflict between Khymer Rouge Cambodia and Communist Vietnam ran much deeper and lay far closer to the surface than was commonly appreciated at the time. The dust of America's withdrawal from Vietnam had hardly settled when the Khymer Rouge launched a series of vicious raids across the Vietnamese border in order to provoke an uprising among the Khymer minority in the Mekong Delta and regain Cambodia's lost provinces there.[9] That helps to explain the presence of a surprisingly heavily armed and well-trained *Khmer Kraham* (Khymer Rouge Army) garrison on a seemingly insignificant offshore island.[10] But such considerations are strategic rather than tactical assessments, and—as the ensuing story makes clear—there is a double irony here. It was tactical, not strategic, factors that gave us fits in the *Mayaguez* affair, yet U.S. intelligence had a sound grasp of Khymer Rouge tactical capabilities on Koh Tang.

In assessing the motives of the Khymer Rouge, President Ford and his advisers had little to go on. Even the identity of Cambodia's rulers was uncertain. The only real manifestation of their foreign policy was the xenophobic totality with which they had expelled Westerners from Phnom Penh along with the indigenous populace. Also, there were several incidents involving harassment of shipping in the Gulf of Siam, including the seizure and release of a Panamanian vessel the previous week.[11] Ford and his inner circle considered the possibility that the *Mayaguez* might have been seized on the initiative of a local commander, but this alternative was not pondered until the afternoon of 14 May, scant hours before the Koh Tang assault force took off. That realization apparently prompted Ford to scale back retaliatory action by ruling out the use of B-52 bombers.[12] It had no other perceptible effect on U.S. strategy, nor is it easy to see how it might have. If the Khymer regime did not actually order the *Mayaguez* seized, it immediately assumed control of ship and crew and showed every indication of keeping them, so the point is moot. Ford and his advisers thus assumed that the Khymer Rouge would oppose efforts to retake the ship and crew with military force. Their logic was sound. It did not, however, percolate downward with uniform effectiveness.

The planners in Washington were haunted from the beginning by the specter of a repetition of the *Pueblo* crisis. This crisis was precipitated by the seizure of the U.S. Navy intelligence-gathering ship USS *Pueblo* by boarders from North Korean gunboats on 23 January 1968. Locally available U.S. air and naval forces were not used promptly, and by the time the Johnson administration reacted, the North Koreans had secured the vessel in port and removed the crew, rendering effective military intervention impossible. The deep humiliation inflicted by brutal North Korean exploitation of *Pueblo's* crew and the diplomatic price of securing their release had left their mark. Scowcroft, in particular, drew the parallel between the two incidents explicitly.[13] Although the seizure of a merchant ship was a different matter from that of a naval vessel, in either case the feasibility of military response on a manageable scale could be expected to diminish rapidly with time.

These considerations argued compellingly for a swift operational response, and it was here that advanced communications technology made its initial mark. In the years since the *Pueblo* incident communications satellites had become a reality, and instant radiotelephone contact between the White House and major U.S. military headquarters overseas was routine. The deployment of specialized aircraft as radio relay platforms could quickly extend this capability to forces in the field and had done so in the Saigon evacuation. Early in the *Mayaguez* crisis, high-altitude U-2 strategic reconnaissance planes specially modified to serve as radio communications relays were put on station to link USSAG headquarters at Nakhon Phanom with U.S. forces off the Cambodian coast. Similarly, EC-130 ABCCC command and control aircraft were placed in orbit over the Gulf of Siam to manage their commitment to combat.[14] Ford and his advisers, in short, could be and were kept abreast of developments in the Gulf of Siam almost from the outset.

Politically, the need for urgency was framed by the provisions of the War Powers Act of 1973. This measure required presidential consultation with Congress before U.S. forces could make war and a written justification of the commitment within forty-eight hours.[15] During the event, Ford did consult with Congress, but only in the most perfunctory manner and at the eleventh hour. When the marines hit the beach at Koh Tang, key congressional committees were receiving an administration briefing "on the impending action." The briefing started at precisely three o'clock in the afternoon on 15 May, eastern daylight time, five minutes before the assault helicopters were scheduled to lift off from U Tapao.[16] It is unlikely that the timing was a coincidence.

Although congressional leaders rewarded the president with applause when he later appeared before them to explain his actions,[17] it was not preordained that his behavior would be so well received. Ford and his advisers were clearly and understandably anxious to resolve matters before congressional politics began to play an active role in the crisis. The need for a speedy resolution was thus to exert an overriding operational influence. We can only speculate as to how much time Ford and his inner circle of key advisers believed they had, in part because operational factors beyond their control helped to determine how much time was available. (The Khymer failure to take the *Mayaguez* into Kompong

Som was critical in this regard.) On balance, though, the evidence suggests that the timing of the operation was determined by the president
himself and that technical military considerations did not play a central
role. Air force General David C. Jones, acting chairman of the Joint
Chiefs of Staff during the National Security Council meetings that preceded the commitment of forces, repeatedly advised delay to permit
more thorough military planning. But in the end, he and the JCS went
along with the timing of the assault.[18]

On balance, it appears that military action was begun somewhere
near the outside limits of the president's tolerance; that is, he and his
inner circle waited about as long as they felt they could. That suggests
a deadline for effective crisis resolution of about seventy-two hours
from first notification of the ship's seizure.

Ford and his close advisers quickly settled on three overlapping objectives: first, to recover the ship and crew; second, to avoid the possibility of hostage negotiations; and third, to mount a demonstrative use of
U.S. force to bolster America's international credibility. This was at a
low ebb in the wake of the collapse of South Vietnam and the ignomini-
ous evacuation of Saigon less than two weeks before.[19] The balance that
they struck between the three, with the recovery of ship and crew ac-
corded clear priority, is of pivotal importance, for it drove the commitment of forces. Although the application of demonstrative force in
bombing the Cambodian mainland played large in the response of do-
mestic media and in international reaction, it clearly occupied a subsidiary position in the decision-making process. For this reason, and
because it entailed minimal operational and strategic risk, the demonstrative use of force is a matter of incidental concern to us here. Although the point is not central to my analysis, I agree with Jon Lamb's
conclusion that Ford's operational decisions were not driven by concern
for his personal political fortunes.[20] My focus will be on the recapture of
the *Mayaguez,* the recovery of her crew, and on the Koh Tang invasion. It
was there that tactical and operational events most directly impinged
on the pursuit of policy goals—predictably so, for it was there that the
enemy ability to interfere was greatest.

Ford and his advisers recognized that their first two objectives might
conflict. Their actions suggest, therefore, that if necessary they were
prepared to give priority to the avoidance of hostage negotiations at the
expense of the crew's welfare.[21] However that may be, recapture of the
ship and crew and avoidance of hostage bargaining, in whatever order,
clearly took precedence over a demonstrative application of force. The
latter could be orchestrated at leisure, given the overwhelming air
power available to deliver it and the virtual nonexistence of Khymer
Rouge antiaircraft defenses.

OPERATIONAL CONSIDERATIONS

If recovery of the ship and crew was the driving operational objective, then the job would have to be done by armed men. If it was to be accomplished within the president's time criteria, those men would have to be carried to their objectives by Thailand-based U.S. Air Force helicopters. There were no amphibious assault ships nearby, and the carriers that supported the Saigon evacuation were out of the area, out of commission, or both. They would not be available in time. Counterbalancing this reality was a fortuitous happenstance. The attack carrier *Coral Sea,* the core of TF-73, was transiting Indonesian waters en route to an Australian port of call for a belated celebration of the anniversary of the World War II victory of 3–8 May 1942 over the Japanese Navy off New Guinea, for which she was named. *Coral Sea* was thus within striking distance and an obvious candidate for retaliatory raids but offered no help with the troop lift problem: she carried only two helicopters, unarmed and unarmored SH-3s, which were unsuited for assault operations.[22] Marine infantry was available on Okinawa and in the Philippines and could be quickly ferried to U.S. bases in Thailand by Military Airlift Command transports, but marine helicopters were unavailable.

Consequently, the operation was to hinge on the 21st SOS and the 40th ARRS at Nakhon Phanom. Both units were trained for long-range combat operations; both were equipped with the H-53, having ten and nine on strength, respectively.[23] These were well-armed helicopters with limited armor protection, capable of carrying some twenty to twenty-seven fully equipped infantrymen each. For gross planning purposes in light of the demands of the forthcoming operation, the two units appeared to be virtually identical. There were, however, significant differences between them, and these were to prove pivotal.

During the Vietnam War, air force special operations CH-53s (the *C* is for cargo, the *H* for helicopter) were used to insert and recover patrols and road-watch teams. The latter were small patrols sent behind enemy lines to observe road traffic, particularly along the Ho Chi Minh Trail. The CH-53s were also used to provide logistical support for anti-Communist guerrillas in Laos and, as a residual mission, to give similar support to government antiguerrilla and civic actions efforts in Thailand. Rescue HH-53s (the first *H* is for rescue) were used to recover shot-down U.S. aviators from Laos and North Vietnam.[24] Special operations helicopters normally penetrated hostile airspace unsupported, depending on surprise and precise premission planning to reach their LZs (landing zones) undetected. Rescue helicopters scrambled from alert or diverted from precautionary orbit to rescue downed aviators whose locations were only approximately known. They were supported by

dedicated RESCORT (rescue escort) ground attack fighters flown by specially trained pilots and by ARRS HC-130s, flown by crews trained in
rescue mission coordination. The HC-130s had an extensive communications suite and radio direction-finding gear. To permit penetration
deep into enemy territory and to provide loiter time for precautionary
orbits, HH-53s were equipped for probe and drogue aerial refueling.
Most rescue HC-130s were modified as HC-130P tankers. Combat rescue missions generally received whatever air support was needed, and a
great deal often was.

Special operations CH-53s might have air support on call, but it was
not ordinarily required or even desired. As a rule, special operations
helicopters worked independently, either individually or in small formations. By contrast, long-range rescue helicopters usually operated as
part of an integrated team. Experience over North Vietnam and Laos
showed that close tactical coordination between RESCORT fighters and
rescue helicopters was critical to mission success and that the requisite
skills were demanding. This was particularly true for the fighter pilots.
As noted above, an A-7 squadron at Korat was assigned the RESCORT
mission and trained with the 40th. The latter's crews regularly practiced
aerial refueling with Korat-based HC-130Ps of the 56th ARRS.

By nature, special operations missions were covert and planned in
detail well in advance, while combat rescue missions were overt and
reactive. The special operations mission was conducted in the shadows;
the combat rescue mission was conducted in the limelight. The two
missions called for different mind-sets: that of the stalker and sniper
for special operations, that of the barroom brawler for rescue. The variations in outlook and training were captured in the aircraft radio call
signs of the two squadrons: Knife for the 21st SOS and Jolly Green, short
for Jolly Green Giant, for the 40th. The Knife call sign was of uncertain
origins but had obvious aggressive implications. The Jolly Green call
sign was inspired by the mythical green giant whose bumptious, good-
natured image helped sell vegetables. Products of the 1965–68 air war
against North Vietnam, these call signs persisted not so much for operational reasons—permanent call signs have disadvantages as well as advantages—as for historical ones. Members of the two squadrons carried
the attitudinal baggage of those who had flown their missions before
them, and the call signs were potent reminders of that baggage. The
men of the 21st SOS were Knives, and those of the 40th were Jolly
Greens. Both units were intensely proud of their unit identities, but the
Jolly Greens were more outgoing and boisterous—many would have
said obnoxious—in expressing it. This was most notably demonstrated
by spray painting stylized Jolly Green footprints on everything from the
bare asses of newly assigned officers and visitors to the 40th's informal

officer's club to the engine nacelles of visiting Military Airlift Command C-141 transports and the base water tower.[25]

A final detail underlines the point: the party suits worn at squadron social functions. A distinctive feature of U.S. Air Force life in Southeast Asia during the Vietnam War, the party suit was a short-sleeved jump suit in distinctive unit colors. It was embroidered with the wearer's name, unit identity, and radio call sign and was decorated with an array of serious and mock-serious patches celebrating individual and unit accomplishments. The suits were de rigueur for officers, particularly in flying units; they were also worn by enlisted aircrew and, in the case of the Jolly Greens, maintenance personnel. The 21st's party suits were a muted light gray; the 40th's were a bright kelly green. Many individuals deviated from the squadron stereotypes, and the point is a subtle one, but the customs and social trappings were accurate reflections of distinctly different unit personalities.

The point can never be proved, but I am convinced that those differences in unit personality were real and operationally significant. I believe that they shaped the way in which the Knives and Jolly Greens went about their business when it counted. Some will argue that their willingness to persist in the face of danger on 15 May 1975 stemmed from discipline and obedience to orders, but if military history teaches us anything, it is that simple willingness to die is not enough. Quite the contrary. Misdirected bravery is generally counterproductive. Defenders of aircrew standardization would argue that firm adherence to regulations and procedures is the basis of combat effectiveness and was in this case. There is truth in that argument. But procedures for operating equipment, however valid and important, fall short in combat against an armed, aggressive, and intelligent foe. In fact, certain aircrew procedures proved inadequate—as they always do. The lack of training in tactical approaches is the most obvious example but is by no means the only one. Procedures take the machine into account and, to a degree, the weather. Tactics must consider the enemy. As a result, there are a multitude of possible approaches to any tactical problem. When such a problem is not effectively anticipated in training, as was the case here, improvisation is the only route to success—or survival.

Successful improvisation in combat depends on accurate expectations of individual and group behavior. If you have no idea how your wingman or crew will behave when facing imminent death, you cannot intelligently improvise. If, however, you have a reasonable notion of what they will do, how well, and how quickly, you can. The mechanism is self-reinforcing. Units with confidence in the will and ability of their members to perform under stress assume competence and rise above it. If they have practiced some of the options in training, the self-reinforcing mechanism is stronger still. Units in which no such confidence exists tend to assume individual incompetence, a lack of will, or both, making group incompetence a self-fulfilling prophecy.

These expectations flow from the cohesive mechanism that holds units and crews together in combat. That mechanism is a group phenomenon, not an individual one. It follows that each unit has a distinctive tactical style, and history affirms that such styles exist. History also affirms that the unit personalities from which tactical styles flow can be strikingly different and remarkably stable. At the macro level, the Marine Corps is a prime example, and the performance of Battalion Landing Team (BLT) 2/9 on Koh Tang confirms the hypothesis. If ever an infantry unit was set up by circumstances for failure, 2/9 was it. Yet 2/9 did not fail. The same point applies to the two air force helicopter squadrons.

It is my contention that the best of the 21st's and 40th's contrasting styles can be seen in their performance in the Koh Tang operation. The technical vocabulary to describe the behavioral patterns in question has not yet been invented, but we can try. To me, the Knives' tactical style exemplified grim determination to see the thing through. The Jolly Greens' came across as a kind of perverse optimism: if you keep your cool, get things coordinated, don't do anything really stupid, and keep plugging away, sooner or later *something* will work.

Turning to more tangible factors, there were significant differences in equipment between the two squadrons beyond those already mentioned. The most basic of these involved the fuel system. The HH-53s were air-refuelable, but even with air-to-air refueling the internal fuel capacity of the H-53 was inadequate for the long-range rescue mission. The HH-53 was therefore fitted with two 450-gallon, jettisonable auxiliary tanks. CH-53Cs were not equipped for aerial refueling and achieved the range required for special operations with larger, 650-gallon external tanks. Fully loaded, a CH-53 thus carried some twenty-six hundred pounds more fuel than an HH-53. Since the H-53 was weight limited instead of power limited, the HH-53 could convert the lighter fuel load into more cargo, passengers, armament, or protective equipment. The 450-gallon external fuel tanks of HH-53s were filled with a remarkably efficient, explosion-retardant polyurethane foam. Vaguely resembling a bright orange plastic kitchen scouring pad, the foam rendered fuel tank explosions impossible regardless of the source of ignition. Fires caused by incendiary or explosive bullets were quickly extinguished by gases evolved from the foam. The weight and performance penalty of the foam was minimal: it reduced tank capacity by 3 percent, less than six minutes of fuel at normal cruise settings, and added only forty-seven pounds to the weight of the aircraft.[26] The 650-gallon external tanks carried by CH-53s were simple, unprotected aluminum shells. USSAG had identified the unprotected tanks as extremely vulnerable and requested that foam be installed in anticipation of Eagle Pull. The request was rejected by Headquarters PACAF in the summer of 1974.[27]

As mentioned earlier, both HH- and CH-53s were armed with 7.62-mm miniguns. These offered the gunner a choice of two cyclic rates of fire, two thousand or four thousand rounds per minute, and were highly effective in delivering close-in suppressive fire.[28] Both versions mounted miniguns in the crew door and left forward cabin window. HH-53s carried a third minigun in an armored gun tub on the cargo ramp. Both versions had self-sealing internal fuel tanks. Both were provided with over a thousand pounds of quarter-inch titanium armor plate to shield crew positions, engines, gearboxes, and vital flight control components. Special operations units, however, traditionally stripped much of the armor from their helicopters to increase useful load and power margins. By Rescue Service regulation, HH-53s flew with all armor installed.

In our brief discussion of these two squadrons, a final point must be made: by interservice agreement, air force helicopters—unlike army and marine helicopters—were not used to insert infantry in combat. Air force crews were therefore not trained in vertical assault tactics. This was to play a significant role in the *Mayaguez* battle, because marine infantrymen were accustomed to working with marine helicopter crews who were not only trained in vertical assault tactics but were trained in infantry tactics as well.

COMMAND AND CONTROL RELATIONSHIPS

Whatever the president ordered, it was clear from the outset that the critical action would be in the Gulf of Siam. As with Eagle Pull, General Burns would therefore exercise operational control as commander of USSAG, COMUSSAG in military parlance. This alignment made all the more sense, because Burns had operational authority over tactical air assets in Thailand as commander of the Seventh Air Force. It would, however, be a joint operation involving not only air force, navy, and marine forces but the army as well. The U.S. Army strategic intelligence site at Ramusan, Thailand, would be involved, and in addition to intelligence support, army interpreters and aircraft would be pressed into service. It is therefore worth noting that in accordance with normal practice, Burns's deputy as COMUSSAG was an army officer, Maj. Gen. Ira A. Hunt, Jr. Burns's deputy as commander of the Seventh Air Force was Maj. Gen. Earl J. Archer, Jr., USAF.

In theory, Burns's operational command relationships were simple and straightforward. They extended upward through Admiral Gayler, as commander in chief of the Pacific (ordinarily referred to by the full abbreviation CINCPAC), to Secretary of Defense Schlesinger, who would exercise control through the National Military Command Center, and thence to President Ford as commander in chief.[29] In practice, they were anything but. As COMUSSAG, Burns reported operationally to CINCPAC, but as commander of the Seventh Air Force he fell administratively under Headquarters PACAF. To further complicate matters, air force forces in Thailand were administratively under the Thirteenth Air Force in the Philippines, with the important exception of Strategic Air Command forces at U Tapao, which fell under CINCSAC in Omaha, Nebraska.

By law, the role of the Joint Chiefs of Staff was purely advisory, but the chiefs' access to information needed by the military commanders quickly brought them into the decision-making process at levels subordinate to CINCPAC, if only—in theory—indirectly. Matters were complicated by the fact that Admiral Gayler was in Washington when the crisis broke and worked closely with the Joint Chiefs throughout. A take-charge leader by nature, Gayler was not one to stand passively by and let matters take their course.[30] In consequence the Joint Chiefs, through their control of the machinery of the National Military Command Center, acted as an intermediate level of command from beginning to end. As the final link in the chain of higher-echelon command relationships, Burns was to exercise operational control over USAF forces and issue direction and tasking to naval forces and marines. In both cases he was acting through Cricket Airborne Battlefield Command, Control, and Communications aircraft orbiting off the Thai coast (see figure 1).

To further confuse matters, the command and control of rescue units in Southeast Asia fell partly outside the structure just described. These units reported administratively to the 41st Aerospace Rescue and Recovery Wing in Hawaii and thence through Headquarters ARRS at Scott AFB, Illinois, to Headquarters Military Airlift Command, also at Scott. They fell under the Seventh Air Force operationally. Control of rescue missions, however, was exercised by the Joint Rescue Control Center at Nakhon Phanom, acting through an HC-130 on-scene command and mission coordination aircraft, in effect a rescue-dedicated mini-ABCCC. Rescue HC-130s used the radio call sign King, which, like Jolly Green, was a permanent call sign associated with combat aircrew recovery.

The rescue of aviators downed in enemy territory had enjoyed high priority during 1965–73, and an involved set of command and control procedures peculiar to the combat rescue mission had evolved. Under these procedures, once a rescue mission was begun and designated as such, the aircraft commander closest to the scene and most able to influence the outcome would assume on-scene command. This command was passed on in rotation, with the final hand-off going to the pilot of the helicopter committed for the pickup. The process typically began with King assuming on-scene command or assigning it to a fighter pilot capping—that is, maintaining a protective "cap" over—a downed wingman. The next step was normally a hand-off to a RESCORT element leader, who would locate and cap the downed aviator or aviators pending the arrival of helicopters. The radio call sign assigned to dedicated RESCORT fighters, Sandy, was also permanent.[31] The system was decentralized, complex, and sophisticated, but it worked. Relevant to the issues at hand, it required aircraft commanders at the lowest level to exercise an unusual amount of initiative.

Our brief discussion of command and control touches only the high points of a complex, confused, and confusing situation that is probably beyond meaningful reconstruction. Many technicalities alluded to above—the distinction between operational control on the one hand and direction and tasking on the other, for instance, though a fertile breeding ground for interservice turf wars at the upper levels of command—are arcane and largely irrelevant to a meaningful analysis of the *Mayaguez* affair concerning policy inputs and operational outcomes. We need only recognize them as potential sources of friction and note that they were dealt with effectively.

Communications are another matter. An appreciation of the capabilities possessed by the various headquarters in communicating with one another and with the national command authorities is necessary to understand the flow of events. With this in mind, the basic architecture of the electronic command and control communications net is illustrated in figure 1. Single service links have been omitted for simplicity. The central reality is that Burns was responsible for combat operations in the Gulf of Siam and was given the authority and means to exercise effective command over the forces provided to conduct them. Although it was reasonable to expect that higher echelons might intervene directly, as indeed they did, Burns had full statutory authority over the forces employed. In the end, he was responsible for the results.

Command and control relationships at the level of forces engaged merits more detailed attention.[32] General Burns exercised control of combat opertions from the USSAG facility at Nakhon Phanom through Cricket. As related below, these began during the night of 12–13 May. At the same time, Burns dispatched Brig. Gen. Walter H. Baxter III, commander of the Thirteenth Air Force Advanced Echelon representing Thirteenth Air Force interests at Udorn, to U Tapao to serve as senior facilitator in the planning process. Baxter was joined by his vice com-

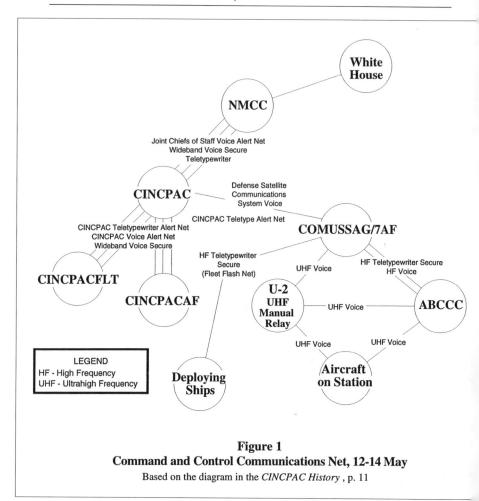

Figure 1
Command and Control Communications Net, 12-14 May
Based on the diagram in the *CINCPAC History*, p. 11

mander, Col. R. B. Janca,[33] who was reassigned and given command of the 635th Combat Support Group at U Tapao at noon on the thirteenth.[34]

Burns also dispatched Col. Robert R. Reed, USAF, USSAG deputy chief, Operations Plans Division, to U Tapao to serve as USSAG/Seventh Air Force coordinator and liaison officer.[35] Col. Loyd J. Anders, 56th SOW deputy commander for operations, was dispatched from Nakhon Phanom to U Tapao to serve as helicopter mission commander. Lt. Col. William P. Pannell accompanied him as his operations officer. Anders and Pannell had served in a similar capacity aboard USS *Midway* during the Saigon evacuation, although the air force helicopters fell under navy-marine operational control once airborne. Anders's operational background was in fighters, and Pannell was a navigator. Baxter's background was also in fighters, and neither he nor Reed had helicopter experience. These men formed the nucleus of a tactical planning and execution cadre that was rounded out by the arrival at U Tapao of Col. John M. Johnson, USMC, designated ground force commander, on the morning of the fourteenth.[36]

ORDER OF BATTLE

The deployment of U.S. forces in response to the seizure of the *Mayaguez* began without orders from Washington. In our account of Frequent Wind, we left the guided missile destroyer *Henry B. Wilson* en route to a liberty call at Kahosiung, Taiwan. In the early morning hours of 13 May she was outbound from Kahosiung for Subic Bay. Commander Rodgers was preparing to turn in for the night when he overheard a BBC report concerning the *Mayaguez* incident on a personal short-wave radio that he kept in his cabin. He ordered all four boilers on line and headed for the Gulf of Siam at maximum speed of thirty-three knots, calling ahead for a tanker to meet *Wilson* off Subic.[37]

As noted above, *Coral Sea* was also within striking range. So were the frigate *Harold E. Holt* and the stores ship *Vega*, posted 100 nautical miles south-southwest of Subic to screen refugee ships fleeing Vietnam. Aboard *Holt* was Rear Admiral Donald P. Roane, commander of Destroyer Squadron 23.[38] At twelve minutes past one on the morning of 13 May local time in the Gulf of Siam, Admiral Weisner's Pacific Fleet Headquarters, in a precautionary move made without approval from Washington, ordered *Coral Sea* and her escorts to proceed to a point 40 nautical miles south-southwest of the Poulo Wai archipelago at best speed.[39] The orders were immediately amended to include *Holt* and *Vega*.[40] The need for swift action in accordance with the first two of President Ford's objectives determined which U.S. forces were available to deal with the crisis. TF-76 had dispersed, and several fleet units potentially within striking distance had maintenance problems. The assault carrier *Okinawa* was limited to eighteen knots by an out-of-commission boiler. The attack carrier *Hancock*, used as a helicopter carrier in the Saigon evacuation, was disabled by a steam valve failure.[41] Neither would be available if President Ford's stringent time criteria were to be met.

We have already addressed the equipment and readiness of the two

Thailand-based American Air Force helicopter units that, by the inexo-rable logic of time, space, and location, were destined to play a central role in whatever military undertaking the president might order. At six o'clock in the evening of 13 May, all available 21st SOS helicopters plus five from the 40th were ordered to deploy to U Tapao. The 40th had two HH-53s on alert at Korat, and one of these was first off, launching at twenty past seven. The other three 40th aircraft launched in formation from Nakhon Phanom at ten minutes past eight, and the first of seven 21st CH-53s to depart that night left at eight-thirty.[42]

Servicing and maintaining the big helicopters called for skills and matériel that were not available at U Tapao. The departing H-53s there-fore carried maintenance personnel with the appropriate specialties and levels of qualification plus an assortment of maintenance stands, tow bars, servicing equipment, spare parts, and bench stock. As a tenant unit with organic maintenance, the 40th was self-sufficient. The squad-ron launched according to a deployment plan in which loads were set up so that maintenance assets would arrive at the deployment destina-tion in order of importance.[43] The 21st and 56th SOW followed proce-dures similar in principle but implemented and supervised at wing level by staff officers not conversant with helicopter operations and mainte-nance. Coordination, therefore, was not as close.[44] The departing 21st SOS helicopters carried volunteer air force security policemen from the 656th Security Police Squadron for use as a boarding party to retake the *Mayaguez*.

Air force tactical strength in Thailand consisted of a mix of fighters, tactical reconnaissance aircraft, side-firing AC-130 gunships, and OV-10 forward air control (FAC) aircraft. Those forces are summarized in table 1 below. In addition, Strategic Air Command (SAC) KC-135 tank-ers based at U Tapao were used to refuel fighters under standard PACAF/SAC operating procedures. U Tapao, the logistic and operational hub of the ensuing operation, was a SAC base. This was significant in several particulars. Base support facilities—air traffic control, communica-tions, maintenance, refueling, munitions, intelligence, briefing facili-ties, and the hospital, for example—were under SAC control. They were consequently oriented to SAC priorities and methods of operation. Fi-nally, there were ARRS local base rescue detachments at Udorn and U Tapao equipped with two HH-43F helicopters each; these were unarmed and could carry only six or eight men or the equivalent in cargo. They lacked the range to reach Koh Tang or the *Mayaguez*.[45]

Logistics and maintenance imposed no significant operational con-straints on fighter, reconnaissance, and gunship units. In-commission rates were good, and there was no shortage of fuel or ordnance.

Air Force Tactical Forces in Thailand [46]	
Udorn RTAFB	
432nd Tactical Fighter Wing (TFW)	
14th Tactical Reconnaissance Squadron (TRS)	*24 X RF-4C*
25th Tactical Fighter Squadron (TFS), 421st TFS	*36 X F-4E*
4th TFS, 13th TFS	*36 X F-4D*
Korat RTAFB	
347th Tactical Fighter Wing	
428th TFS, 429th TFS	18 X F-111A
388th Tactical Fighter Wing	
3rd TFS	18 X F-4E
34th TFS	24 X A-7D
16th SOS	9 X AC-130A, 8 X AC-130H
41st Aerospace Rescue and Recovery Wing	
56th ARRS	5 X HC-130P
Nakhon Phanom RTAFB	
56th Special Operations Wing	
23rd Tactical Air Support Squadron (TASS)	40 X OV-10
21st SOS	10 X CH-53C
41st Aerospace Rescue and Recovery Wing	
40th ARRS	9 X HH-53C

Thailand-based air power does not seem to have been considered for the demonstrative strike role; that mission was allocated to navy carrier-based aircraft or Guam-based B-52s from the outset. In consequence, the number of available fighters and tactical reconnaissance aircraft was more than adequate for any conceivable requirement. Given the preeminence of the first two presidential priorities—recovery of ship and crew and the avoidance of hostage negotiations—any application of aerial firepower in the critical phases of the operation to come would be limited and precise. The limiting factor for fighters under such circumstances would not be numbers. They would be constrained instead by airspace saturation and the ability of crews to see and engage targets.

The AC-130A/H side-firing gunships assigned to the 16th Special Operations Squadron at Korat RTAFB merit additional attention, for the

AC-130 was to prove peculiarly well suited for the ensuing operation. The tactical heart of the AC-130 was a battery of side-firing cannon that fired out of the left side of the aircraft, maneuvered by a sophisticated sensor and fire-control system.[47] The AC-130 had been successful in locating and destroying small, elusive targets at night in interdiction operations over the Ho Chi Minh Trail in southern Laos during 1969–72.[48] In addition, gunships had proved highly effective in providing close support to troops in combat.[49] The large and relatively slow AC-130s were vulnerable to antiaircraft artillery but were equipped with a full passive electronic countermeasures suite and had been able to work effectively at night in a radar-controlled antiaircraft artillery environment along the Ho Chi Minh Trail. The SA-7 Grail surface-to-air missile had posed problems in 1971–72, but the Khymer Rouge were not known to possess them.[50]

The AC-130A was armed with a pair of 20-mm M61 cannon and a pair of 40-mm M2A1 Bofors guns, while the AC-130H carried a pair of 20-mm cannon, a single 40-mm gun, and a 105-mm M102 howitzer. Both versions had a sophisticated fire-control system operated by the pilot, a digital system on the H model and a less reliable and capable analog system on the A. The most significant difference between the two versions was the H model's 105-mm gun.[51] A standard field artillery piece on a specially designed carriage, the 105-mm howitzer was—and is—the largest gun ever mounted on an operational aircraft. AC-130 crews had repeatedly demonstrated its effectiveness in combat. Both versions of the AC-130 were fitted with infrared viewing devices, low-light-level television (LLLTV), and side-looking aerial radar (SLAR) for target acquisition at night. These systems worked equally well in daylight, as did the fire control system. Known as Spectres from their radio call sign, the AC-130 crews were odd men out in the 388th: they were special operations personnel assigned to a tactical fighter wing. If anything, the rivalry between fighter and gunship crews at Korat was more intense than that between rescue and special operations helicopter crews at Nakhon Phanom.

There were more than enough aircraft, fuel, and ordnance available for any conceivable mission or target, and with one exception, logistics were not a problem. That exception was helicopter maintenance. The number of H-53s available was barely adequate, and the H-53 was a notoriously difficult aircraft to maintain.[52] The 21st SOS was able to launch seven CH-53s on the evening of the thirteenth on initial notification and had another one flyable pending maintenance. The 40th had launched three, with another three in commission and two more flyable pending maintenance.[53] It was a creditable showing.

Unless American ground forces were to be committed on the Cambodian mainland, an option that does not seem to have been seriously considered, the firepower represented as described above seemed overwhelming compared to the forces available to the Khymer Rouge. In the end, however, that firepower would assume strategic relevance only as it affected the Americans' ability to place armed men aboard the *Mayaguez* or in a position to rescue her crew. Just what armed men were to be used changed as planning and deployment proceeded. There were no U.S. ground combat units in Thailand, and time was needed to deploy marines. Elements of the 1st Battalion, Fourth Marines (1/4) in the Philippines and the 2nd Battalion, Ninth Marines (2/9), based in Okinawa, were alerted for deployment during the evening of 13 May.[54] A reinforced company from 1/4 (five officers and 115 men) departed Cubi Point by C-141 at a quarter to two in the morning of 14 May and arrived at U Tapao at a quarter to five the same morning. Men from 2/9, organized as a battalion landing team (BLT) under the command of Lt. Col. Randall Austin, USMC, began departing Okinawa at six-fifteen on the morning of the fourteenth and trickled into U Tapao as the day progressed. They arrived between nine-thirty in the morning and eight-thirty that evening.[55] The young marines were keyed up, and few slept on the flight to U Tapao.

The alert order caught G Company of 2/9 in the field, dispersed over three thousand meters of training area. It was between half-past midnight and one o'clock in the morning before the company commander and gunnery sergeant, Capt. James H. Davis and Gy. Sgt. Lester A. McNemar, respectively, could get Golf (marine companies are commonly referred to by their designating letter in the phonetic alphabet) assembled and trucked back to their billets at Camp Schwab. Once there, Davis found a personnel decision awaiting him. It involved one of Golf's marines, a private named K. O. Taylor, who had been in and out of trouble from the time he reported in to the company. Taylor, a black from the Chicago ghetto, had clashed with the first sergeant and done two stints in the brig. The company had submitted Taylor's name for an undesirable discharge, and Davis found it in his "in" basket marked approved. It was an open-and-shut case, but for reasons he could not quite put his finger on, Davis was not convinced that Taylor was a lost cause. The first sergeant with whom Taylor had had problems had rotated, and the young marine had not had problems with Golf's new first sergeant, Larry Funk. In any event, Davis decided to give Taylor the benefit of the doubt. In utter disregard of regulations, he sat on the discharge papers. When Golf deployed, K. O. Taylor went along.[56]

Upon arrival at U Tapao, the marines fell under Colonel Johnson's command. For operational purposes, Johnson reported directly to Lieutenant General Burns at Nakhon Phanom. Technically, navy and marine units were placed under Burns's headquarters for direction and tasking. Otherwise, they remained under their own chain of command extending up through CINCPACFLT to CINCPAC, an arrangement that formalized an appeal channel that would have existed informally in any case.[57]

CHAPTER 4

Plans and Preliminary Operations

BY THE EARLY MORNING HOURS of 15 May, command relationships were established and forces in place that would drive the outcome of the operations to come. But those in command had no way of knowing this, for the situation was fluid. Forces assembled, and command relationships sorted themselves out in a shifting operational scenario that demanded the full concentration of those in charge and those being ordered about. Neither group did as well as they might have: those in charge, because they were saturated with information and requests for facts; those being ordered about, because they assumed that their leaders knew more than they did. That scenario and the way in which it unfolded did much to shape the outcome of the crisis. The Khymer Rouge had little opportunity to redeploy their forces, and we can only speculate on the way in which their policy goals and operational objectives changed during this critical period. With regard to the U.S. forces, however, the record is relatively clear. It is apparent that the initial U.S. actions undertaken in response to the seizure of the *Mayaguez* not only set the stage for the operations of the fifteenth but were the source of much of the information that went into planning them.

PRELIMINARY OPERATIONS

The salient events are quickly summarized.[1] A navy P-3 patrol aircraft at U Tapao on detachment from its home station at Cubi Point in the Philippines was launched on orders from its parent squadron shortly after nine o'clock in the evening on the twelfth. It was followed by a second P-3 from Cubi several hours later.[2] The night was dark, and the squadron commander, J. A. Messegee, had imposed a minimum altitude restriction of six thousand feet. This boundary was established to provide safe clearance from the heaviest antiaircraft guns, 40-mm Bofors, which the Khymer Rouge patrol boats were thought to carry. These disadvantages notwithstanding, the P-3s quickly located two vessels that answered the *Mayaguez's* general description. One of them was dead in the water seven nautical miles off Poulo Wai with two patrol boats tied up alongside.[3] It was the *Mayaguez*. Shortly after dawn, a third P-3 from the Philippines descended to three hundred feet and made a single low-altitude pass one thousand yards off the ship's port side. The navy patrolmen could clearly read *Mayaguez* on the vessel's stern and bow and made positive identification. During the pass the P-3 crew observed small-arms and antiaircraft fire directed at them from patrol boats and the *Mayaguez*. The aircraft sustained a single .50-cal. hit.[4]

At about eight-thirty in the morning on the thirteenth, the *Mayaguez* weighed anchor and got underway in the direction of Kompong Som. Some two hours later, however, the ship slowed and anchored a mile off the northeast tip of Koh Tang, a small, heavily jungled, crucifix-shaped blob of land.[5] The first tactical U.S. Air Force planes, a pair of Korat-based F-111As, arrived in the area several hours later. They were launched in response to Messegee's request for a fighter escort for his P-3s, which was passed on to USSAG through the Joint Chiefs of Staff.[6] Diverted shortly after noon by COMUSSAG/Seventh Air Force as they were preparing to take off for a training mission, the F-111As were armed with practice bombs. They departed on the assumption that the *Mayaguez* was still near Poulo Wai.[7] The escort planes were followed in rotation by flights of F-4 and A-7 fighter-bombers from Korat and Udorn as well as additional F-111s.

Later that afternoon, a small fishing vessel and a patrol boat tied up alongside the container ship. Shortly after 1700, the navy aviators observed some thirty to forty people—a group the size of the *Mayaguez's* crew—sitting on the deck of the fishing vessel with their heads on their knees. Doubts up the chain of command concerning the group's identity were relieved by the observation that they appeared to be Caucasian.[8] There was an element of unconscious irony in this statement, because many of the *Mayaguez's* crew were Asian. Escorted by the patrol boat, the vessel proceeded toward Koh Tang and anchored off the east beach. About 1730 the P-3 crew observed small boats transferring personnel to the beach. Some forty-five minutes later, the crew of a rescue HC-130 saw them moving toward the interior of the island.[9]

Throughout the day, U.S. aircraft continued to receive fire from

Khymer patrol boats and antiaircraft guns on the island. Based on the altitude of tracer burnout, about thirty-five hundred feet, the navy patrol aviators concluded that the largest weapons firing were .50-cal. machine guns. Messegee had imposed his six-thousand- foot altitude restriction on a worst case assumption that some of the Khymer boats mounted 40-mm cannon. Learning that none did, he lowered the altitude limit for his squadron to forty-five hundred feet. But by then the six-thousand-foot restriction had taken on a life of its own. It remained in effect for other units.[10]

During the night AC-130 gunships from Korat joined the P-3s in maintaining surveillance, putting their sophisticated sensors and night-viewing equipment to good use. American aircraft continued to receive fire from Cambodian gunboats and the island throughout the night. By this time, USSAG/Seventh Air Force at Nakhon Phanom, CINCPAC, CINCPACAF, and CINCPACFLT in Hawaii were linked to one another and to the National Military Command Center by the communications net outlined in figure 1 in what amounted to a continuous, secure conference call.[11] USSAG/Seventh Air Force was in continuous contact with aircraft on the scene through Cricket EC-130s and a manual UHF (ultrahigh frequency) relay aboard an overhead U-2. This setup provided what amounted to real-time voice communications within the command net and, on a selective basis, with tactical aircraft on scene (see Appendix A).

By implicit agreement, the navy patrol planes assumed responsibility for tracking ship traffic, and the air force aircraft were responsible for cordoning off the *Mayaguez* and Koh Tang. Orders from the White House to the Department of Defense, relayed by Lieutenant General Scowcroft, were to sink anything coming off Koh Tang. Secretary Schlesinger, concerned with the potential implications of these orders if literally implemented, issued them with an important qualifier. "We should be *prepared*," he ordered, "to sink anything coming off Koh Tang."[12]

To prevent transfer of the crew to the mainland, U.S. aircraft were authorized to fire warning shots ahead of ships departing the island. In the early morning hours of the fourteenth, fire from an AC-130 prompted a patrol boat to run aground on a small islet near Koh Tang. It was the first of many sunk or beached by American air power. The deployment of USAF helicopters and marines to U Tapao had already begun, and *Coral Sea, Harold E. Holt,* and *Wilson* were converging on the Gulf of Siam.

A-7 fighter-bombers relieved the AC-130s at dawn and were on station when a fishing boat escorted by gunboats made a run for the mainland. The fighters dropped bombs in the water ahead of the boat, but to no effect. The A-7s sank the escorting patrol boats and doused the fishing boat with riot-control gas, but it maintained its course toward Kompong Som. Orders from the White House to sink anything coming off Koh Tang remained in effect, but Secretary Schlesinger "kept [his] hand on the phone," stalling for time. At one point a fighter pilot offered to shoot off the vessel's rudder with cannon fire—an impressive feat if he could have pulled it off—only to be refused. Finally, a navy pilot reported that he saw Caucasians on deck, presumably the *Mayaguez's* crew. With the acquiescence of the highest authorities, presumably by a direct presidential order, the fishing boat was allowed to proceed. Schlesinger's hard-nosed skepticism, grasp of operational reality, and refusal to act in a manner he considered premature and imprudent had allowed the boat to continue. As Schlesinger put it later, he had "fluffed off the White House for three hours."[13] It was a critical judgment call, for the crew of the *Mayaguez* was in fact aboard the vessel. Two A-7s watched it enter the port of Kompong Som and dock at about 1015.[14]

During the day, U.S. Marines began to arrive at U Tapao. That night, AC-130 gunships damaged or destroyed several more patrol boats near Koh Tang. Meanwhile, USSAG/Seventh Air Force had come up with a contingency plan: to use air force security policemen to retake the *Mayaguez* by direct helicopter assault at first light on the fourteenth.[15] In response to this plan or in anticipation of it, seventy-five volunteers from the 656th Security Police Squadron at Nakhon Phanom under the squadron commander, Capt. Charles J. Huebusch, were deployed to U Tapao on CINCPAC orders during the evening of the thirteenth.[16] When Major Porter's marines of 1/4 arrived from the Philippines during the morning of 14 May, they replaced the security policemen and were put on standby for the operation. They actually boarded helicopters at noon, only to be told to deplane two hours later.[17] The plan was aborted, and the marines went back on standby.

We can only speculate about the reasons for the abandonment of plans for a direct helicopter assault on the ship and for the use of security police, but the salient considerations are clear: placing troops on a defended ship by helicopter in the teeth of enemy fire would have been an extremely dangerous undertaking. One source maintains that President Ford personally rejected the plan on this basis.[18] The option was definitively put to rest when research determined that the cargo containers on the *Mayaguez* were not strong enough to support the weight of an H-53. The ship would instead be retaken by a boarding party from *Holt*—or, according to later, persistent rumors, by a SEAL team that would depart before the marines came aboard.

Preliminary planning in Thailand was severely disrupted at 2130 hours when the third 21st SOS helicopter to take off, Knife 13, crashed thirty-six miles east of Nakhon Phanom. All five crew members and eighteen security policemen aboard were killed. Beyond the loss of life and a badly needed helicopter, the crash dislocated deployment plans through the diversion of H-53s for rescue and to investigate the crash site. The first Knife reached U Tapao at 2330. The sixth, Knife 51, was brought into commission with a night maintenance check flight and arrived at about 0300 on the fourteenth, flown by a crew led by 1st Lt. Richard Brims.[19] Knife 51 was preceded by two 40th helicopters scrambled from alert at Korat by the Joint Rescue Coordination Center (JRCC) on receiving news of the crash.[20] Overlooked in the confusion, their scramble orders to proceed to the crash site remained in effect, despite their requests for clarification, long after 21st helicopters had landed near Knife 13's wreckage and determined that there were no survivors. The 40th helicopters were diverted on the insistence of the 40th Squadron commander, Lt. Col. Joseph P. McMonigle, only minutes before depleting their fuel reserves below the amount needed to reach U Tapao.[21] They landed at U Tapao sometime before three in the morning.[22] At that point, most of the Knives had been without sleep for twenty-four hours, and the Jolly Greens weren't much better off.[23]

Finally, and probably most important, it became evident that most if not all of the *Mayaguez's* crew had been removed from the ship. There was evidence that they might still be on Koh Tang.[24] If recovery of the crew were to take place ashore, trained infantry would be needed. The security police were only partially trained as infantry, particularly for offensive operations, and lacked heavy weapons. It is probable, of course, that interservice politics played a role in the decision to use marines, and legitimately so: the excellent communications between Nakhon Phanom, the Philippines, Pearl Harbor, and Washington no doubt facilitated the necessary negotiations. However this may be, the decision to use U.S. Marines was justified for the reasons given above.

It was against this backdrop that USSAG/Seventh Air Force, in consultation with higher authorities in Washington, CINCPAC, CINCPACFLT, and CINCPACAF, settled on the final plan: a simultaneous marine assault on the *Mayaguez* and Koh Tang, timed to begin at dawn on 15 May. The time was specified to the minute: 0542G. This was apparently in accordance with JCS planning guidance, transmitted at 1345G (G for Gulf, meaning local time in the Gulf of Siam) on the fourteenth, which called for execution at sunrise.[25] The planning group at U Tapao was given no reason for the insistence on this precise time, which raises two questions: why specify the assault time to the minute? Why specify that particular time?

The first question is easily answered. The specification of a not-earlier-than time to begin combat operations was clearly appropriate because the commanders and staffs involved needed a common reference datum for planning. That datum had to be specified early in the planning process and would unavoidably be arbitrary to a degree. There is no easy answer to the second question. The time chosen would have to meet the president's deadline for decisive action, as it did. It would also have to satisfy the operational and tactical demands of the actions envisioned. Although there was inevitably a certain amount of tension between these two requirements, there were no factors present to make reconciling them particularly difficult. Simply put, the president's requirements were measured in days and hours, not minutes, and the exact timing of the assault was part of a tactical problem best dealt with by those charged with solving it.

In fact, the Joint Chiefs seem to have understood the issue in those terms. The JCS execute order to *Coral Sea* for raids on the Kompong Som naval complex made it plain that they were to occur after the seizure of the *Mayaguez* and the landing of the first marines on Koh Tang.[26] This order provides clear if indirect evidence that the JCS, at least, understood that the helicopter assault was the most critical tactical facet of the operation and should drive the timing in detail. This argument, however, begs the question of why specific times were assigned to specific events. It also does not address the issue of why the planning group at U Tapao was not allowed a degree of flexibility in implementation.

The ability to specify well in advance the initiation of operational events to the minute—or even to the second as, for example, in time-on-target artillery preparations—is part of the profession of arms. There is, moreover, nothing unusual in higher headquarters specifying starting times to the minute where such precision is required to avoid conflict among collateral organizations and to coordinate their actions. The need for such precision in this case is not readily apparent. The principal maneuvers contemplated were the recapture of the *Mayaguez*, the assault on Koh Tang, and retaliatory raids on the Cambodian mainland. The need for simultaneous execution in attacking the ship and island is clear: the *Mayaguez* was anchored within sight of Koh Tang, and an attack on one would alert the defenders of the other. This, however, was a tactical issue best addressed as close to the scene as feasible. So long as the attacks were simultaneous, the precise timing was inconsequential. A competent on-the-scene commander could coordinate the operation, and tactical air power could be held overhead until needed.

Whatever requirement there may have been to precisely synchronize the retaliatory raids with the helicopter operations was clearly not in the tactical or operational domain. It was probably inadvisable to begin bombing before the assault began; the Khymer Rouge, after all, had radios, and surprise would be lost. This, however, was more of a policy and strategy consideration than a tactical one. If the Khymer Rouge was able to intercept and analyze U.S. radio transmissions, or if a friendly power passed such intelligence on to them, the U.S. preparations at U Tapao must have been transparent. Moreover, the helicopters would have to fly over or near Khymer Rouge patrol boats and outposts en route to their objectives. Because the timing of a tactical surprise would be all but impossible to achieve, the operational and tactical interaction between the retaliatory bombings and helicopter assaults was effectively nonexistent. So long as the bombing did not politically compromise the helicopter attacks, precisely when it began was irrelevant. The tactical issue was not so much how to preserve surprise but what to do when it was lost.

Military history has few tactical lessons of enduring value specific to arms and method. One of those few is that although assaulting infantry can benefit enormously from surprise, assault tactics designed to fully exploit surprise are by nature risky. If surprise is lost, the infantry almost invariably pays a high price in casualties unless supported by immediate, heavy, and effective firepower. Surprise can be obtained by doing the unexpected in an almost limitless number of ways—notably through tactics and direction—but timing is a key ingredient. This returns us to the relevance of the specified assault time. Our only clue is the association with sunrise in the JCS message cited above: sunrise at Koh Tang on 15 May was at 0546G, four minutes later than the time specified. Barring an attempt to exploit the glare of the rising sun to blind the enemy—and the marines would attack the island from east and west simultaneously—the relevant factor for the aviator and infantryman is dawn, when the pilot can fly visually and the soldier can see the terrain. On 15 May, dawn broke at Koh Tang twenty to thirty minutes before sunrise.[27] At Koh Tang's latitude on that date, 0542G corresponded to sunrise at a point precisely one degree of longitude east of Koh Tang. This raises suspicions of a simple error in calculation in the basement of the Pentagon or the antechambers of the NMCC. The question remains unanswered.

Whatever the rationale, the specified assault time drove the entire planning process, and the reasons for it should have been made clear to the planners at U Tapao. Moreover, if those reasons were compelling, they should have become apparent after the fact. That they were not, and are not, suggests an unpardonable rigidity on the part of those who specified the time to begin with. Ironically, the helicopters were ready to launch on time but were held on the ground at U Tapao at the last minute, apparently by high echelon intervention.

INTELLIGENCE AND ENEMY ORDER OF BATTLE

The forces available to the Khymer Rouge to oppose the U.S. military action were limited: a handful of patrol vessels, mostly former U.S. Navy Swift boats, small craft intended for inshore work; and a company-sized force of infantry on Koh Tang. Against these sparse resources the Khymer Rouge could, if they were so inclined, balance the fact that they had control of both ship and crew and could probably conceal the location of the latter.

By the evening of the fourteenth, U.S. planners could be reasonably certain that most if not all of the *Mayaguez's* crew were no longer aboard the vessel. It must also have been apparent that some of the crew, and perhaps all, had been taken from Koh Tang to the mainland: that much was clearly implied by air force pilots' reports on the fourteenth. But it was by no means clear that the entire crew had been taken from the island or from the ship. Confusion on the point is partially attributable to the fact that two vessels were used to transfer the crew from the vessel to Koh Tang, while the Americans were taken to Kompong Som by only one. In either case, the possibility that some members might be still on Koh Tang could not be excluded. We are hampered in our analysis by lack of access to classified intelligence reports, particularly those involving intercepted radio communications, but less so than might be supposed. If such reports gave, or appeared to give, definitive information about the crew's location, it would have been difficult or impossible to verify their credibility in the time available. Because some of the crew might still be on Koh Tang, seizing and searching the island was thus a valid operational objective. Seizure of the island was also a meaningful goal in policy terms, since the commitment of U.S. ground forces would signal American resolve far more eloquently than aerial bombardment. In short, it is difficult to imagine intelligence that would have dismissed the invasion of Koh Tang as a legitimate objective.

Two independent intelligence estimates of Khymer Rouge strength on Koh Tang were available to U.S. planners. These varied in detail but closely agreed in their essentials. The first, by Commander Intelligence Pacific (IPAC), estimated that the island was held by between ninety and one hundred infantry supported by a heavy-weapons squad of ten to fifteen, armed with an 82-mm mortar, a 75-mm recoilless rifle, three machine guns, and RPGs (rocket-propelled grenade launchers). The second, by the Defense Intelligence Agency (DIA), estimated a force of one hundred fifty to two hundred with a somewhat larger complement of heavy weapons—an understrength battalion in prevailing *Khmer Kraham* tables of organization.[28] Given the limited number of helicopters available and the fact that some of them would be needed to carry a boarding party to *Holt* to recapture the *Mayaguez*, the size of the assault force that could be placed on the island in the first lift was barely larger than the force they were attacking, even according to the more optimistic IPAC estimate. This was in clear violation of a marine rule of thumb: in offensive ground combat, the attacker should outnumber the defender by at least three to one.

In light of the enormous amount of supporting aerial firepower available, the problem should have been manageable with proper planning. That having been said, the similarity in size between assault force and defenders that intelligence indicated would surely have caused second thoughts about the operation had it been known to Baxter's planning group. As it happened, the intelligence was irrelevant: neither the IPAC nor DIA estimate was briefed to Baxter's group or to the assault force, and there is no evidence that it was available to the ABCCC battle staff. This is bitterly ironic, for the information was surprisingly accurate—indeed remarkably so, given the rapid development, unexpected nature, and unanticipated location of the crisis. After the battle, Lieutenant Colonel Austin, who commanded the marines on the island, estimated that he had been opposed by about one hundred fifty professional soldiers, well equipped with small arms, machine guns, recoilless rifles, and mortars. This was a thoroughly credible appraisal in light of his experience as a company commander in Vietnam and well within the range set by the two estimates.[29]

Nor was the failure to disseminate the IPAC and DIA estimates—which will be discussed further later on—the only U.S. intelligence lapse. During the previous twenty-four hours, American aircrews had observed and reported fire from guns of .50 caliber or larger from Koh Tang at least twice. During the afternoon of the fourteenth, a flight of two Jolly Greens was dispatched from U Tapao on a rescue mission with ill-defined objectives, apparently to "rescue" the survivors of a sunken Khymer patrol boat. Unaware of the plan to assault Koh Tang the next morning, they flew directly over the island and observed tracers, which they reported as 23-mm, rising from the island.[30] The crews in question had worked the maximum number of hours permitted by U.S. Air Force regulations in a twenty-four-hour period and were released from duty. They were asleep when the assault force briefed and took off the next morning. Their report was lost in the absence of arrangements at U Tapao for intelligence debriefing of the helicopter crews. During the night of 13–14 May, the crew of an AC-130 orbiting above the island observed large tracers rising toward their aircraft from a position near the cove on the northwestern corner of the island (map 3). The aircraft commander, Lt. Col. David Mets, operations officer of the 16th SOS, requested permission to return fire but was refused by Cricket.[31]

Unknowingly echoing Commander Messegee's earlier suspicions, Mets reported the gun as 40-mm, based on the size of the tracers and their velocity. This was markedly slower than that of rounds from heavy machine guns in the .50-cal. class with which he was familiar from gunship experience in Vietnam. The size of antiaircraft tracers can be deceptive, especially at night, when visual cues for size comparison and distance estimation are obscured. Similarly, the apparent rate of fire, which Mets observed to be low, is inconclusive in differentiating between fire from a heavy machine gun—in this case, most likely a 12.7-mm weapon of Soviet design (the projectile sizes and capabilities of .50-cal. and 12.7-mm weapons are effectively the same)—and that of a larger, slower-firing piece in isolation. This is true because only a fraction of machine-gun rounds are tracers, and what that fraction might have been is unknown. Still, Mets's combat experience makes it difficult to discount his estimate. What is clear is that *something* bigger than small arms was firing up from the island. Moreover, whatever that something was, it was firing from an antiaircraft mount, a carriage designed for all-around traverse emplaced in an open pit for overhead fire.

Mets's observation was reported to 388th Tactical Fighter Wing intelligence at Korat. It never reached the planning group at U Tapao.

In retrospect, it is unlikely that the *Khmer Kraham* defenders of Koh Tang were equipped with antiaircraft artillery; that is, specialized antiaircraft weapons with bore diameters of 20-mm or larger firing explosive shells. That conclusion, however, is based on information that was unavailable at the time; namely, after-action reports and inspection of battle damage sustained by surviving aircraft. The conclusion applies, moreover, only to ordnance that actually engaged American aircraft on 15 May. We cannot, therefore, categorically rule out the possibility that one or more of the reports cited above was accurate.[32] More directly, technical debates over the presence or absence of antiaircraft artillery on Koh Tang miss the point: there was abundant and unequivocal evidence from the beginning that antiaircraft weaponry of at least .50-cal./ 12.7-mm *was* present.[33] Weapons in this category are brutally effective against helicopters. Indeed, most professional observers would have considered a helicopter assault against a position defended by .50 cal./ 12.7-mm machine guns firing on antiaircraft mounts from open pits near suicidal unless heavy suppressive fire were employed.

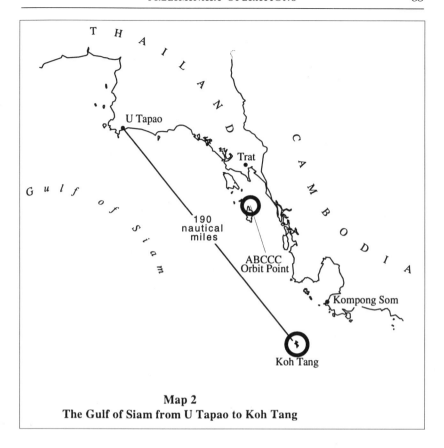

Map 2
The Gulf of Siam from U Tapao to Koh Tang

TIME, SPACE, AND GEOGRAPHIC FACTORS

The overriding spatial consideration in the operation was the distance of 190 nautical miles from U Tapao to Koh Tang. By pushing the normal cruise speed of 120 knots, an H-53 could reach the island an hour and thirty-five minutes after takeoff from U Tapao. This translated into a cycle time of about four hours to reach the island, off-load, and return.[34] This was a significant constraint, because the available helicopters could carry only about a third of the assault force in a single lift.

In addition, the helicopters were fuel limited. Special operations CH-53s, unable to refuel in flight, were constrained by a total endurance of six and a half hours. The equivalent figure for the HH-53s was four and a half hours. The distances are depicted on map 2.[35] Because helicopter fuel consumption varies as a function of gross weight instead of with airspeed and altitude, as with fixed-wing aircraft, the helicopters would consume a disproportionate amount of fuel on the outbound leg.[36] The CH-53s would have about two hours of loiter time over the island. Unless they topped off by aerial refueling on the way in, the HH-53s, with smaller external auxiliary tanks, would have none at all. The Jolly Greens would refuel en route to Koh Tang as a routine precaution, but aerial refueling complicated coordination between the Jolly Greens and Knives.

The dependence of both special operations and rescue H-53s on external fuel to reach the objective also had important ramifications concerning vulnerability to battle damage. H-53s carry only about an hour and thirty minutes of fuel in their internal tanks, not counting a small reserve for approach and landing.[37] The rest is carried externally. External fuel is transferred from the tanks by pneumatic pressure bled from the compressor stages of the turbine engines, and an external tank with even a small hole in it cannot be pressurized. Therefore, a single 7.62-mm hit in an external tank would render the fuel inside unusable. An H-53 over Koh Tang could make it back to U Tapao without external fuel, but only just—and only if it started back immediately. If it had to land first, and especially if it had to hover for an extended period, it would probably be unable to make the return flight unless it were an HH-53 and could refuel in flight.

The critical importance of the thinness of helicopter fuel reserves, particularly if encountering hostile fire, does not seem to have been appreciated by the planners. During the event, the helicopter crews coped with this problem with uniformly professional competence, ably assisted by the HC-130 King crews in the case of the rescue helicopters. Ironically, the very competence with which the aircrews managed their fuel has obscured the narrowness of the margin between success and failure.

Weather was not a major factor. The *Mayaguez* was seized during the transition from the northeast to the southwest monsoon, and sustained periods of heavy rain and low ceilings were not in prospect. Isolated thunderstorms were a possibility and might interfere with flight operations or even halt them for a time—as nearly happened during the Saigon evacuation—but generally good flying weather and reasonably dry ground conditions could be expected and, in fact, prevailed. The tidal rise and fall in the Gulf of Thailand is only about two and a half feet.[38] Perhaps for this reason, the planners did not take the tides into account. This oversight, together with the lack of good maps, affected the operation. The planning group's visual reconnaissance of the island on the afternoon of the fourteenth took place not long after low water. It showed Koh Tang's shallow beaches to be relatively wide.

An H-53 rescue helicopter, spring 1975. Though difficult to maintain, the H-53 was a highly capable machine, respected by its crews for its power and survivability. Air force versions of the H-53, however, were flawed, leading to the destruction of three aircraft by May 1975. A fourth air force H-53 would go down on the night of 13 May with no survivors. (USAF photo)

Air force H-53s of the 21st Special Operations Squadron and 40th Aerospace Rescue and Recovery Squadron landing aboard USS Midway, 20 April 1975. Note the generous deck space given the air force helicopters by Midway's deck crew: normal Navy tolerance was two feet between rotor tips. (USAF photo)

An H-53 coming aboard **Midway**, *20 May 1975. Note the open cockpit side window at left: The cockpit windows were closed in flight, and emergency exit involved jettisoning the entire window and frame. The cockpit window was a tight fit, particularly for a broad-shouldered pilot wearing a parachute. (USAF photo)*

The deck of the USS **Midway**, *loaded with air force H-53s, replenishing at sea before Frequent Wind. Unlike Marine Corps H-53s, the air force birds lacked mechanisms for folding and stowing the blades and tail rotor on the fuselage. As a result, air force H-53s required an inordinate amount of deck space by Navy standards. (USAF)*

Vietnamese refugees deplaning an Air America UH-1 aboard USS Midway, *29 April 1975. Few Americans who participated in the evacuation were unmoved by the experience. (USAF photo)*

The Mayaguez *at anchor, probably taken from a Navy P-3 on the morning of the 13th. (USAF photo)*

The author, second from right, and his crew aboard USS **Midway** shortly after the Saigon evacuation. S.Sgt. Robert G. Bounds, far right, served as a flight mechanic aboard Jolly Green 44 during extraction operations from Koh Tang on the night of 15 May. Capt. Martin A. Nickerson, in sunglasses behind author, was copilot of Jolly Green 12 during the second wave insertions on 15 May. Pararescueman S.Sgt. Steven W. Lemminn, far left, was ramp gunner aboard Jolly Green 13 during the first, unsuccessful, attempt to extract the isolated group from the east beach on the morning of the 15th; he saved his aircraft by jettisoning a burning flare case. Pararescueman A1c David Reich is second from left, and flight mechanic A1c George Hodges is third from left. Neither flew in the Koh Tang—Mayaguez operation. (USAF photo)

View of a Rescue KC-130 tanker from the cockpit of an HH-53 prior to aerial refueling. Note the drogue on the end of the refueling hose at right: The doughnut-shaped fabric ring with its heavy wire supports stabilized the hose and provided a target for the refueling probe. Since the probe was on the right side of their fuselage, helicopters normally refueled from the left drogue providing about six feet additional clearance between the main rotor and the tanker's horizontal stabilizer. (USAF photo)

The village off the east beach, taken by a low-flying RF-4 probably about noon on the 14th; the shadow of the reconnaissance aircraft appears in the lower right. Before the fall of Phnom Penh, the village was a radio communications site and a small fishing community. (USAF photo)

The specified assault time of 0542 local time in the Gulf of Siam drove the planning from beginning to end.[39]

Tactically, the single most important geographic factor was the nature of the terrain on which the assault force would land and fight. Koh Tang was a small, irregularly shaped island just under three and a half nautical miles long and two nautical miles across at its widest point. The only inhabited area was a small fishing village adjacent to the cove on the northeastern corner of the island. The cove, the village, and a cove on the northwestern side of the island were connected by a strip of cleared land approximately four hundred meters long. Except for the cleared strip and the beaches, the island was covered with an extremely dense jungle, which restricted visibility on the ground to between ten and fifteen feet.[40] The vegetation was effectively impenetrable to aerial photography, and coverage by Udorn-based RF-4Cs produced no useful order of battle information.[41] The beaches were rocky in most places, especially on the western side, sloping abruptly upward into the jungle. The east beach could accommodate H-53s, but the west beach was appreciably narrower. An H-53 could land on the west beach when the tide was low, as it would at dawn on the fifteenth, but barely. When the tide was high, as it would be later that day, the big helicopters could load and unload only by landing in the water or by backing up to the island to present their cargo ramps to the beach.

A final, critical geographic factor about the island concerned maps: tactically speaking, there were none.[42] On aeronautical charts, Koh Tang appeared as a small, misshapen crucifix with no information beyond its approximate outline and the maximum elevation of 440 feet MSL (above mean sea level). No other published maps were available. Koh Tang was photographed by American Air Force reconnaissance platforms before the assault, and outline maps were developed from the photographs. Raw aerial photographs and sketch maps, however, are no substitute for proper tactical charts. The lack of gridded charts with the terrain information essential to infantry maneuvers and naval gunfire support would pose major problems throughout the operation.

PLANS

By late evening of the thirteenth, it was clear that recapture of the *Mayaguez* by air force security policemen would not work. But the situation was changing rapidly, and plans for a security police helicopter assault on the ship had not been ruled out when the first marines began touching down at U Tapao.[43] At the same time, the problem of landing H-53s on the *Mayaguez's* cargo containers surfaced, and the option of boarding from *Holt* was broached. Ship-to-ship boarding operations

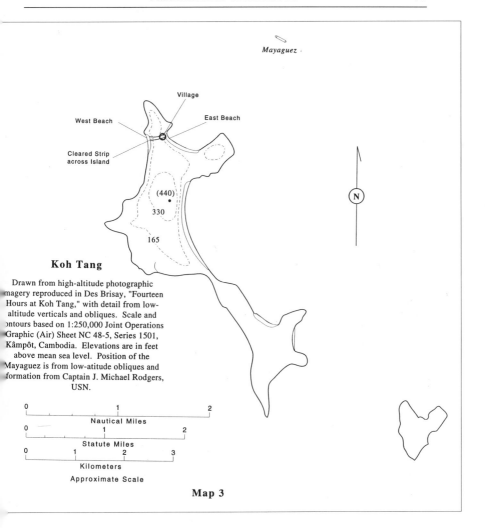

Mayaguez

Village

West Beach

East Beach

Cleared Strip
across Island

(440)
•
330

165

Koh Tang

Drawn from high-altitude photographic
imagery reproduced in Des Brisay, "Fourteen
Hours at Koh Tang," with detail from low-
altitude verticals and obliques. Scale and
contours based on 1:250,000 Joint Operations
Graphic (Air) Sheet NC 48-5, Series 1501,
Kâmpôt, Cambodia. Elevations are in feet
above mean sea level. Position of the
Mayaguez is from low-atitude obliques and
formation from Captain J. Michael Rodgers,
USN.

N

0   1   2
Nautical Miles
0   1   2
Statute Miles
0   1   2   3
Kilometers
Approximate Scale

Map 3

posed their own hazards: the *Holt* was a single-screw vessel, unable to use opposed propellers to control heading at low speed, and her bridge crew would be faced with a difficult ship-handling problem.[44] But *Holt* was far less vulnerable to small-arms fire than the helicopters, and that choice seemed safer. The boarding party could be transferred to *Holt* by helicopter from U Tapao, despite limited air force familiarity with shipboard operations and the small size of *Holt's* helicopter pad.[45]

The prospect of landing ground forces on the mainland was apparently never seriously entertained, and the initial planning at U Tapao revolved around recapture of the *Mayaguez*.[46] The idea of landing troops on Koh Tang surfaced late—no earlier than the afternoon of the four-teenth for those who would have to plan and execute the undertaking. By that point, it was clear to Johnson and Austin that BLT 2/9 would conduct the Koh Tang operation. Austin picked Golf Company to lead the attack and charged Captain Davis with preparing the assault plan. Marine Corps doctrine was attuned to such operations and schedules but assumed marine or navy air support. Neither was available, and the time to work out the alternatives was running short. The lack of rele-vant information became starkly evident at the first planning meeting following the decision to attack Koh Tang, when Davis asked for photo-graphs of the island. There were none. Baxter had been offered the ser-vices of an army U-21 twin turboprop (the military version of the Beechcraft King Air) for a reconnaissance of the island, but it had no cameras either. Davis volunteered his own 35mm Minolta, and an air force enlisted man was dispatched to the Base Exchange for high-speed Ektachrome film.[47]

Late that afternoon the U-21 flew over Koh Tang, carrying Baxter; Anders; Johnson; Austin; Maj. John B. Hendricks, 2/9's operations officer; Davis; 1st Lt. John J. Martinoli and 1st Lt. Terry Tonkin, the battalion's two forward air controllers; and McGowin. Descending to forty-five hundred feet despite the still-standing six-thousand-foot alti-tude restriction, they could make out little more than the outline of the island.[48] Davis took some photographs with his Minolta.[49] These were quickly developed but were of little value, serving only to confirm that the island was heavily jungled and the beaches were narrow. The prem-ission planning was done on outline maps prepared from aerial photo-graphs, probably U-2 imagery.

Meanwhile, preparations to get the marines to their objectives, what-ever they might be, proceeded. At the same time that the first H-53s arrived at U Tapao, a small ad hoc helicopter maneuvers section was set up in the base operations building adjacent to the flight line. Manned by a combination of 56th SOW and 40th officers and NCOs (noncom-missioned officers), it became the focal point for flight scheduling and for coordinating aircraft maintenance and servicing. The section had minimal communications: a portable HF single-sideband radio, access to the base telephone system, and the normal aggregation of "bricks": short-range, hand-held radios for flight-line coordination.[50] Helicopter operations and preparations were Colonel Anders's responsibility, but he and his principal deputy, Lieutenant Colonel Pannell, spent the bulk of their time with Baxter's group. The helicopter operations section functioned more or less autonomously.

Johnson's orders to Austin were straightforward: BLT 2/9 was to seize, occupy, and search Koh Tang while 1/4 boarded the Mayaguez.[51] The inexorable logic of airframe availability and H-53 in-commission rates decreed that there would be only a dozen or so H-53s available for the first wave, each capable of carrying between twenty and twenty-seven men. Three of these would take the boarding party to *Holt*. The remainder would transport the Koh Tang force.

When he chose G Company to lead the attack and charged Davis with drawing up the plan, Austin envisioned a four- to five-day campaign involving his entire battalion landing team. Austin considered Captain Davis a good leader, but he had no compelling reason for selecting Golf.[52] His choice left an indelible mark on the operation, for Golf had its particular strengths, weaknesses, and tactical style.

Frequent Wind had hit Golf by temporarily drafting forty-seven of its men to fill out other units. Shortly before the *Mayaguez* was seized, forty-two of the borrowed men had been returned, but they had not trained with the unit. Of G Company's officers, only Davis had seen combat. Just nine of Golf's NCOs had combat experience: the company first sergeant, Funk; the company gunnery sergeant, McNemar; First Platoon's platoon sergeant, Seferino Bernal, Jr.; Second Platoon's platoon sergeant, Fofo T. Tutele; S.Sgt. Francis L. Burnette; S.Sgt. Clay Pruitt, and three other sergeants.[53] In the business at hand, McNemar played a key role: as company gunnery sergeant (the term is a job description and title as well as a rank), he had primary responsibility for training. As the company commander's executive agent, he was responsible for operational planning and execution. McNemar and Davis had rotated together in November.

In the process of learning the unit and its men, Davis and McNemar found that they functioned well together as a team. They worked Golf's young marines hard, keeping them in the field and out of Kadena's bars and bathhouses to maximize training and minimize disciplinary problems. They had no illusions about the state of training of their men: in Davis's view, the company was just beginning to come together as a cohesive unit. Nevertheless, Davis and McNemar were confident that Golf was as good a company as 2/9 possessed.[54] Their confidence would soon be tested.

Marine planning for the attack on Koh Tang began with the realization that 2/9's infantry would be totally dependent on the air force for fire support. A battery of 4.2-inch mortars had been deployed to U Tapao, but the bulky tubes and heavy ammunition would displace a disproportionate number of infantry. This was a particular problem in light of the limited number of troops that the available helicopters could carry in a single lift. In any case, carrying such heavy firepower could not be justified while the logistic penalties and tactical disadvantages of deploying the big mortars were clearly apparent. Their use does

not seem to have been considered. The heaviest firepower available to
2/9 on Koh Tang would be the battalion's organic 81-mm mortars.[55]

The original marine plan was for an assault on the center of the
cleared strip across the northern tip of the island. With the full benefit
of hindsight it was a good plan, assuming that the entire first wave could
be inserted quickly. But U.S. Air Force sources rejected the idea on the
grounds that the cleared area was too small and had too many obstacles.
Several air force C-130s equipped with AWADS (adverse weather aerial
delivery systems) had been deployed to U Tapao carrying fifteen-
thousand-pound BLU-82 bombs, which could be used to blast landing
zones out of the jungle. Their use was rejected, however, out of concern
for the safety of the *Mayaguez's* crew.[56] Austin therefore directed Davis
to plan for an insertion on the northern beaches. Those along the eastern cove were appreciably wider. They were also closer to the village,
which was to be the initial focus of search operations, so most of the
first wave would go into the east beach. Davis designated five LZs along
the eastern beach and two along the western one.[57] His plan was to put
a platoon-sized blocking force on the western side of the island and use
the bulk of G Company to drive across from the east beach. After seizing the northern peninsula as a base of operations and bringing the rest
of the battalion ashore, 2/9 would drive south to seize Hill 440, the
highest point on the island.

In retrospect, the suitability of the east beach for helicopter LZs was
as apparent to the Khymer Rouge as it was to the American Marines.
The *Khmer Kraham* were well dug in along the beaches on both sides
of the northern neck of the island, but the defenses on the east beach
were heavier. They were supported by a patrol boat sitting on the bottom of the cove with decks awash and guns functional. Sunk earlier, it
had been crossed off the enemy order of battle by U.S. intelligence. The
planners at U Tapao discussed preparatory fire support, but to no avail—
and in the haste of the moment, misunderstanding was born. The marines thought that preparatory fire would be provided, or at least on
immediate call. During the event, it was not. The only workable arrangement for providing fire support on call depended on the BLT 2/9
air liaison team, which was to be inserted into the east beach with the
initial assault. Aside from emphasizing concern for the safety of the
Mayaguez's crew, a valid consideration, air force sources are noncom-
mittal about the reasons for the failure.

The air support plan was developed by USSAG/Seventh Air Force:
the 432nd at Udorn and 388th at Korat would provide tactical air coverage with formations of fighters flying in rotation over the island. In accordance with standard American Air Force procedures, the details were
worked out in advance and transmitted to the flying squadrons through

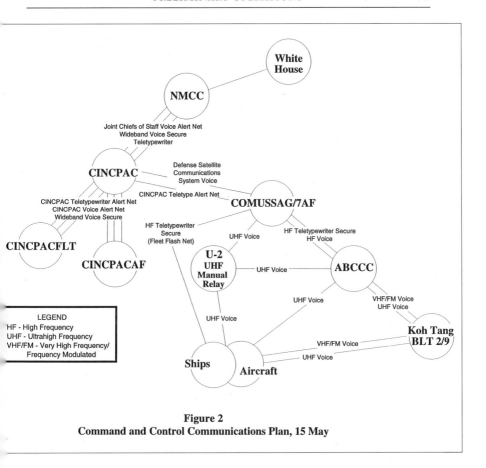

Figure 2
Command and Control Communications Plan, 15 May

their parent wings by means of detailed fragmentary orders (so called because each unit's order was a fragment of the total, comprehensive order) specifying takeoff times, ordnance loads, times on target, and aerial refueling information. Inherent in the plan was the concept of an on-scene commander. At all times, a pilot designated as on-scene commander would be over Koh Tang to control the air battle and to serve as a link between ABCCC and tactical air elements. The Korat-based A-7s had VHF/FM radios compatible with marine tactical radios and were tasked to provide on-scene command. Plans were made to load A-7s with canisters of riot-control gas to suppress resistance on the *Mayaguez* before boarding. The communications plan, outlined in figure 2, was elaborated to provide linkage between the tactical forces and USSAG.

The OV-10s of the 23rd Tactical Air Support Squadron remained at Nakhon Phanom. This, like the absence of immediate on-call air support for the assault force, is not easily explained. Experience in Vietnam led most professional military observers to conclude that in general, jet fighters could not provide ground forces with effective close support unless controlled by a forward air controller (FAC). Jets moved too fast for pilots to see ground targets clearly enough to distinguish friend from foe in dense jungle and hit the latter without endangering the former. The same considerations applied to fire support for helicopters and had prompted the formation of dedicated RESCORT units, originally formed with propeller-driven A-1s. Ground FACs were an effective solution but required special training and special radios, and there were never enough of them. Interservice communications difficulties, not least among them the incompatibility of tactical radios, added to the problem.

The solution was the airborne FAC flying a slow-moving aircraft. Military fixed-wing pilots, especially fighter pilots, possessed most of the necessary skills ab initio, and the airborne FAC was an obvious and tactically elegant solution. In Clausewitzian terms, it was an effective means of reducing friction. In Vietnam, air force FACs flying piston-engined Cessna O-1s and O-2s, and later turboprop OV-10s, served as an effective link between air force jet fighter-bombers and ground troops in contact. It was against this background that squadrons such as the 23rd TASS were formed.

The problem and solution described above were essentially an army-air force matter, but the Marine Corps had arrived at the same basic solution by another route. Marines routinely used their own ground and air FACs to regulate naval gunfire and tactical air power in close support of troops in combat (the OV-10 was developed in response to a marine requirement). Austin's force included a naval gunfire liaison/FAC team. But air force and marine doctrines and procedures differed. Also, BLT 2/9 had only one such team. The arrangement was workable, but only if things went according to plan, as they rarely do in combat. An element of OV-10s on station would have been reasonable insurance.

When 2/9 went in, on-scene command over Koh Tang was assigned to FAC-qualified A-7 pilots who had trained with the Jolly Greens. Their tactical orientation, however, was as fighter pilots instead of specialized FACs. Even their hands-on RESCORT training was sketchy. Most combat-experienced Jolly Green pilots questioned the effectiveness of the A-7 in that role because of the difficulty in maintaining continuous visual contact with low-flying helicopters and acquiring and quickly engaging targets on the ground from a fast-moving jet.[58] The A-7's limited low-altitude loiter time, a product of high jet-engine fuel consumption at low altitudes, was a consideration as well. These factors figured prominently in the Koh Tang assault.

There was a final option: the AC-130 Spectre. Although Spectre flights over the Ho Chi Minh Trail had been confined to darkness by high-firing antiaircraft artillery, the aircraft's fire control system worked equally well in daylight. It was, moreover, deadly accurate (jokes about placing 105-mm rounds in enemy soldiers' hip pockets were not entirely specious). The AC-130 could fire effectively from ten thousand feet, safely above the range of anything possessed by the Khymer Rouge on or near Koh Tang. But fighters were at the top of the tactical air force pecking order and gunships were at the bottom, just above helicopters and well below FACs. Perhaps for this reason and perhaps because Spectre was traditionally considered a specialized weapon of night combat, AC-130s would not be overhead when the assault force went in. When dawn broke on 15 May an AC-130, Spectre 61, was on station above Koh Tang. It departed for Korat minutes before the helicopters started their approaches, relinquishing on-scene command to a flight of A-7s.[59]

FINAL PLANS AND PREPARATIONS

The 0542 assault time meant that the helicopters would have to launch from U Tapao at about 0400, so final planning activities were rushed. Brigadier General Baxter's planning group at U Tapao held a final meeting at seven in the evening of the fourteenth. Anders, having spent some thirty hours on the go, was absent.[60] The group reviewed the situation and finalized plans. Eleven helicopters were available: six Jolly Greens and five Knives. The *Holt* would be in position to accept the *Mayaguez* boarding party, which would be taken out from U Tapao by three Jolly Greens. The boarding party was to consist of fifty-nine marines of 1/4 plus six Military Sealift Command volunteers, two air force experts on explosive ordnance disposal, and an army Cambodian linguist.[61]

In accordance with Austin's orders, Davis finalized the Koh Tang attack plan. He would lead a reinforced platoon onto the west beach as a blocking force. The balance of G Company, supported by a section of 81-mm mortars and accompanied by Austin's command group and the BLT forward air control party, would go onto the east beach.[62] Five Knives and three Jolly Greens would land the first wave on Koh Tang: 177 men of BLT 2/9 plus three army translators.[63] The main force under Austin would drive along the cleared strip across the northern neck of the island to link up with the blocking force. The combined force would then clear the northern peninsula before driving south to seize Hill 440 and sweep the island. Meanwhile, the helicopters would recycle, bring-

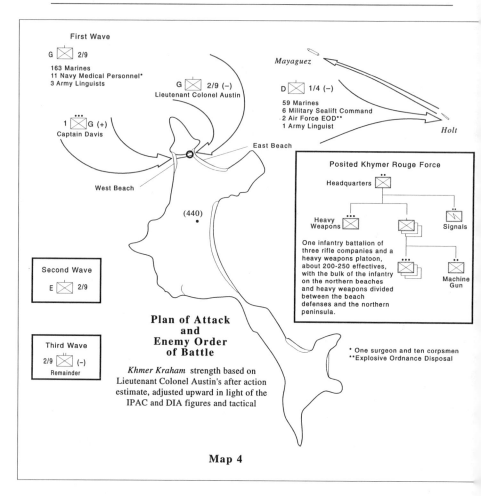

First Wave

G ⊠ 2/9

163 Marines
11 Navy Medical Personnel*
3 Army Linguists

G ⊠ 2/9 (–)
Lieutenant Colonel Austin

Mayaguez

D ⊠ 1/4 (–)

59 Marines
6 Military Sealift Command
2 Air Force EOD**
1 Army Linguist

Holt

1 ⊠ G (+)
Captain Davis

East Beach

West Beach

(440)
•

Posited Khymer Rouge Force

Headquarters ⊠

Heavy
Weapons ⊠   ⊠   Signals

One infantry battalion of
three rifle companies and a
heavy weapons platoon,
about 200-250 effectives,
with the bulk of the infantry
on the northern beaches
and heavy weapons divided
between the beach
defenses and the northern
peninsula.

Machine
Gun

Second Wave

E ⊠ 2/9

Third Wave

2/9 ⊠ (–)
Remainder

**Plan of Attack
and
Enemy Order
of Battle**

Khmer Kraham strength based on
Lieutenant Colonel Austin's after action
estimate, adjusted upward in light of the
IPAC and DIA figures and tactical

* One surgeon and ten corpsmen
**Explosive Ordnance Disposal

Map 4

ing E Company to the island in the second wave and the remainder of
2/9 in the third. To maximize the fighting strength available to Austin
in the first wave, Johnson elected to hold his command group at U Tapao until later. In doing so he recognized that he was in effect turning
over command of the force to ABCCC.[64]

Gunnery Sergeant McGowin briefed intelligence: the expected opposition on the island consisted of some twenty to thirty Khymer Rouge
irregulars.[65] In accordance with air force custom and regulation, the helicopter crews had been put in crew rest to conserve them physically
and mentally for the morrow. None was present at the meeting.[66] The
40th had detailed an experienced Jolly Green pilot, Capt. Vernon Shef-

field, as squadron operations coordinator. But as part of the ad hoc section at base operations, he was fully absorbed with preliminary flight planning, air refueling coordination, tracking aircraft maintenance status, matching crews and projected loads against aircraft, and other duties. Sheffield was not invited to the meeting.[67] Neither were ABCCC representatives, a curious omission considering Cricket's key role in the operation.

At this point, control over operations in the Gulf of Siam was being exercised through an ABCCC aircraft. It had launched from U Tapao shortly after four in the afternoon following some twelve hours on the ground and was to remain on station until 0435 on the fifteenth.[68] Although the official unit history skirts the issue, a second EC-130 and battle staff under Col. James M. Shankles, deployed ABCCC force commander, landed at U Tapao about six o'clock in the evening of 14 May and did not take off again until about two o'clock in the afternoon on the fifteenth.[69] Shankles and his battle staff were thus on hand when the critical briefings occurred and attack plans were finalized. That they were not included speaks poorly for all concerned, particularly Shankles, whose responsibility it was to apprise those in charge of planning the operation how his men and aircraft could help.

In the interim, Baxter and Johnson sought information about defenses on the island, going so far as to locate and interview a former Lon Nol Khymer Navy officer in the refugee camp near U Tapao. He told them that the normal population of the island consisted of some twenty to thirty armed irregulars defending a communications site. It wasn't much to go on, but the numbers coincided with those of preliminary intelligence estimates, reinforcing their credibility. It was this figure that McGowin briefed. The IPAC and DIA assessments were available to USSAG and 307th Strategic Wing intelligence at U Tapao on the fourteenth but were never passed on to the assault force.[70] The reasons are unclear. Col. Alfred Merrill, 307th director of intelligence, approached Baxter in the early morning hours of the fourteenth with current information. Merrill, apparently believing that an infantry assault on the mainland was being contemplated, was deeply concerned with the overwhelming strength of Khymer Rouge ground forces there. Baxter, preoccupied with the problems confronting him and struck by Merrill's negative attitude, dismissed him.[71] There is no convincing evidence that Merrill or his staff made any serious attempt to brief Baxter or other members of his planning team afterward. Although it is perhaps stretching a point, Merrill's concern with Khymer Rouge force on the mainland suggests that he suspected or knew that the *Mayaguez's* crew had been taken into Kompong Som as was, in fact, the case.

During the afternoon of the fourteenth, Johnson's executive officer,

Lt. Col. John Hopkins, approached 307th intelligence. He wished to obtain information about the nature of denial agents used by the U.S. Air Force (CS tear gas, as it turned out) and the adequacy of the protective filters against them in his men's gas masks, a vital detail. One of Merrill's briefers later claimed that he had used the occasion to apprise Hopkins of the IPAC estimate.[72] This, too, is suspect. Although Merrill's briefer may have mentioned the estimate, it is all but certain that he did not discuss it in meaningful detail. Hopkins, an infantryman, would have remembered. Captain Huebusch, the security police commander, had obtained the IPAC estimate through back channels and claimed later to have briefed it to Maj. Raymond E. Porter, officer in charge of the *Mayaguez* boarding party. Porter, while vaguely remembering Huebusch, had no memory of receiving an estimate of enemy strength on Koh Tang. Both men's recollections are probably accurate. Their encounter took place in the U Tapao MAC passenger terminal on the afternoon of the fourteenth as Huebusch, saddened by the death of eighteen of his men and disappointed at losing the mission, awaited air transportation back to Nakhon Phanom. Their conversation was brief, and—the critical detail—Koh Tang had not yet been selected as a marine objective.[73]

As the plan took form, the helicopters on which it depended assembled. The process was even more confused and confusing than the above narrative suggests and is best left to the reader's imagination. Some of the Jolly Greens were at first held in reserve as a rescue force, and two were launched on a rescue mission during the fourteenth. The 21st SOS was apparently slated to lead the attack from the beginning, and the possibility that it might go in on the fourteenth remained alive until that morning. The Knife crews at U Tapao were held in readiness until six in the morning, when they were released—only to be recalled for a noon briefing. They were then held until two-thirty, when they were released again with instructions to be ready to report for an 0230 briefing the next morning.[74] The seventh and final 21st helicopter, Knife 52, came into commission at Nakhon Phanom during the early morning hours of the fifteenth and was flown south by a crew led by 1st Lt. Robert Rakitis. It arrived at four in the morning out of commission, just before the assault force launched.[75]

Having finalized the attack plan, Davis and McNemar checked the number of men they would be able to send in the first wave. It was evident that some of the company would have to be left behind. A dozen or so of Golf's marines had committed infractions of one kind or another, mostly involving drinking and fighting in Kadena's tenderloin district, and had disciplinary action pending. Combat is a poor place for rehabilitation, and Davis called them aside. He told them that they would not go in with the first wave and why but that they were still members of the team and would be brought to the island later. Pvt. K. O. Taylor, his approved undesirable discharge sitting on Davis's desk at Camp Schwab, was a charter member of the group. But Davis had a positive feeling about the man. Taylor would go in with the first wave.

Davis and McNemar then organized Golf Company into helicopter teams according to the number of seats available on each of the H-53s, keeping platoons, squads, and fire teams together as much as possible. It was an almost automatic drill that the two had done many times in Vietnam and required little thought. Having made the helicopter assignments, they then distributed ammunition and pyrotechnics to the troops, breaking into a prepackaged deployment container provided for the purpose. The gravity of the situation dawned on the troops when Davis and McNemar started passing out hand grenades "like popcorn."[76]

CHAPTER 5

Assault

BY MIDNIGHT on 14 May, the principal elements that were to establish the location, scale, and intensity of the battle to come were in place. Policy objectives had been clearly established. President Ford and his de facto advisory staff had developed a military strategy and made it clear to those charged with implementing it. Command and control relationships were set. Military objectives were assigned and had been briefed to the satisfaction of those in charge. Operational plans had been made. The forces on which the outcome of the day's events would depend were either in place or on the way. We know this to have been the case for U.S. forces. We can reasonably surmise that it was true for the Khymer Rouge as well, if for no other reason than because U.S. air power had constrained the possibilities for reinforcement and redeployment to the vanishing point.

Tactical plans and adjustments were another matter altogether. They could change and did. Those of the American forces are clear: we will address them in detail below. About those of the Khymer Rouge we can say little. The evidence suggests that by the fourteenth, if not before, the *Khmer Kraham* commander on Koh Tang had identified the island as the probable site of a helicopter-borne infantry assault and adjusted his dispositions accordingly. His troops were well dug in and their positions skillfully chosen. Marines on the island would later report that some of the Communist bunkers showed signs of recent construction and improvements.

None of this should be taken to suggest that the leaders on either side were fully aware of the effective strengths, dispositions, and states of readiness of the forces at their own disposal, let alone those of the enemy. Uncertainty in all of these areas represented sources of risk to

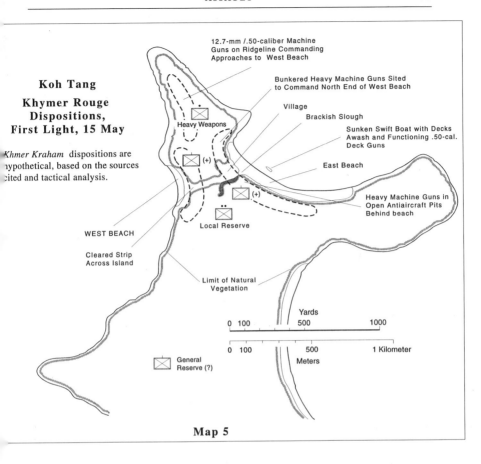

Koh Tang

Khymer Rouge Dispositions, First Light, 15 May

Khmer Kraham dispositions are hypothetical, based on the sources cited and tactical analysis.

12.7-mm /.50-caliber Machine Guns on Ridgeline Commanding Approaches to West Beach

Bunkered Heavy Machine Guns Sited to Command North End of West Beach

Village

Brackish Slough

Heavy Weapons

Sunken Swift Boat with Decks Awash and Functioning .50-cal. Deck Guns

East Beach

Heavy Machine Guns in Open Antiaircraft Pits Behind beach

Local Reserve

WEST BEACH

Cleared Strip Across Island

Limit of Natural Vegetation

Yards

0   100   500   1000

0   100   500   1 Kilometer

Meters

General Reserve (?)

Map 5

be considered and dealt with in the operation to come. This is always the case in war, and experienced soldiers take it as a given. But from the American standpoint the *Mayaguez* affair, particularly the Koh Tang invasion, was fraught with uncertainty and unanticipated risk to an unusual degree—although many in the chain of command do not seem to have appreciated the extent to which this was true. Quite the contrary, in fact.

The degree to which uncertainty was anticipated and the manner in which measures were taken to guard against its effects deserve particular attention in order to more closely examine the cause-and-effect relationships involved. Indeed, the Koh Tang invasion provides a concise case study of the way in which tactical uncertainty and unanticipated risk can interact to drive the flow of events once battle is joined. Cumulatively feeding on and reinforcing one another, these elements created new sources of operational and strategic risk, overturning calculations that predicted the easy attainment of policy objectives.

EXECUTION

The assault force helicopter crews and marine commanders and staff briefed at about 0100 on the fifteenth.[1] This was the key tactical players' first and only chance to meet face-to-face to work out problems in the plan. It was also the last chance for those in charge to ensure that all understood what was required of them. Anders conducted the briefing. No intelligence personnel were present. Neither were representatives from Cricket: the ABCCC crew on station when the assault went in would have to base its decisions entirely on information transmitted to them in flight.

The briefing was an impromptu affair conducted in a room without chairs or tables. The briefers stood and the aircrews sat on the floor, oddly primitive accommodations for a fully operational base of the Strategic Air Command, well known for excellence of physical facilities. The atmosphere was relaxed and off-hand, almost casual.[2] The helicopter crews were given formation assignments, radio call signs, and LZs. Times, radio frequencies, weather, and intelligence were briefed. Porter's force was to be put aboard *Holt* by Jolly Green 11, 12, and 13. A combined formation of Knives and Jolly Greens would carry the Koh Tang assault force with the Knives leading. The formation leader was Lt. Col. John Denham, 21st SOS commander. The blocking force for the western beach, 1st Platoon, G Company (reinforced), was aboard Denham's aircraft and that of his wingman, 1st Lt. Terry D. Ohlemeier. Ohlemeier's load included Captain Davis and Gunnery Sergeant McNemar.

Denham's formation briefing was sketchy in the extreme if he conducted one at all. The radio call signs designated indicate that Anders and Pannell organized the Knives and Jolly Greens in elements of three with the Knives leading as they had for Frequent Wind, apparently imitating marine practice.[3] During the event, the crews carrying the Koh Tang assault force organized themselves into elements of two en route to the objective. The call signs given out by Anders and Pannell thus had little bearing on tactical reality, which was to be a source of confusion.[4] Pannell was later to claim that Col. Robert R. Reed, USSAG deputy chief, Operations Plans Division, briefed intelligence, but the evidence suggests otherwise: Anders conducted the intelligence portion of the aircrew briefing himself.[5] He told the assault force that they could expect to be opposed by between eighteen and thirty irregulars.[6]

Meanwhile, 56th SOW maintenance workers stripped much of the protective armor plate from 21st SOS helicopters to lighten the aircraft.[7] The Knives would launch with crews of four: two pilots and two flight mechanic-gunners. The 40th helicopters would launch configured for combat rescue operations with full complements of guns, ammunition, and armor. All but one Jolly Green carried an extra enlisted crew member besides the normal cabin crew of a flight mechanic and two PJs. This measure had earlier proved its value as insurance against the unexpected in Frequent Wind. The mission would tax the helicopters' range and endurance to the limit, and all carried full fuel loads. With their 650-gallon external tanks, the Knives would take off carrying some twenty-six hundred pounds more JP-4 jet fuel for their their turbine engines than the Jolly Greens. The fuel cut into the Knives' useful loads. Each Jolly Green carried an average of seven more marines than the Knives: about twenty-six as opposed to nineteen.[8]

The Cricket EC-130 that was to be on station when the assault began took off from U Tapao at a quarter past three in the morning. The onboard ABCCC battle staff was informed by radio of the plan for the operation at four-thirty. Working in the tight confines of the C-130's cabin, the staffers had only an hour and a half to assemble and organize the information necessary to do their job: objectives and initiation times for the helicopters and marines, on-station times and ordnance loads for the fighters and gunships, radio frequencies and call signs, intelligence, and all the rest. The ABCCC unit history describes their preparations as feverish, no doubt with considerable understatement.[9]

The assault force was ready to take off at the planned departure time of 0405,[10] only to be held on the ramp by orders from above. The reasons for the delay remain obscure, but the close correlation between the scheduled takeoff time and the start of the Ford administration's briefing of congressional leaders, noted earlier, is suggestive. It is worth noting, too, that the communications available to the key decision makers would have made it possible to delay takeoff until positive confirmation was received that the briefing was actually in progress. That presumably would ensure that the requirements of the War Powers Act of 1973 were satisfied, however technically.

In the final moments before departure, as the marines were standing by their assigned helicopters waiting to load, Captain Davis was approached by a noncommissioned officer with large, glossy, black-and-white aerial photographs of Koh Tang. Gunnery Sergeant McNemar, who was standing next to Davis, remembers the individual as an air force NCO; Davis later thought he might have been a marine. Whatever his service—it was dark and the ensuing encounter was brief—the man handed the photos to Davis.[11] Davis and McNemar scanned the photos by flashlight as the NCO pointed out details to them, including a struc-

ture he identified as a barracks. The two marines had used aerial photographs in planning helicopter assaults many times before and quickly
went beyond their anonymous briefer's analysis. They saw unmistak-
able signs of Communist bunkers sited in defense of the beaches. That
was bad. They also saw open gun pits adjacent to the east beach: antiaircraft positions.[12] That was worse. "It was then," McNemar was to say
years later, "that we knew we were going into shit."[13]

Davis and McNemar briefly considered the situation: there was no
time to rework the attack plan, which in any case was about as good as
any they could come up with under the circumstances. After a brief
internal debate, Davis concluded that sharing the information with his
troops would accomplish nothing beyond making them more nervous
on the way in. He stuffed the photographs in the pocket of his flak vest
and passed the word for the men to expect enemy fire. Davis and
McNemar kept their secret to themselves.[14]

The first element of three Jolly Greens took off at four-fourteen, followed by the other helicopters between four-twenty and four twenty-
five.[15] As a result of the predeparture hold, they would reach *Holt* and
Koh Tang some twenty minutes later than the specified assault time of
0542. About thirty minutes after takeoff, the helicopter crews observed
tracers and flares rising from the ocean below them in the darkness,
apparently from Khymer Rouge patrol boats. One helicopter pilot later
compared the flares and tracers arcing upward toward the helicopters
with a ragged fireworks display—a cheap Fourth of July, as he put it.[16]
Captain Davis in Knife 22 saw a glow beneath the aircraft. Remembering Vietnam, he thought to himself, Here we go again![17] Surprise had
surely been compromised.

The helicopter armada reached the vicinity of Koh Tang without further incident, and Jolly Green 11, 12, and 13 began putting Porter's force
aboard *Holt* at about two minutes after six. Off-loading the marines was
a tedious operation, requiring the big H-53s to hover over the vessel's
small helicopter pad while the marines deplaned one by one through
the crew door. There were communications problems. Neither Cricket
nor the Jolly Greens had *Holt*'s radio frequency, and the ABCCC controllers made initial contact with the vessel on UHF Guard, the common distress frequency. From that point, the operation went relatively
smoothly. Each of the Jolly Greens took just under ten minutes to unload, and the boarding party was aboard *Holt* by six-thirty.[18]

The assault on Koh Tang began perhaps a minute after U.S. Marines
started transferring to *Holt*. The eight helicopters approached the island
in the sequence depicted in map 6, led by Denham in Knife 21 with
Ohlemeier in Knife 22 close behind. As Denham began his final ap-

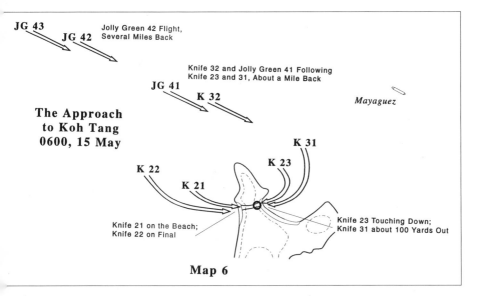

JG 43

JG 42   Jolly Green 42 Flight,
         Several Miles Back

                        Knife 32 and Jolly Green 41 Following
                        Knife 23 and 31, About a Mile Back
            JG 41
                                                              Mayaguez
               K 32

**The Approach
to Koh Tang
0600, 15 May**
                                              K 31

   K 22   K 23

         K 21
                                         Knife 23 Touching Down;
Knife 21 on the Beach;   Knife 31 about 100 Yards Out
Knife 22 on Final

Map 6

proach, Knives 23 and 31 were several hundred yards out from the
west beach.

Denham brought Knife 21 to a hover above the narrow beach, turned
the helicopter 180° to present the open ramp to the shore, and landed.
Ohlemeier followed him in, using a side flare and slewing the big helicopter sideways to slow down before turning the ramp to the beach. It
was about 0603. As the marines began unloading from Knife 21 and
Knife 22 came to a hover, a storm of small-arms and heavy automatic
weapons fire erupted from the jungle, accompanied by RPGs (rocket-
propelled grenades) and bursting mortar shells in the LZ. Knife 21
immediately lost an engine. Ohlemeier aborted his approach to cover
Denham with minigun fire. His call of "Hot LZ!" on the Cricket UHF
helicopter control frequency at 0605, followed by the announcement
that he had wounded aboard, was the first indication of trouble to those
in control.[19]

Denham and his copilot, 1st Lt. Karl Poulsen, jettisoned external
tanks and dumped fuel to lighten the aircraft. They got Knife 21 off the
beach despite heavy damage but were unable to maintain altitude and
ditched three-quarters of a mile off the west side of the island. The helicopter almost immediately rolled over and sank. Ohlemeier made a second firing pass into the maelstrom to cover Denham's withdrawal. As
he ran in, Knife 22's right-door gunner fell back from his position,
clutching his stomach. The marines watched as he raised his hands to

his face, looking for blood. Finding none—he had taken a nearly spent round in the buckle of his gunner's restraining harness—he went back to his gun and continued firing. Captain Davis took a spent round in the face at the same time.[20] Knife 22 sustained heavy damage.

On the east beach, Knife 23 was just touching down when an even more intense fire erupted, probably triggered by the sound of gunfire to the west as the *Khmer Kraham* opened up on Knife 21. Knife 23 immediately lost an engine, and the tail pylon was shot off: the pilot, 1st Lt. John Schramm, managed to set the helicopter down despite the loss of yaw control. The marines from Golf's 3rd Platoon, including the platoon commander, 2d Lt. Michael Cicere, scrambled down the ramp and headed for the tree line to the north. Knife 31, less than fifty yards out on its final approach to the beach, sustained hits from small arms, heavy automatic weapons, and probably RPGs. Aboard Knife 31 was BLT 2/9's forward air control (FAC) team. The copilot, 2d Lt. Richard Vandegeer, was killed almost immediately. As the pilot, Maj. Howard Corson, tried to abort the approach and climb away, the aircraft exploded in a ball of fire fueled by JP-4 jet fuel from a ruptured 650-gallon external fuel tank. Corson managed to retain control long enough to put the helicopter down in some four feet of water. At six minutes after six Knife 32, about a mile out, transmitted on UHF, "Looks like somebody went in on the LZ." The transmission was supplemented to confirm an explosion and a large fire on the east beach. The pilot of Knife 32, 1st Lt. Michael Lackey, aborted his approach, followed by Jolly Green 41. Cricket received the first transmissions from the island on the marine VHF/FM tactical net at about the same time: they were garbled but contained clear reference to enemy opposition.[21]

Observing the fireball from Knife 31, the commander of the HC-130 rescue squadron at Korat, flying overhead as pilot of King 21, intervened. In accordance with standard rescue procedures, he transmitted on Guard, identifying himself—the King call sign was automatically associated with rescue—and asking for any RESCORT-trained A-7 pilot to contact him on rescue frequency.[22] An A-7 element leader responded and assumed rescue on-scene command. He focused his attention on the east beach, looking for survivors and forming the nucleus of a search-and-rescue task force.

Ohlemeier, with fuel pouring from Knife 22's punctured external tanks and control of the aircraft problematical, abandoned attempts to insert and orbited over Denham's helicopter as it went down. Lackey, acting on his own initiative, diverted to rescue Denham's crew with Jolly Green 41 as backup. He and his crew had to dump fuel to keep the heavily laden helicopter in a hover but succeeded in pulling Denham, Poulsen, and one flight mechanic from the water by rescue hoist. The second flight mechanic, S.Sgt. Elwood Rumbaugh, disappeared after exiting the aircraft and apparently drowned. The hoist operations and a fruitless search for Rumbaugh occupied Knife 32 for over twenty minutes. Meanwhile Jolly Green 42, piloted by 1st Lt. Philip Pacini, followed Lackey's lead: he aborted his approach to the east beach and went into an orbit north of the island with Jolly Green 43 on his wing.

With smoke rising from the primary LZ and at least three H-53s down, the helicopter crews tried to sort out what had happened and to whom on VHF/FM and intercom. At the same time, the Cricket controllers struggled to make sense of the situation, confused by the discrepancy between the helicopters' radio call signs and formation assignments. Logically, for example, they assumed that Jolly Green 41 was the leader of an element of three and that Jolly Green 42 and 43 were her wingmen. The controllers' frantic attempts to sort things out and the helicopter crews' efforts to make sense of the situation were complementary. On two occasions between ten and fifteen minutes after six, Cricket endorsed helicopter pilots' individual decisions to terminate insertions and told them to hold pending further instructions.

At about ten minutes past six, hearing repeated attempts by 2d Lt. James McDaniel, the commander of 1st Platoon, G Company, to contact his battalion commander on the marine VHF/FM tactical net using internal BLT 2/9 call signs, a Cricket controller came up on the BLT 2/9 net. He asked McDaniel for his position and if he desired reinforcement. McDaniel stated that he was on the west side of the island and replied emphatically in the affirmative. He was in a bind: not only was his small force isolated and under heavy pressure but he had no one to report to. Standard operating procedures called for a spot report to company or battalion headquarters, but McDaniel had no one to talk to but Cricket. Three minutes later, in a spot report to Cricket, he reported that he and his marines—there were only twenty counting himself, and he pointedly declined to state a number—had been under continuous small-arms fire since disembarking. They had, however, managed to push inland a short distance—at a guess some forty meters—from the water, overrunning a 60-mm mortar position in the process.[23]

The next twenty minutes were critical. Although the precise chronology is in doubt, the basic sequence of events is clear. Several minutes before McDaniel submitted his spot report to Cricket, Pacini, in Jolly Green 42, orbiting seven miles north of the island with Jolly Green 43, checked in as a flight of two. Pacini announced that his two Jolly Greens were ready to insert and requested instructions. At about 0620 Cricket cleared them in and they started for their briefed LZs on the east side of the island. At that point, Knife 32, holding two miles north of the

island with fifteen marines and the survivors of Denham's crew on
board, checked in and requested instructions. Like Pacini, Lackey was
told to insert.

At this point, communications on primary tactical frequencies were
being intermittently blocked by transmissions on UHF Guard, associated with rescue attempts off the east beach, and confusion was endemic. It was apparently not clear to the entire ABCCC battle staff that
McDaniel and his group were on the west side of the island. But Lackey,
in Knife 32, smelled a rat and requested clarification in unequivocal
terms. Did Cricket, he asked, want him to insert his marines in the
same LZ where Knife 23 and 31 had gone down? After a quick check,
the controller directed him to go into the west beach instead of his
briefed LZ on the east. Still unsure that Cricket had it straight, Lackey
again requested explicit confirmation and received it. Jolly Green 42
and 43 had already begun their run-in to the east beach, but the exchange between Knife 32 and Cricket got Pacini's attention. He requested clarification as well. After another quick check, the controller
reversed his field and sent the two Jolly Greens into the west beach.
Beyond a reasonable doubt, Lackey's request for clarification, the two
heads-up calls by anonymous ABCCC controllers, and Pacini's situational awareness averted disaster.

At some point Cricket, apparently in response to orders from
USSAG, ordered Spectre 61, which had departed Koh Tang about ten
minutes before the first wave went in, to land at U Tapao, refuel, and
return to the island as soon as possible.[24] It was a good call and was to
have far-reaching consequences.

As Knife 32, Jolly Green 42, and Jolly Green 43 began their run-ins,
the situation on the island was grim. Of the twenty-six men aboard
Knife 31, eight died in the aircraft and five in the water nearby. Corson
exited through the cockpit window and dropped into the water; the two
flight mechanics and eight marines left the cabin by smashing out windows with M16 butts or swimming underwater through the crew door.
Three of the marines charged the tree line and were killed by enemy
fire.[25] Among them was Lance Cpl. Gregory Copenhaver, a veteran of
Frequent Wind.[26] The rest of the small party emptied their M16s and
aircrew revolvers at the hostile tree line and, with no place else to go,
made their way out to sea and started swimming.

As related earlier, the twenty marines aboard Knife 23 under 2d Lt.
Cicere had deplaned through the open ramp and headed for the nearest
available cover, just inside the tree line to the north. The pilots stayed
aboard long enough to shut down the aircraft and inform Cricket of
their situation before following the marines. Astonishingly they all
made it, though one of Cicere's men was wounded. They set up a small

perimeter just inside the trees, dug in, and called for help. 1st Lt. John Lucas, Knife 23's copilot, took charge of the group's communications and repeatedly attempted to contact aircraft overhead on his UHF personal survival radio. At first he went unnoticed in the cacophony of noise on primary tactical frequencies and then was unable to get anyone's attention. Ironically, Lucas's coolness was the apparent cause of his frustration. According to a story later current at Nakhon Phanom, when Lucas made initial contact with Cricket, the airborne controller, fooled by his calm, unhurried voice, told him to stop transmitting and stand by—that he was attempting to establish contact with the survivors from a downed helicopter![27]

Among the survivors of Knife 31 in the water off the east beach was a marine FAC, 1st Lt. Terry Tonkin. He broke out an air force survival radio, made contact with A-7s overhead, and directed them in strikes against whatever enemy positions he could observe until his radio's batteries ran out. Tonkin's actions served to further focus attention on the east beach and were apparently responsible for the first expenditure of ordnance by the fighters: strafing runs by A-7s, at about 0620.[28]

The evidence suggests that Jolly Green 42 and 43 began their run-ins shortly before Knife 32; that is, at about 0620. Pacini's element went in as a flight or two, trying for a simultaneous insertion with 42 to the south and 43 to the north. This was apparently done on the basis of the sketch map on the wall of the U Tapao helicopter operations section, which showed two discrete LZs on the west beach: one on each side of the cleared strip of land across the island. The fighters were little more than spectators as chaos erupted beneath them. Unaware that Cricket had shifted the insertions to the west beach, the pilots queried controllers about helicopters going "the wrong way" as the three H-53s started in from the west.[29] As Jolly Green 42 made her run-in, Pacini, monitoring the A-7 VHF/FM interplane frequency, heard A-7 after A-7 call, "I'm dry," "I'm dry," in sequence as they screamed overhead—meaning that they were not prepared to deliver ordnance. At first it struck him as funny, then it angered him.[30] The Knives and Jolly Greens could use some help. So could the marines on the beach.

Pacini and his crew went in south of the main LZ and saw neither marines nor signs of activity as they flew over the beach. Pacini concluded he was in the wrong place and pulled off for a second try. Meanwhile Jolly Green 43, piloted by Capt. Wayne Purser and carrying Lieutenant Colonel Austin and the BLT 2/9 command group, approached the main LZ, only to be driven off by intense small-arms fire. Knife 32 got her marines into McDaniels's perimeter at about 0623, increasing the size of the tiny force on the beach from twenty to thirty-three. The aircraft sustained heavy battle damage, however, including an RPG hit in the tail section that left a gaping hole in the fuselage. Critically low on fuel, Knife 32 made it back to U Tapao, running on fumes with a wounded marine and an army linguist who had refused to leave the aircraft on board. Knife 32 was out of commission and out of the fight.

After their unsuccessful attempt to unload their marines, Pacini and Purser pulled off, regrouped, talked things over, and went in again. On the second try, Pacini's crew made it into the primary LZ. Jolly Green 42 exchanged fire with nearby Communist positions using her ramp minigun while landing and inserted the men some three minutes after Knife 32. Aboard Jolly Green 42 was 1st Lt. Dick Keith, Golf Company's executive officer.[31]

Keith could hear small-arms fire, heavy automatic weapons fire, and mortar fire as the helicopter came to a hover. As he exited the aircraft, the marine in front of him was hit by enemy fire. Keith helped him to cover and found a medic; it was the start of a long day. McDaniel found Keith shortly thereafter and informed him that he had only about thirty marines with him, that he had heard nothing from the second or third platoon, that the helicopter carrying Captain Davis had been shot off the LZ, and that he believed Davis to be dead. The perimeter was under constant small-arms fire, and there was a particularly troublesome machine gun off the northern end of the perimeter, firing from the ridge running along the tip of the island.[32]

Keith began tightening the perimeter and considered the human resources at his disposal. Among them was S.Sgt. Fofo Tutele, the assistant platoon sergeant, or guide, of the second platoon. A six-foot-two-inch Samoan weighing some two hundred fifty pounds, all muscle, Tutele was a respected leader. The limited capacities of the air force helicopters had forced Davis and McNemar to split up platoons. To ensure that no fragment of a platoon would be without NCO leadership, they had assigned platoon sergeants and guides to different helicopters. Tutele's platoon was on the opposite side of the island, making him essentially a free agent.

Keith directed Tutele and S.Sgt. Seferino Bernal, McDaniel's platoon sergeant, to take out the machine gun off the northern end of the perimeter. They went. Shortly thereafter, the machine gun stopped firing. Keith, relieved of one problem and beset by many more, stopped thinking about it.

While on the LZ, Jolly Green 42 had sustained damage from small arms and mortar fragments. Pacini and his crew cleared the island with damage to the airframe, a malfunctioning flight control system, and a punctured external fuel tank. Jolly Green 42 was able to return to U

Tapao only by aerial refueling and landed out of commission.[33] Keith's marines in the western perimeter numbered about sixty.[34]

Purser and his crew in Jolly Green 43 inserted a few minutes after Jolly Green 42, probably in the same spot Pacini had rejected earlier. The location was well south of the primary LZ. Austin, his command group, and the mortar section, totaling twenty-nine marines, were separated from Keith and his group by from nine hundred to twelve hundred meters, nearly three-quarters of a mile.[35] They felt especially vulnerable because many in the group, including most of the mortarmen, had only .45-cal. pistols as personal arms.

From the air force perspective, the operation had turned into a series of rescue missions that demanded immediate attention.[36] Jolly Green 11 and 12 were detailed to escort Knife 22, spewing fuel from punctured external tanks and with flight control difficult, to the Thai coast. If the damaged aircraft went down in the water, the survivors would have to be recovered by rescue hoist. The limitations to hovering performance meant that more than one helicopter would be required. After unloading her marines on *Holt*, Jolly Green 13 refueled with King 21. Cricket ordered Jolly Green 13 to hold near the island to support rescue efforts on the east beach.[37] At some point in this interval, Lucas finally managed to make contact with friendly aircraft overhead, confirming that there were survivors from the crash of Knife 23.[38]

By seven o'clock the situation on the island had begun to consolidate, but hardly along the lines expected in preattack planning. The marines on the west beach, fighting against fierce opposition, had pushed their perimeter out to fifty meters; this gave them breathing space but not a secure LZ.[39] Austin's group was under no immediate pressure, for the *Khmer Kraham* did not seem to have anticipated marines coming ashore where they did—the only conceivable benefit of being inserted in the wrong place. But his party was small and vulnerable: only a few of the men in the group were armed with M16 rifles, and others were burdened with 81-mm mortar barrels, bipods, and baseplates. Worse, Austin was isolated from his command. Twenty marines of Golf's 3rd Platoon under 2d Lt. Cicere and five helicopter crewmen were holed up off the east beach. Some thirteen survivors were swimming for it off the eastern cove. Overhead, flights of A-7s scrambled to make sense of the tactical situation. In the words of the official CINC-PAC history, the fighters "were unable to pinpoint locations of friendly units and suppress enemy fire because of the confines of, and confusing situation on, the battlefield."[40] In plain language, they were unable to see and engage tactically meaningful targets.

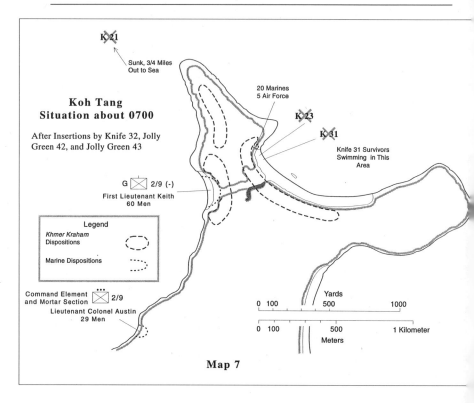

Map 7

The loss of the marine FAC team in Knife 31 was particularly damaging because it eliminated the only UHF link with aircraft overhead. Radio contact between the A-7s and marines was not the problem; the VHF/FM radios were compatible, and the pilots were trained as FACs. But the dense vegetation and absence of clearly defined landmarks combined with the lack of gridded tactical charts to render precise location of the marine positions impossible. Repeated efforts to mark the marine locations with smoke grenades set off on request failed to define them accurately enough to permit putting in ordnance nearby. To make matters worse, the marines had received only a partial issue of signal pyrotechnics and smoke grenades and were running short.[41] The A-7s tried to locate Communist positions by trolling for ground fire, flying low and slow to present easy targets and to induce the enemy to give away its positions with muzzle flash and tracers, but the *Khmer Kraham* weren't biting. They displayed excellent fire and camouflage discipline from beginning to end and saved their fire for the helicopters.[42]

The diversion of effort to support rescue operations on the east beach

and the high fuel consumption caused by sustained low-altitude maneuvering forced repeated handoffs of on-scene command as flights of
A-7s went to KC-135 tankers to refuel—and ultimately back to Korat
to rearm. At about seven o'clock, on-scene command over Koh Tang
fell briefly to a flight of F-4s, unequipped with VHF/FM radios and man-
ifestly unsuited for the job.[43] Austin established radio contact with the
main body at 0712, and his group began working its way north. Their
progress was slow, for the terrain was difficult and the dispositions of
the enemy unknown.[44] Keith was not in touch with Cicere's isolated
group on the east side of the island or even aware of its existence.

Concerned with Austin's isolation and his own lack of manpower, at
about eight o'clock Keith ordered McDaniel to take a patrol south to
bring the command group into the perimeter. McDaniel's patrol had
gone only a few yards when the southern side of the perimeter, hitherto
quiet, erupted with fire.[45] McDaniel's point man, Lance Cpl. Ashton
Looney, was killed, and McDaniel and other members of the patrol were
wounded. As the patrol recoiled and fell back into the perimeter, Keith
braced himself for a counterattack.[46] It came on the heels of the repulse
of McDaniel's patrol.

The marines responded aggressively, engaging the attacking *Khmer
Kraham* in intense fighting. In the process, a forward movement organized and led by Staff Sergeant Bernal silenced the stronghold that had
repelled McDaniel's patrol.[47] The force of the counterattack and the
density of the jungle carried the *Khmer Kraham* to within fifteen yards
of the marine perimeter where the two forces remained locked in combat, neither willing to give ground.[48] Plans to dispatch a force to link up
with Austin's group were abandoned for the moment.

In the wake of the counterattack, the *Khmer Kraham* seemed satisfied to consolidate its position, and pressure on the marine perimeter
eased. For the next few hours, Communist fire against the perimeter
slacked off, picking up only when helicopters approached. Keith was
later to hypothesize that the *Khmer Kraham* commander was deploying
his reserves during this interval. His hypothesis makes sense.

The situation in the air was no better than that on the ground. Of
the eleven helicopters in the first wave, two were smoking wreckage on
the east beach, and another was sunk off the west side of the island.
A fourth, Knife 22, unable to insert its marines, was headed for the
nearest reasonably secure point on the Thai coast. It landed on the
beach eighty-three nautical miles east of U Tapao shortly before eight
o'clock.[49] Knife 32 and Jolly Green 42 had suffered heavy battle damage.
Both would make it back to U Tapao but would be out of commission
for the duration of the operation. Jolly Green 41 was in commission but

as yet had been unable to insert her marines. She would remain committed and unavailable until she did so. The three helicopters involved in the *Holt* insertion were all in commission, but one, Jolly Green 13, had been diverted to rescue operations by ABCCC. Jolly Green 11 and 12 were escorting Knife 22 to the Thai coast, and Jolly Green 43 was escorting 42 back to U Tapao. Only three helicopters of the first wave, Jolly Green 11, 12, and 43, were available for the second wave.

Two more helicopters were added to this meager total while the events described above were unfolding. Knife 52 came into commission after the first wave launched and was made ready to depart with Knife 51. The latter was still out of commission with the problem that had delayed its departure from Nakhon Phanom two nights before. Brims and his crew cleared Knife 51 on a maintenance check flight at 0720, only to be immediately launched on a rescue mission mounted in response to news of the first wave debacle.[50] Included in Brims's crew were two volunteer 40th pararescuemen, T.Sgt. Wayne Fisk and Sgt. Ronald Cooper. This was an unusual measure because 21st and 40th personnel did not ordinarily fly as crew members on one another's aircraft; that it was adopted speaks volumes for the perceived urgency of the situation.

The details of what happened next and why are uncertain, but the outlines are clear. Jolly Green 11 and 12 escorted Knife 22 to the Thai coast, where they landed near Knife 22. There they were joined by Knife 51. Jolly Green 11 then returned to U Tapao while Jolly Green 12 stayed behind to pick up Davis and his marines plus Ohlemeier's crew.[51] It took some time for the marines to transfer their equipment to the Jolly Green. Meanwhile Knife 51 departed for Koh Tang, apparently in accordance with her original orders, only to be recalled to U Tapao when three-quarters of the way there.[52] Jolly Green 11 landed at U Tapao at a quarter past eight, refueled, launched again fifteen minutes later,[53] and proceeded southeast to rendezvous with Jolly Green 12, which, in a final wrinkle, had been instructed to return Ohlemeier's crew to its aircraft. The men were later picked up by an army UH-1.[54] Jolly Green 43 landed at U Tapao in commission at nine o'clock. Jolly Green 11 and 12 landed together just before nine-thirty, by which time Knife 52 was serviced and ready to launch. Knife 51 landed shortly before ten.[55] There were now five H-53s available for the second wave.

Helicopter availability was a critical factor when the operation began and became progressively more so as it proceeded. A brief recapitulation of H-53 status is therefore in order. When the deployment to U Tapao was ordered during the late afternoon of 13 May, the 21st had ten CH-53s on strength. The 40th had nine HH-53s, of which three were deployed to the squadron's operating location at Korat. Each squadron had one helicopter disassembled in the phase dock, undergoing exhaustive phased inspection. These inspections involve the removal of major airframe, power train, and flight control components—gearboxes, rotor hubs, servo assemblies, and the like—and there was no hope that either helicopter could be brought into commission within a reasonable time. An estimate of seventy-two hours to make either helicopter airworthy would have been highly optimistic. When the crisis broke, the 40th, at least, reassigned the members of its phase dock crew to other tasks where their efforts would have immediate effect.[56] One CH-53 and one HH-53 were therefore unavailable within the time constraints imposed by President Ford.

Six 21st helicopters departed Nakhon Phanom during the night of 13–14 May in response to the initial deployment order. Of these, one crashed en route, and the other five arrived safely. That evening, three 40th helicopters reached U Tapao from Nakhon Phanom and three more from Korat. That left five H-53s at Nakhon Phanom potentially capable of being made airworthy within the president's time constraints. Although maintenance and check flight aircrews had no idea of what those constraints were, it was clear on the basis of queries from above that time was of the essence. Of those five helicopters, three belonged to the 21st and two to the 40th. Four of the five, two from the 40th and two from the 21st, were brought into commission in time to participate in the Koh Tang invasion. The intervention of two of the four was to prove critical and perhaps decisive.

Knife 51 came into commission in the early morning hours of 14 May after a night maintenance check flight, almost surely to test the flight control rigging (see Appendix B). It arrived at U Tapao about five in the morning. Knife 52 came into commission the following night and arrived at U Tapao at four o'clock in the morning of the fifteenth. The 56th SOW thus went two for four, a creditable showing. It was to take the 40th longer, for major maintenance was required. But as the second wave prepared to launch from U Tapao, 40th maintenance was within minutes of having the first HH-53 ready for a check flight and was within striking distance on the second.[57]

Colonel Johnson, out of the tactical communications net, was largely unaware of the details of the aerial ballet that determined the availability of helicopters for the second wave and brought Davis and the rest of Knife 22's marines back to U Tapao. More substantively, he remained ignorant of tactical developments on Koh Tang beyond what he could learn from returning helicopter crews and marines. But none of the former were infantrymen, and none of latter had set foot on the island, so their testimony was of limited value. Johnson was, however, keenly aware of the urgent need to reinforce the marines on Koh Tang. By the time helicopters began recovering at U Tapao, it was clear to the operations team, to the helicopter crews, and to maintenance—let alone Johnson and his small marine staff—that it was vitally important to cycle as many marines as possible to Koh Tang as quickly as it could be done. They were, however, operating in isolation. There is little evidence to suggest that Cricket or USSAG/Seventh Air Force appreciated just how tenuous the tactical situation on the island was or how urgently the marines needed reinforcement. The impetus behind the effort to get a second wave of marines onto the island came from below. The OV-10s sat on the ramp at Nakhon Phanom.

Meanwhile, the *Mayaguez* was retaken. At 0714, a flight of A-7s saturated the ship with CS tear gas dispensed from underwing canisters,[58] and *Holt* put in the boarding party shortly thereafter. It was a tricky bit of seamanship, but *Holt's* skipper, Comdr. Robert Peterson, managed it nicely despite the fact that the bridge crew was wearing gas masks. Major Porter's marines scrambled aboard and at 0725 reported the ship deserted with neither captors nor crew aboard.[59] *Holt* attached a tow and began pulling the vessel clear of Koh Tang while the Military Sealift Command volunteers went to work to raise steam and get her underway on her own. This took time. *Holt* was out of the action until dark.

At about twenty minutes after seven, the situation began to change for the better, although not to the immediate benefit of the hard-pressed marines. *Henry B. Wilson* arrived off Koh Tang, having maintained thirty-one knots continuously since refueling off Subic Bay. It was a remarkable performance. Not only had her engineering plant held up— all four boilers remained continuously on line—but she hit her estimated time of arrival, by now forty-eight hours old, within fifteen minutes.[60] *Wilson's* skipper, Comdr. Mike Rodgers, sensed disorganization even before his lookouts spotted the island. When *Wilson* checked in with Cricket, the controller asked what kind of aircraft she was and assigned her an orbit point at ten thousand feet.[61] Rodgers's radioman informed ABCCC that a ten-thousand-foot orbit was beyond *Wilson's* capability. As the destroyer arrived off the east beach, her lookouts spotted men in the water, the survivors of Knife 31. There had been no warning of their presence. Rodgers immediately ordered his gig and motor whaleboat into the water. As rescue procedures got underway, he spotted a helicopter trailing smoke that appeared to be descending into the water on the opposite side of the island. It was Jolly Green 41, piloted by 1st Lt. Tom Cooper, climbing out from the west beach after the first of five attempts to insert her marines.[62]

The *Khmer Kraham* had waited until Jolly Green 41 was in a hover before opening up, and when they did, their fire was intense and accurate.[63] The heaviest fire was from the one o'clock position (that is, slightly to the right of the nose: twelve o'clock is dead ahead, three o'clock is 90° off the right wing, and so on). With an inoperative right-door minigun, Cooper swung the tail of the helicopter toward the beach as he aborted. The smoke that Rodgers observed from *Wilson's* bridge was a combination of fuel spewing from a punctured external fuel tank, muzzle smoke from the ramp minigun covering the withdrawal, and the exhaust of the helicopter's turbine engines at full power.[64]

Wilson was occupied with rescue operations until about nine-thirty, when she was ordered to intercept a boat that a P-3 had reported coming out of Kompong Som headed for Koh Tang. Rodgers was worried about the possibility of armed Khymer intervention from the mainland—the initial report described the vessel as a missile boat[65]—and proceeded cautiously. But *Wilson's* radar showed the vessel moving slowly and ex-hibiting no signs of aggressive behavior. It neither radiated nor made rapid changes of direction or velocity. *Wilson* held her fire and closed the range. Finally, a fire control technician working a television camera with zoom telephoto capability mounted on the masthead brought the deck of the vessel into view. He reported Caucasians and a white flag. It was the *Mayaguez's* crew sent out by the Khymer Rouge aboard a seized Thai fishing boat.[66] *Wilson* confirmed the men's identity and had them aboard by 1005.[67] Word was immediately passed to Washington.

From a policy standpoint, the recapture of the *Mayaguez* and the re-turn of her crew was unalloyed good news. White House photographer David Hume Kennerly captured the euphoria of the moment in a mem-orable photograph. The shot shows an exuberant White House Chief of Staff Donald Rumsfeld and Lt. Gen. Brent Scowcroft cheering an ebul-lient President Ford as a broadly smiling Henry Kissinger looks on.[68] There would be no repetition of the *Pueblo* fiasco: the president and his advisers had hung tough, acted decisively, and achieved their policy objectives. Viewed from Washington, it was all over but the shouting. The wisdom of additional retaliatory bombing would be debated, a de-bate that Kissinger would win by overruling Secretary of Defense Schle-singer and obtaining approval for additional strikes. But the initial attacks by *Coral Sea's* aircraft had encountered no opposition, and the operational risks were minimal.[69] From Washington's perspective, it seemed logical to wrap things up and disengage as quickly as possible to cut political and military risks still further.

But although the release of the *Mayaguez's* crew was good news in policy terms, it was operationally and tactically irrelevant, for the Khmer Rouge on Koh Tang continued to fight with unabated ferocity. The *Khmer Kraham* were proving to be tough soldiers who stayed in their holes and fought to the death. As Captain Davis later put it, they had to be "killed, and killed again" to take them out of the fight. Well-armed with AK-47s and captured American M16s and M26 fragmentation grenades, the *Khmer Kraham* infantrymen were skilled and resourceful in taking advantage of the available cover.[70] The only discernible chink that the marines found in their tactical armor was a minor one: only recently equipped with U.S. equipment taken from the defeated Lon Nol Army, the Koh Tang garrison was unfamiliar with the characteristics of the M26 hand grenade. Accustomed to stick grenades of Chinese Communist manufacture that were notorious for their unpredictable time delay and prone to explode in the user's hand or face, the *Khmer Kraham* consistently threw their M26s prematurely to protect themselves against fast-burning fuses. This afforded enterprising marines familiar with the M26—and its reliable five-second delay—time to field the grenades and throw them back.[71] Lieutenant Colonel Austin was later to describe these exchanges as resembling a lethal game of tennis.[72]

Despite the return of the *Mayaguez's* crew, the predicament of the U.S. Marines on Koh Tang was highly relevant in policy terms. An embarrassing defeat on Koh Tang—a real possibility—would largely erase whatever policy gains had been made. That possibility and its implications were not apparent to all concerned.

The situation on the island deteriorated following *Wilson's* departure. Nothing had happened to improve the marines' situation on the ground since the repulse of the Khymer Rouge attack shortly after eight o'clock. The air force fighters were still unable to locate and engage worthwhile targets. Air force after-action reports indicate that a flight of three A-7s responded to ground fire with 20-mm strafing between 0615 and 0715. Also, three A-7s and two F-4s put 20-mm fire, 2.75-inch rockets, and three bombs on structures and troops, probably in the village off the east beach, at about the same time. At 0830 an AC-130 fired ten 40-mm rounds against enemy troops.[73] This first, tentative AC-130 fire mission was probably in support of Jolly Green 13, which had been committed to rescue the survivors of Knife 23 off the east beach about ten minutes earlier.[74]

Going in without an assigned backup helicopter—a sharp departure from combat rescue doctrine—Jolly Green 13 landed on the north end of the east beach and was immediately plastered with small-arms and automatic weapons fire. Looking north, the copilot, 1st Lt. Charles Brown, could clearly see the muzzle flashes of nearby bunkered heavy machine guns.[75] Multiple 12.7-mm hits damaged the flight control and fuel systems and set a flare case and an external fuel tank on fire. Knife 23's crew and Cicere's marines, pinned down and doubtful that the helicopter could survive the storm of fire, held their position. Neither of

Jolly Green 13's pilots had been under fire before, and they kept the helicopter on the ground, mistaking the thuds and bumps of Communist rounds hitting the aircraft for the impact of marine boots on the cabin floor. Shattered glass from cockpit instruments hit by small-arms rounds coming up the open ramp disabused them of their error and convinced the pilot, 1st Lt. Charles Greer, to abort the attempt.

On the infrared imagery of the orbiting AC-130 overhead, the helicopter seemed engulfed in flame. Explosion-retardant foam extinguished the external tank fire, however, and an alert pararescueman, S.Sgt. Steven Lemminn, jettisoned the burning flare case.[76] Jolly Green 13's armor and protective equipment had saved her crew, but the aircraft was no longer battle worthy, and the punctured external tank left insufficient fuel to return to U Tapao. Greer tried aerial refueling but abandoned the attempt as fuel poured into the cabin from ruptured overhead lines. Jolly Green 13 proceeded to the Thai coast, out of the fight. Stretching their fuel for all it was worth, Greer and his crew made it to within twenty-five miles of U Tapao, landing near the road from U Tapao to Rayong.

Meanwhile, Jolly Green 41 made a second attempt to insert its troops at about eight o'clock. This effort was coordinated with the marines on the beach at Cricket's suggestion, only to be driven off by heavy fire.[77] Aware that they were the last survivors of the first wave and that there would be no backup if they were shot down, Cooper and his copilot, 1st Lt. Dave Keith worked systematically. On VHF/FM, they contacted the A-7s that had earlier supported the *Mayaguez* boarding operation and were now trying to help the marines on the west beach. By 0835, Jolly Green 41's crew had finished a second aerial refueling—the punctured external tank sharply reduced endurance—and was coordinating fire support for the marines' insertion directly with the A-7s.[78] Given their rescue training, that might have been expected. But the crew members worked the A-7s on marine tactical frequency and included the marines in the coordination—that was not. Cooper and Keith had also established contact with Spectre 61 on UHF at 0704 before their first insertion attempt[79] and almost surely remained in contact thereafter.

After refueling with King 21, Cooper and his crew made a third attempt at 0915, running in parallel to the beach to suppress Communist fire with their operative left minigun. By the time Jolly Green 41 began her run-in, Spectre 61 and Lieutenant Keith on the island were working together on marine tactical VHF/FM frequency, orchestrating a well-coordinated effort to get 41's marines in.[80] Their efforts did not bear immediate fruit. Jolly Green 41 reached a hover over the LZ, only to be driven off by intense small-arms fire with hits in the fuselage, engine cowling, and rotor blades. Keith, watching from inside the perimeter, was struck by the intensity of Communist fire directed against the helicopter.[81]

Cooper and his crew tried again at ten o'clock, but this time things had changed—in no small measure because of their efforts. By 0938 Spectre 61 was providing direct fire support to the marines on the west side of the island and by 1000 was knocking out bunkers at marine request.[82] The American Marines working with the gunship knew nothing of the aircraft's destructive capacity and accuracy until Spectre 61 showed them graphically by putting 105-mm shells though the tops of Communist bunkers.

According to a story, no doubt colored by repetition, current among 16th SOS crews after the operation, Spectre 61 had identified itself to a marine on VHF/FM—almost surely Capt. Barry Cassidy, the FAC with Austin's group—and asked if he had targets.[83] The marine replied in the affirmative. Spectre asked him to identify his location and the relative position of the target—a bunker—which he did. Spectre then fired a 40-mm spotting round and asked for a correction, which the marine provided. Spectre fired another spotting round, which hit the bunker, and the following dialogue ensued. Spectre: "How was that?" Marine: "Right on, but it didn't do much." As the marine replied, Spectre fired a 105-mm round, which demolished the bunker in a shower of logs and dirt. Marine: "Jesus *Christ*, What was *that*? Have I got targets for *you*!"[84]

The bunkers in question lay between Austin's group and the main perimeter.[85] Their reduction was essential to the subsequent linkup and perhaps to the marines' survival.

Meanwhile, Jolly Green 13's unsuccessful rescue attempt on the east beach had yielded unintended benefits: Greer and his crew had unequivocally established the location of Knife 23's survivors by landing next to them and making positive identification. Of more immediate value, when the *Khmer Kraham* gunners opened up, they revealed their firing positions to the watchful fighters overhead. The A-7s had clear targets for the first time. One of the four on station, acting as an FAC, brought in a flight of F-4s to strike targets on the east side of the island. There was, however, another unanticipated wrinkle: Jolly Green 13 had gone in without a backup, and an A-7 diverted to escort the damaged helicopter. This stretched A-7 assets past the breaking point, and Spectre was the only tactical aircraft on station capable of communicating with the marines.[86]

When Jolly Green 41 went in for the fourth time at ten o'clock, Spectre 61 had assumed on-scene command by default. Cooper and his crew again encountered heavy small-arms fire, and mortar rounds began fall-

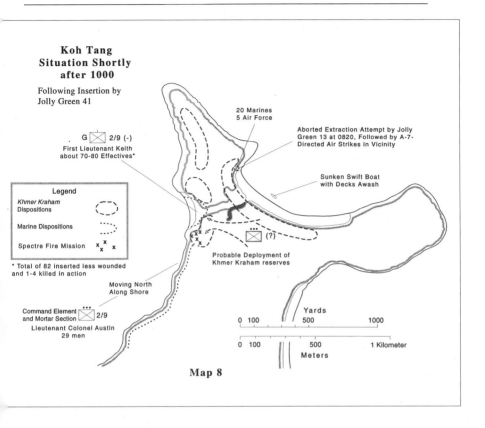

**Koh Tang
Situation Shortly
after 1000**

Following Insertion by
Jolly Green 41

20 Marines
5 Air Force

G ⊠ 2/9 (-)
First Lieutenant Keith
about 70-80 Effectives*

Aborted Extraction Attempt by Jolly
Green 13 at 0820, Followed by A-7-
Directed Air Strikes in Vicinity

Sunken Swift Boat
with Decks Awash

Legend
Khmer Kraham
Dispositions

Marine Dispositions

Spectre Fire Mission

* Total of 82 inserted less wounded
and 1-4 killed in action

⊠ (?)

Probable Deployment of
Khmer Kraham reserves

Moving North
Along Shore

Command Element
and Mortar Section ⊠ 2/9
Lieutenant Colonel Austin
29 men

Yards

0 100   500   1000

0 100   500   1 Kilometer
              Meters

Map 8

ing in the LZ as the marines headed down the open ramp. Cooper and
his crew were able to off-load twenty of their twenty-five marines—part
of G Company's 2nd Platoon, including the platoon commander, 2d Lt.
Richard H. Zales—before they were forced to abort. The helicopter was
damaged, but Cooper and his crew came back in to off-load their last
five marines and take on wounded. It was their fifth attempt.[87] They got
back into the LZ before their luck finally ran out. The helicopter suffered heavy damage before the remaining marines could deplane, and
Jolly Green 41 headed back to U Tapao with five marines still on board,
aerial refueling en route. With damage to the tail pylon and two main
rotor blades and a hole in the belly the size of a man's head, Jolly Green
41 would not fly again that day.[88] Cooper and his crew were out of the
fight, but their intervention had been pivotal. In the words of a later
analysis sponsored by the Marine Corps, the twenty marines were
"badly needed because the situation was critical at the time."[89]

Beyond adding a vital increment of manpower to Keith's force defending the west beach, Zales's marines brought badly needed supplies of ammunition. Keith reorganized his defenses, assigning the southern half of the perimeter to Zales's platoon and shifting McDaniel's to the north. The *Khmer Kraham* responded to the reinforcement by increasing the intensity of their fire.[90]

The evidence suggests that the incredible persistence of Cooper and his crew—the copilot, Keith, was a standout—accomplished much more than increasing the strength of the beleaguered marines on the west beach by a badly needed one-third and replenishing their supply of ammunition. Air force after-action reports show that at 0940 Spectre 61 began a heavy fire mission, laying in no fewer than fourteen 105-mm rounds along with 20-mm and 40-mm fire.[91] Logic and analysis of the sequence of events suggest that this fire mission relieved pressure on the U.S. Marines at a critical time and perhaps preempted a counterattack. The causal relationship between the fire mission and Jolly Green 41's self-initiated coordination efforts is clear, for Spectre 61 had been over Koh Tang since her return from U Tapao, probably no later than seven-thirty, and had not previously entered into the ground battle. Nor was the delivery of effective ordnance at a critical time the only benefit of Spectre's intervention. During the fire mission, Spectre's sensor operators had accurately located all friendly forces on the island for the first time. This was all the more critical because the marines in the main perimeter off the west beach had run out of smoke grenades to mark their positions.[92]

CHAPTER 6

Battle

THE SECOND WAVE was a catch-as-catch-can operation. As H-53s touched down at U Tapao, they were quickly evaluated by their flight crews and maintenance. If airworthy, they were refueled, rearmed, loaded with marines, and launched. Word of the first-wave debacle had spread quickly, lending urgency to the effort. This critical part of the battle was fought mostly in isolation by the small, ad hoc helicopter operations section and the 56th SOW and 40th ARRS maintenance staff, with Colonel Johnson looking anxiously on as his tiny staff matched marines with helicopters. Some critical, base-provided requirements of the undertaking, notably fuel, could be obtained without deviating from routine day-to-day procedures. But others could not, and the seeming unwillingness of U Tapao base personnel to accept the reality of the drama taking place before their eyes presented problems. The failure of 307th Strategic Wing intelligence to pass on enemy order of battle information was the most dramatic example of this. A member of the operations section later characterized the prevalent reaction of U Tapao staff to the situation in the following words: "A war? Wow! That can't be! That was all over in '73!"[1]

There were, however, notable exceptions to the general pattern: the members of the small U Tapao base operations staff wholeheartedly threw themselves behind the effort from the outset. The base hospital responded with alacrity, mobilizing surgical resources and providing ambulances and medical personnel to meet returning helicopters. After his initial requests for 7.62-mm ammunition to replenish depleted minigun canisters were rebuffed for lack of proper authorization and paperwork, the 40th's Capt. Vern Sheffield contacted a junior officer from the munitions storage facility. The officer, learning what the problem was, unequivocally placed himself and his men at Sheffield's disposal on the spot. There were problems with minigun reliability in the operation but none with ammunition supply.[2]

The base operations in-flight kitchen kept pumping out lunches, a small but important detail. Air force in-flight lunches typically contained either two sandwiches or one sandwich and a piece of fried chicken; a small bag of chips; a hard-boiled egg; an apple or orange; a small can of juice; a container of milk; packets of salt, pepper, mayonnaise, and catsup; and a packet of cookies. They were surprisingly tasty when fresh. The kitchen quickly ran out of chicken, but everything else held out. In a sharp departure from normal procedures the kitchen did not charge the crews for their lunches, and nothing was said about paperwork.[3] The Knives and Jolly Greens did not have to fight on empty stomachs, and the benefits went beyond nutrition. The ritual of opening the lunches, trading contents back and forth—white meat for dark, ham for cheese, cookies for an apple—and eating would help fill the anxious hours between launch and arrival over Koh Tang.

As the second wave launched, the Knives and Jolly Greens were well aware that tactical air support would be of little value to them. They departed in mutually supporting pairs when possible, planning to use their miniguns to suppress Communist fire during their insertions. These tactics, a departure from both rescue and special operations practice, were worked out by the helicopter crews entirely on their own initiative. It is difficult to avoid the suspicion that intense discussions on the beach between Ohlemeier and his crew and the crews of Jolly Green 11 and 12 and Knife 51 played a catalytic role in their development and adoption. This was the first face-to-face contact among helicopter crews following the initial shock of combat and the first eyewitness debrief to come back from the island concerning the situation on and above the LZs.

There was no attempt to launch the second wave as a single formation. Judging from landing and takeoff times and the recollections of those involved, launch times were driven by aircraft availability and the determination of the crews to go in as two-ship elements if at all possible. Departures were staggered accordingly. Knife 52 and Jolly Green 43 left from U Tapao at about nine-thirty, followed by Jolly Green 11 and 12 at ten o'clock. Delayed by the diversion toward Koh Tang, Knife 51 returned to U Tapao as the others were taking off and launched independently ten minutes after Jolly Green 11 and 12.[4] By a quarter after ten, the second wave was en route to Koh Tang with 127 marines.[5] Captain Davis and his men from Knife 22 were among them. The reinforcement was substantially smaller than expected and the situation on the island substantially worse, but it was the best that could be done under the circumstances and would have to suffice.

Based on the planning factors outlined earlier, the helicopters of the second wave should have reached Koh Tang beginning about a quarter past eleven. In fact, they did not start touching down until shortly before noon. The reason was a JCS order to CINCPAC to cease offensive operations and prepare an extraction plan. The order was issued between ten-thirty and a quarter to eleven and apparently passed on to the second wave by USSAG and Cricket without further ado. The substance of the order was spelled out in a JCS message to CINCPAC transmitted at 1155, directing "all concerned to immediately cease all offensive operations against the Khymer Republic . . . [and to] disengage and withdraw all forces from operating area as soon as possible."[6] These orders made perfect sense in policy terms. Their strategic implications were another matter, for their operational and tactical ramifications were counterproductive. If carried out literally and immediately, strategic disaster might have ensued. The manner in which they were transmitted and executed is indicative of the way in which command and control was exercised and is worth pursuing further.

There is no doubt that the disengagement order originated with the president and that it was driven primarily by policy considerations— framed and phrased with them foremost in mind. That, of course, is how things were supposed to work. The evidence, however, suggests that the order was passed down the chain of command with little or no interpolation to allow for situational contingencies. It was apparently issued as a tactical execution order without full consideration of its strategic and operational implications. *Wilson's* message that the crew of the *Mayaguez* was accounted for went out at five minutes after ten. Some ten to fifteen minutes must have been needed for the White House staff to confirm the accuracy of *Wilson's* report and for the good news to sink in. Additional time, perhaps ten to fifteen minutes more, would have been needed to translate the presidential order into military terminology and transmit it on the command and control net.

The evidence thus suggests that the disengagement order was issued from the White House almost immediately upon receipt of news that the crew had been recovered. Just how and by whom it was passed to the forces in battle is unclear. The most likely path, however, is from the White House to the National Military Command Center and thence to Admiral Gayler's headquarters in Hawaii, Lieutenant General Burns's headquarters at Nakhon Phanom, and Cricket in turn. In light of the many channels of communication and the absence of written records, we may never know. Most of the key orders were issued and confirmed by voice on secure nets, and after-the-fact teletypewriter retransmissions for the record rarely capture the flavor of the moment. Nor is the question terribly relevant: the same multiplicity of communications made all higher headquarters privy to whatever orders went out and thus, in some measure, responsible for them.

Perversely, the very excellence of electronic communications and the abundance of channels tying the higher echelons of command together had become a major source of operational uncertainty. To begin with, that excellence and multiplicity supported, and therefore indirectly created, a flood of information and queries. In the words of the CINCPAC history, the net "was sometimes encumbered with statistical information and extraneous high level queries not appropriate for a command and control net."[7] In simple terms, the straphangers (a term of approbation applied to higher-echelon observers by soldiers in the field) in Washington, Hawaii, the Philippines, and God-only-knows where else were flooding the channels with requests for superfluous information. This presented problems at the top, where staffs were hard-pressed to come up with the desired information in a timely fashion. The more senior the source of the query the more preemptive the efforts to produce a response. There can be little doubt that considerable amounts of time, effort, and energy were devoted to answering questions of dubious relevance that might better have been devoted to planning and analysis.

But if the variety and excellence of communications presented problems at the top, they threatened to produce disaster at the bottom. The operational and tactical realities of combat had severely curtailed communications between those in command and their forces battling the enemy. The flood of messages and queries for information from on high was brought to bear on a small number of combatants, potentially disrupting vitally important transmissions.

An example makes the point eloquently. A query from USSAG/Seventh Air Force was passed on by Cricket to the marines on Koh Tang just before ten-thirty in the morning, almost exactly coincident with Spectre 61's critical fire mission on the western side of the island and Jolly Green 41's final attempt to insert. USSAG/Seventh Air Force wanted to know whether the marines had a Khymer linguist and bullhorns with them.[8] Perhaps mercifully, the marine reaction to this request was not recorded.

For reasons having more to do with tactics and the uncertainties of combat than with strategy or policy, Cricket had become a bottleneck in the command and control net. In a mechanical sense, the primary culprit was the loss of BLT 2/9's forward air control team and its UHF radios in the first minutes of combat. Examination of the geometry of the command and control communications net as shown in figure 3 makes the point clearly. But sheer communications saturation was a factor as well. The command and control net had become exceedingly top-heavy, and ABCCC, as the primary link between those in command

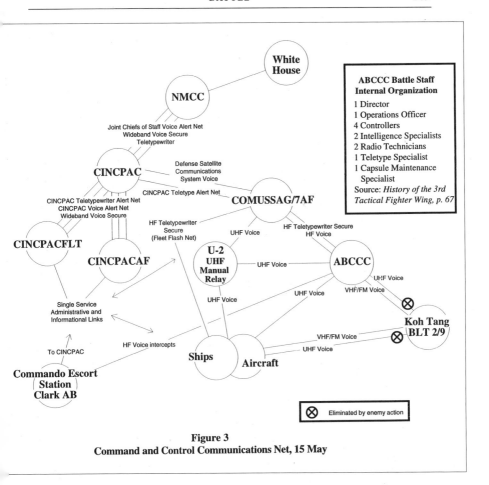

Figure 3
Command and Control Communications Net, 15 May

and those in combat, came under heavy pressure. Whatever weight we assign to the various causes—and fatigue was surely a factor—the EC-130 battle staff was plainly pushed to and beyond the limits of its ability to absorb, analyze, and pass on information and at the same time make time-critical tactical decisions.

The ABCCC battle staff had performed remarkably well all morning. This was an impressive achievement, considering the novelty of the operation and the late hour at which the controllers had learned of the plan. Their performance, however, slacked off during the afternoon.

At the same time, agencies out of contact with the enemy and pressed from above for information had to improvise to overcome communications blockages and facilitate the flow of information. Paradoxically, intelligent higher-echelon improvisation, praiseworthy in its own right, compounded the problems caused by the top-heaviness of the command and control net. Some of the effects were strikingly negative. The fact that Admiral Gayler's headquarters was better provided with reception, transmission, and processing facilities than Lieutenant General Burns's played a major role in this regard. A radio communications intelligence center at Clark Air Base in the Philippines, codenamed Commando Escort, was able to intercept HF voice transmissions associated with the *Mayaguez*/Koh Tang operation and pass them to CINCPAC by telephone.[9] The transmissions in question included those on the primary COMUSSAG/ABCCC tactical command circuit. Because they were made in voice and in the clear, there was no need for further interpolation: the Commando Escort operators simply patched them in to the CINCPAC switchboard. Similarly, transmissions monitored and passed on by the communications-relay U-2 were transcribed to teletype and loaded into a National Security Agency computer from whence they were immediately available to the CINCPAC staff.[10]

Admiral Gayler's staff at Pearl Harbor could thus listen in on the COMUSSAG/Seventh Air Force command net and second-guess Burns in real time. Although the details remain shrouded by security restrictions, it is clear that this was only the tip of the iceberg. A characteristic of HF single-sideband communications is the need to periodically shift frequencies to overcome atmospheric interference and other disturbances. The Commando Escort monitors and CINCPAC staff, better manned and equipped than their USSAG counterparts, were clearly much better able to follow the shifts. Moreover, other agencies were exchanging relevant information in the clear on HF. The Commando Escort monitors could scan the frequency bands, select whatever was relevant, and pass it on.[11]

An obvious candidate for this treatment was the rescue net that linked JRCC, the Joint Rescue Coordination Center at Nakhon Phanom, to King HC-130s. On a discretionary basis, for UHF and VHF channels were normally used, it was also linked to the Jolly Greens. Those working the Rescue Service net were trained to quickly collect and disseminate at least one category of information that higher headquarters hungered for throughout the day: data on aircraft damaged or shot down. This included identity, time, place, nature of damage, souls on board, and tactical details of rescue efforts. The JRCC's call sign, Joker, is worthy of mention as an ironic footnote.

Which transmissions were intercepted and passed along to Headquarters CINCPAC is probably beyond reconstruction, but it is evident that General Burns and his staff were in the singularly uncomfortable position of having to respond to the queries of senior commanders and staffs in possession of more timely and complete information concerning their forces than their own.[12] In this particular, at least, one cannot but sympathize with Burns and his staff.

More important than the precise timing of the disengagement order or its originating authority was its operational and tactical impact. Official accounts are less than candid on the point, but it is clear that the helicopters were at least briefly turned back from Koh Tang. The order was rescinded, and with good reason: it is exceedingly difficult to disengage from an air assault campaign without control of the LZs and hazardous in the extreme to try. Colonel Johnson's reaction to the order was immediate and forceful. An air force witness recalls him as livid, shouting words that effectively summed up the marines' predicament: "We don't even *own* the beach yet! Let's see us get off a piece of property we don't even own."[13] Johnson's emotional analysis was both succinct and deadly accurate.

Well aware that a safe extraction depended on control of the LZs, Johnson had contacted the deputy commander of USSAG, army Maj. Gen. Ira A. Hunt, Jr., two hours earlier in an attempt to have the 1/4 party aboard the *Mayaguez* transferred to Koh Tang by helicopter. It was to no effect.[14] Johnson clearly understood that if insertion of the second wave were halted, the situation on the island would be desperate. There is no evidence to suggest that Burns, Hunt, or the ABCCC battle staff did.

The U.S. Marines were not alone in questioning the disengagement order. When it was transmitted on the ABCCC helicopter control channel, six H-53s were airborne and monitoring tactical frequencies. These included two Knives and three Jolly Greens of the second wave and Jolly Green 41, fifteen minutes from landing at U Tapao. Two of the helicopter pilots immediately protested the order to Cricket. One was a Knife, probably Dick Brims or Bob Rakitis—my informants could not say. The other was Tom Cooper. At this point Cooper and his copilot, Dave Keith, probably had a better handle on the tactical situation on and above Koh Tang than anyone else not on the ground slugging it out with the Khymer Rouge. It was clear to Cooper that reinforcement was imperative, and his protest was forceful. The transmission stuck in the minds of his squadron mates who heard it.[15]

Just how the disengagement order was rescinded and by whom is uncertain. Johnson did what he could, and the ABCCC battle staff surely considered the helicopter pilots' protests. One source says that Johnson's protest was immediately and independently echoed by the commanding general, Fleet Marine Force Pacific, in Hawaii.[16] The evidence is negative, but Burns and the USSAG/Seventh Air Force staff must have appreciated the validity of the protests as soon as they were raised. The order was rescinded with remarkable swiftness given the coordination required, even with—or perhaps especially with—real-time voice communications. Whoever was responsible and however it was done, cancellation of the disengagement order was secured in less than fifteen minutes.[17]

The second wave proceeded to Koh Tang. Disaster might have ensued had it not.

As the air force helicopter crews proceeded grimly back into the fray, Johnson no doubt heaved a tentative sigh of relief. In the meantime, unbeknown to them, two events had occurred at Nakhon Phanom that were to have a material impact on the ensuing operations. In the first of these, two OV-10s departed for U Tapao at 1047, shortly followed by two more.[18] Who ordered them launched is unclear. Major General Archer, Seventh Air Force chief of staff, passed instructions to prepare a plan for OV-10 employment on the HF voice command net shortly after nine o'clock.[19] A source close to the situation who declined to be named told me unequivocally that the commander of the 56th SOW, Col. Harry Goodall, ordered the launch on his own authority.[20] The official histories are ambiguous on the point, but whoever ordered the OV-10s launched, Goodall was responsible for selecting their pilots. Flying the lead aircraft under the call sign Nail 68 was Maj. Robert W. Undorf, an experienced FAC and fighter pilot. It would be afternoon before they arrived.[21]

The second event was the product of forces set in motion two days earlier. The skeleton 40th ARRS maintenance and functional check flight crew left behind when the squadron deployed south had been struggling to make the squadron's two potentially flyable HH-53s ready since the evening of the thirteenth. Shortly before eleven o'clock, they brought one of the two into commission and turned it over to the squadron commander, Lt. Col. Joseph P. McMonigle. McMonigle took it south, departing shortly before noon and estimating arrival at U Tapao some three hours later.[22]

As the second wave made its way toward Koh Tang, Austin and his group continued their trek north, staying close to the shore and arming themselves with AK-47s and M16s abandoned by the *Khmer Kraham* that they found along the way. By about 1030 they had closed to within striking distance of the main perimeter but were still separated from it by Communist positions.[23] Bolstered by Spectre's earlier bunker-busting and by the reinforcements brought in by Jolly Green 41, Austin and Keith decided to mount a linkup attack from the main perimeter, spearheaded by Zales's platoon and supported by tactical air and mortar fire.

Zales would lead the attack, backed by First Sergeant Funk and the weapons platoon commander, 2d Lt. Daniel J. Hoffman.[24]

As the command group came within striking distance of the perimeter, the mortar section commander, 2d Lt. Joseph J. McMenamin, placed himself at the point. Serving as his own forward observer and coordinating his actions with Keith inside the perimeter, he began his preparation with a spotting round fired out to sea to provide a safe point from which to correct fire. A simple but effective way of compensating for the lack of gridded charts, it was nevertheless an inherently risky expedient: McMenamin's mortars would be firing directly at the marines inside the perimeter.[25]

Air support had declined in effectiveness after Spectre 61's departure. Without smoke grenades to mark their positions, Keith and Captain Cassidy, Austin's air liaison officer, had to be satisfied with simply identifying to the air force fighters as best they could the zone between the two marine groups where it was safe for them to attack. The fighters would make successive passes over the island from west to east until Cassidy reported that he was off their right wing and Keith reported that he was off their left wing. This procedure, requiring three-way coordination, was slow and anything but precise, but it was the best that could be done under the circumstances. Keith and Cassidy called in flights of fighters at intervals, and they raked the corridor between the marine forces with 20-mm cannon fire and 500-lb. bombs.[26] Once McMenamin had his mortars set up and registered, he had them fired for effect as each flight pulled off from its pass. This process had to be repeated with frustrating frequency as successive flights of A-7s ran low on fuel and had to be replaced. It was cumbersome, but it worked.[27]

With the *Khmer Kraham* in the corridor softened up, Zales's platoon jumped off. The attack apparently caught the Communists by surprise, and Zale's men quickly made contact with Austin's group. As had been the case earlier, marine offensive action was swiftly followed by a strong counterattack. As before, the counterattack was broken up by a timely, improvised response. In this case, the riposte was led by McMenamin, who observed a Communist squad moving against the exposed eastern flank of the attacking marines. He led two men forward to take them under fire by surprise.[28]

The linkup was nearing completion as the second wave reached the island. The insertions began with a run into the west beach by Jolly Green 11 and 12 at 1150. The tide was in, and the small LZ could hold only one helicopter at a time, but the two Jolly Greens made their approaches together and took turns landing and hovering offshore to provide suppressive fire. Both successfully off-loaded their marines. Jolly Green 12 delayed in the LZ to take four wounded marines on board before heading back to U Tapao. Their successful trip into the west beach was followed at noon by a Cricket-ordered attempt by Knife 52, Jolly Green 43, and Knife 51 to insert on the east beach. This was eloquent testimony to the degree to which Cricket—or whoever was calling the shots—was out of touch with the situation on the ground.[29] Knife 52 was hit hard by enemy fire in the attempt and aborted the approach, continuing straight across the narrow neck of the island and streaming fuel from ruptured external tanks. The aircraft barely made it to the Thai coast with her marines still aboard. Knife 51 and Jolly Green 43 then diverted—on whose initiative is unclear—to the west beach, where they inserted successfully shortly after noon. Knife 51 delayed in the LZ to take five wounded marines aboard for return to U Tapao.[30]

In sharp contrast to the first wave, none of the helicopters landing on the west beach suffered serious battle damage. The LZ was anything but secure, but a combination of suppressive marine fire and helicopter miniguns had effectively beaten down the enemy response. The helicopters were able to get in and out more or less unhindered. The number of marine effectives in the main perimeter was up to 205.[31] The bulk of G Company was now on the island. More importantly, Golf's company commander and gunnery sergeant were with their men.

Austin's group entered the perimeter while the second-wave insertions were taking place. As they moved into the perimeter, the soldiers passed a knocked-out *Khmer Kraham* 106-mm recoilless rifle position.[32] The precise time is in doubt, but the available evidence suggests that the linkup took place at a quarter to twelve or shortly before.[33] Keith had commanded the marines within the perimeter for six hours; now he finally had relief. He saw Austin first. The older marine grabbed Keith by the helmet, pulled his head against his shoulder, and said, "Good job, kid!" Minutes later, Keith was delighted to see Davis, whom he had thought to be dead.[34] Keith quickly briefed Austin and Davis on the situation within the perimeter.

Between noon and twelve-thirty—the critical interval—responsibility for on-scene command overhead had apparently fallen vacant. This was eloquent testimony to the lack of effective air-to-ground coordination. At five minutes past one, COMUSSAG/Seventh Air Force queried Cricket, asking why fighters were not striking near the marine positions.[35] Higher headquarters briefly flirted with the idea of committing *Coral Sea's* A-7s and A-6s in support of the marines on Koh Tang, but the navy properly rejected the plan. The aircraft were not equipped with VHF/FM radios and could not communicate with the marines on the island.[36]

After assuming command of Golf Company from Keith, Davis and

McNemar took stock of the situation. Most of the men in the perimeter belonged to Golf. Austin delegated tactical control to Davis while he tried to sort things out by radio, appointing Keith his operations officer to replace Major Hendricks, who had dislocated his shoulder. Davis's first priority was to tie in the perimeter and integrate the elements of Echo Company that had come in with the second wave into a coherent defensive position. He and McNemar systematically marked out fighting positions, and the troops started digging in. Davis assigned the northern half of the perimeter to Golf. Elements of Echo under Capt. Mykle Stahl assumed responsibility for the southern half. As Davis moved forward to mark the boundary between Golf and Echo, he encountered Pvt. K. O. Taylor. Taylor, dug in and fighting, had found his element and was prominent among those fielding live Khymer grenades and tossing them back. Davis was favorably impressed and it showed. "Hell, sir," Taylor said to Davis, "this ain't no big thing. We do this kind of shit back home all the time!"

It occurred to Davis that he had not seen Staff Sergeant Tutele, who should have gone into the west beach with the first wave. He inquired to no effect: none of the marines recalled seeing Tutele after the initial insertion. Davis concluded that Tutele had become a casualty, only to observe him several hours later, emerging from the jungle carrying an armload of AK-47s and with a big smile on his face. Shortly afterward, Keith saw Tutele inside the perimeter with several captured weapons and packs. It was about three in the afternoon.[37]

Confronted with terrain and vegetation much like that of his native Samoa and separated from his platoon, Tutele apparently decided early in the fight that he could best serve his fellow marines by thinning out the Communist ranks from within and had gone hunting. Enemy fire against the northern side of the perimeter had diminished significantly during Tutele's absence, and it is difficult to avoid making a causal connection.

The consolidation of marine strength within the main perimeter eased tactical pressure on the ground. Austin, however, had insufficient force to execute his assigned mission, and the landing zones were still under fire. He asked for clarification about 1500, and he and Keith began planning for three contingencies: digging in to spend the night, mounting an attack to seize the island, and extraction. Of the three options, extraction was the most complicated.[38] Back at U Tapao, plans for a third wave were abandoned. Without additional reinforcement the marines' situation on Koh Tang remained marginal, or so it would have seemed to an impartial observer.

At least one competent observer would have disagreed: Gunnery Sergeant McNemar. In the process of laying out and tying in the defensive perimeter, McNemar had taken careful note of the terrain, the volume and nature of enemy fire, and the fighting qualities of the marines. He was concerned about Second Lieutenant Cicere's platoon. Committed to the east beach with the first wave, they not been heard from since. McNemar could hear sporadic gunfire from that direction, but that was all. About three in the afternoon, McNemar concluded that there was no immediate threat to the perimeter and decided to take appropriate action. Accompanied by Sergeant Tutele, he conducted a personal reconnaissance along the cleared strip dividing the northern neck of the island. Moving forward a hundred meters in front of the marine perimeter, the two sergeants encountered no opposition. They threw fragmentation grenades at likely Communist positions in a reconnaissance by fire. The grenades drew no response. That confirmed McNemar's tactical assessment.

The southern half of the cleared strip dividing the island's northern neck was occupied by a gouged-out strip or crater: whether natural or man-made, McNemar was not sure. Whichever, it would impede movement from the south, and almost all of the enemy fire was coming from that direction. McNemar concluded that Golf could leapfrog along the northern edge of the strip, using fire and maneuver to reach the other side of the island.[39] His young marines had taken the initial shock of combat well; they had found their confidence and were fighting effectively. Davis was later to recall that they were edging forward in their fighting positions and had to be restrained. The opportunity was evident to McNemar and the obligation to exploit it clear. He approached Davis, laid out his assessment and his plan, and said, "Captain, let's take this damn island."[40] Davis did not question McNemar's judgment, and he had no doubt that Austin would back whatever decision he made. "Gunny, give me a few minutes, I want to think about it," he replied.

Davis was torn: emotionally he was with McNemar, but intellectually he had his doubts. Golf's green troops had not really slept in three days, and ammunition was becoming a problem; there was no source of fresh water inside the marine perimeter, and the men were drinking brackish water from plastic containers in overrun Khymer Rouge positions. Finally, Davis was concerned with casualties. The prospect of getting the company spread out across the island and then being ordered off and having to fight a retrograde action back to the beach was the deciding factor. "Gunny, this is my decision and I'm gonna have to live with it, but we're not going to take this island," Davis announced. McNemar was outraged.[41]

After the second-wave insertions, Jolly Green 43 and 11 were held near Koh Tang for an attempt to rescue the isolated group on the east beach. This materialized shortly after two o'clock. The plan was for

Jolly Green 43 to go in, shielded from Communist fire by a protective screen of riot-control gas laid down by a flight of A-7s. It was a good idea, the difficulties of flying an H-53 while wearing gas masks notwithstanding.[42] But the plan miscarried when the A-7s released the gas crosswind instead of into the wind, parallel to the helicopter's approach path. Instead of approaching the survivors screened by the gas, 43 plunged into the cloud and then emerged silhouetted against a white backdrop.[43]

Khmer Kraham fire discipline remained solid: the Communist gunners held their fire until the helicopter was well inside their killing zone. As Jolly Green 43 slowed to enter a hover a storm of fire erupted, much of it from lethal 12.7-mm machine guns. A 12.7-mm round severed a main fuel line in the left side of the fuselage. The right engine was protected by an automatic shutoff valve in the cross-feed line, but the left engine immediately failed from fuel starvation. Worse, fuel under pressure from the electric boost pump in the main tank spewed out into the cabin through the ruptured line. Airflow through the open cabin door and windows atomized the fuel, filling the fuselage with a spray of JP-4 that poured out the open ramp. Jolly Green 43 aborted, clawing for altitude on its remaining engine. The helicopter pulled away from the island, trailing a streamer of raw fuel over one hundred fifty yards long.[44]

The unsuccessful rescue attempt left only three of the second-wave helicopters flyable. Based on the experience of the day so far, this number was insufficient for either reinforcement or extraction. Worse, no one in a position to do anything about it had a clear appreciation of the tactical situation. Austin understood the precariousness of his circumstances all too well, but he was operating alone. No one with whom he was in contact outside his perimeter was conversant with the fundamentals of infantry combat or Marine Corps ground doctrine, let alone the tactical specifics of his predicament. Johnson, out of contact with Austin and his marines, was reduced to the status of an operations facilitator. Although he possessed only fragmentary knowledge of the situation on the island, he clearly understood what had to be done operationally. More to the point, Johnson had been effectively removed from the chain of command by the lack of radio and secure telephone communications at U Tapao base operations. He could identify and help to rectify blunders after the fact, as in his reaction to the decision to turn back the second wave, but he was isolated from the decision-making process.

Nor were air force arrangements for tactical command and control working any better. The attention of on-scene commanders above the island had been split by the diversion of A-7s to provide cover for Knife

23's survivors early on. None had been able to stay on station long enough to form a coherent picture of the tactical situation on the ground. The severity of the problem was underlined by the stubborn misconception that the main body of marines was on the east side of the island. The crew of Spectre 61 possessed the raw information needed to correct this assumption when they departed Koh Tang. But although the Spectre crew could no doubt have plotted the marine positions with considerable accuracy, they were untrained in ground combat and thus probably unaware of just how critical the situation was. More to the point, apparently no one thought to ask them to do so after they landed at Korat.

This seemingly hopeless tactical situation was relieved by a series of unrelated events. *Henry B. Wilson* had returned to Koh Tang shortly after one o'clock. Informing Cricket of her willingness to provide gunfire support, she contacted the A-7s covering Knife 23's survivors and serving as rescue on-scene command.[45] By mutual understanding, *Harold E. Holt* was to operate west of Koh Tang and *Wilson* to the east. Rodgers shared the general impression that the marine main body was on the east side of the island, so the cove off the east beach seemed a logical place to bring *Wilson's* weight to bear. For their part, the A-7s had located most of the enemy gun positions on the east side of the island in the wake of Jolly Green 13's unsuccessful rescue attempt but were unable engage them for fear of hitting the small group of Americans. *Wilson's* 5-inch guns had the necessary accuracy, but enemy positions in the interior of the island were not visible from the ship.

Rodgers and the A-7 pilots worked out a solution to the problem. Rodgers ordered *Wilson* down to two boilers and set up a slow circuit up and down the cove, working in as close to the island as possible while keeping ten to fifteen feet of water beneath the keel (map 9). The island was no more than a speck on *Wilson's* hydrographic charts, and leadsmen in the bow began plotting the subsurface contours, drawing their own charts as they went.[46] The procedures that *Wilson* and the A-7s adopted to compensate for the lack of gridded charts mirrored those used by McMenamin on the opposite side of the island. The destroyer would put a round into the water: a prominent rock off the eastern side of the northern peninsula served as a convenient reference point. The A-7s would use the shell splash as an initial point from which to make progressive adjustments to correct *Wilson's* fire onto the target.[47]

The A-7 pilots had no previous experience adjusting naval gunfire, and the improvised solution wasn't elegant, but it worked. By one-thirty *Wilson* was engaging targets on the island and was to put in some 176 rounds of 5-inch fire that day. It is impossible to identify her targets

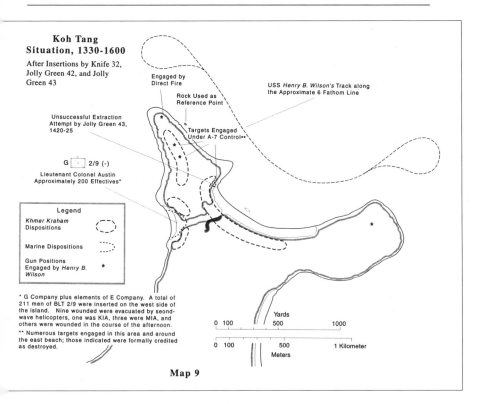

**Koh Tang
Situation, 1330-1600**

After Insertions by Knife 32,
Jolly Green 42, and Jolly
Green 43

Engaged by
Direct Fire

Rock Used as
Reference Point

USS *Henry B. Wilson's* Track along
the Approximate 6 Fathom Line

Targets Engaged
Under A-7 Control**

Unsuccessful Extraction
Attempt by Jolly Green 43,
1420-25

G ☐ 2/9 (-)

Lieutenant Colonel Austin
Approximately 200 Effectives*

Legend

Khmer Kraham
Dispositions

Marine Dispositions

Gun Positions
Engaged by *Henry B.
Wilson* *

* G Company plus elements of E Company. A total of
211 men of BLT 2/9 were inserted on the west side of
the island. Nine wounded were evacuated by seond-
wave helicopters, one was KIA, three were MIA, and
others were wounded in the course of the afternoon.
** Numerous targets engaged in this area and around
the east beach; those indicated were formally credited
as destroyed.

0 100   500   1000
Yards

0 100   500   1 Kilometer
Meters

Map 9

with any precision, for the reported coordinates were plotted on woefully inadequate maps, but fire from her 5-inch guns may have prevented Jolly Green 43's abortive rescue attempt from turning into disaster. *Wilson's* fire was to be instrumental in recovering the isolated body of twenty-five marines and air force crewmen.

Coral Sea, relieved of her punitive strike role by the cancellation of a final launch shortly after one o'clock, began closing the island at thirty knots. By two o'clock, she was reconfiguring her flight deck to support helicopter operations.[48] When Jolly Green 43's rescue attempt failed, *Coral Sea* was within seventy nautical miles. Apprised of the carrier's proximity by Cricket, Purser elected to recover aboard ship, even though he had never before made a shipboard landing. Jolly Green 11 followed him in to refuel and rearm.[49] Once aboard, Purser's flight mechanic, T.Sgt. Billy D. Willingham, contacted *Coral Sea* maintenance personnel and took immediate steps to repair the ruptured fuel line. After consultation with Willingham, a chief petty officer cut away the offending section of fuel line with a hacksaw and replaced it with a piece of rubber tubing secured by radiator hose clamps. The repairs took time and were hardly in accordance with anyone's technical orders. The fuel system was undoubtedly contaminated with aluminum filings, but the filters worked as advertised and it was successful.

An incident took place during this interval that, although not directly germane to the flow of events, conveys the flavor of the moment and bears repeating. While repairs to Jolly Green 43 were in progress, an off-duty *Coral Sea* sailor, bearded, shirtless, and clad in cut-offs and flip-flops in the best traditions of the Zumwalt-era navy, approached the helicopter. After exchanging nods of greeting with the copilot, 1st Lt. Robert Gradle, he slowly eyed the helicopter up and down. Noting numerous bullet holes in the airframe, seeing hydraulic fluid and JP-4 dripping out of holes onto the flight deck, and hearing the rasping of a hacksaw from within, he turned to Gradle and asked, "Where'd you come from?" Gradle, a man of few words, answered, "Koh Tang Island." The sailor looked the helicopter over with renewed interest and, after a considerable pause, asked, "What are you doing?" "Fixing the aircraft," replied Gradle. After more reflective scanning and another long pause, the sailor asked, "Where you going?" "Koh Tang Island," replied Gradle. The sailor slowly rescanned the aircraft and the battle damage, looking up and down. Then, speaking slowly, pronouncing the word with two distinct syllables, and talking more to himself than to Gradle, he said, "Heavy! Heavy!" and cruised off down the flight deck without another word.[50]

As *Coral Sea* closed Koh Tang from the southeast, more help was on the way from the north. Jolly Green 44 had cleared a functional flight check for maintenance shortly before eleven o'clock and launched for U Tapao ten minutes before noon. Another Jolly Green came into commission about one-thirty and left for U Tapao just before three-thirty.[51] The four OV-10s from Nakhon Phanom had arrived at U Tapao. At 1440, about an hour and a half after they landed, USSAG/Seventh Air Force issued a message ordering their launch ASAP (as soon as possible).[52]

How this decision was reached is obscure, but that it was belated there can be no doubt. It should have been clear by midmorning from analysis of radio traffic on tactical frequencies—or from debriefs of returning helicopter crews—that existing arrangements for air support of the marines on Koh Tang were not working. The repeated handoffs of on-scene command over the island, coordinated by Cricket and thus at least potentially known to the USSAG/Seventh Air Force staff, provided more evidence of this fact. OV-10 Nail pilots were specifically trained to control tactical jet fighters in close support of troops in combat and to serve as on-scene commander. Like the A-7s, the OV-10s had the VHF/FM radios needed to communicate with the marines on the ground. But unlike the A-7s, the OV-10s had the maneuverability and cockpit visibility needed to locate, identify, and maintain continuous eye contact with ground targets. They also had the low-altitude endurance to remain on station long enough to provide operational continuity. Indeed, the OV-10 was designed for precisely these characteristics.

Whatever the reason for the delay and whoever was responsible for rectifying the situation, Major Undorf in Nail 68 and his wingman, Capt. Richard Roehrkasse in Nail 47, arrived over Koh Tang about twenty minutes after four.[53] They found a chaotic situation. Assuming on-scene command from a flight of A-7s, Undorf, backed by Roehrkasse, swiftly moved to put it in order. In the process he formed an accurate view of the situation on the ground, the first individual to do so who was in a position to do anything about it. It was a turning point. Working systematically, Undorf contacted the marines in the west perimeter and the survivors of Knife 23 on the eastern side of the island and established their locations. Using smoke rockets to mark targets for the fast-moving jets, he launched suppressive A-7 and F-4 strikes while he considered the situation.

Having taken stock, Undorf's first order of business was the isolated group off the east beach. While he focused his attention there, Roehrkasse kept an eye on the western side of the island. As Undorf was putting in strikes, Rodgers, advising Undorf of his intentions, ordered *Wilson's* gig back into the water to adjust gunfire and serve as a rescue backup. Undorf contacted Lucas and *Wilson* to assess the situation and consider the options. The gig could bring out only fifteen men at a time, and they would have to make their way out through the surf to reach it. Lucas rejected that option: the remaining marines and air force crewmen would not be able to hold off the enemy.[54]

A helicopter pickup would be needed, and the available assets were neither extravagant nor immediately at hand. Jolly Green 11 launched from *Coral Sea* at 1625. She was accompanied by *Coral Sea's* two SH-3s, unarmored and with M16-toting marines their only firepower. They and *Wilson's* gig were the final backup. Jolly Green 12 would land on the carrier shortly after five o'clock, refuel with engines running, and launch for Koh Tang at five-thirty after dropping off maintenance workers and parts.[55] Knife 51 had departed U Tapao for Koh Tang at 1545 but would land en route to drop off fuel and maintenance personnel with Knife 52.[56]

In the course of his three-way exchange with *Wilson* and Lucas, Undorf had discovered a part of the problem not yet addressed: the sunken

Swift boat in the cove. Decks awash, it was manned by a small crew hiding in the pilot house. They would take cover when jets passed overhead, then come out to man the deck-mounted guns when helicopters approached. With an unrestricted field of fire, the Swift boat's twin .50-cal. mount on the forward deck covered the east beach like a blanket. It was clearly responsible for much of the damage to Jolly Green 13 and the likely cause of Jolly Green 43's ruptured fuel line.[57] Sensing the problem, the A-7s had begun a strafing attack on the boat shortly before Undorf and Roehrkasse arrived on station.[58] Information from Lucas convinced Undorf that the Swift boat's guns would be a major impediment to any attempt to get his group out and that strafing hadn't done the job. Overhearing the exchange, *Wilson* volunteered her guns. Undorf agreed. It was 1633. Within minutes, the boat was smothered with twenty-two 5-inch rounds. Racked by secondary explosions, the Swift boat was out of action for good.[59]

By 1635 Jolly Green 11, piloted by 1st Lt. Donald Backlund, was standing by in orbit with the SH-3s. Backlund and his crew had put the first marines aboard *Holt* that morning and had monitored tactical frequencies throughout the day. They provided fire support during Jolly Green 43's failed rescue attempt and were well aware of the outcome of Jolly Green 13's earlier attempt to rescue the survivors of Knife 23. Backlund, quiet but forceful, urged Undorf to speedily resolve the situation on the east side of the island, emphasizing the need to deploy heavy suppressive ordnance before another attempt.[60] Undorf brought in a flight of F-4s with laser-guided Mk-82 bombs to hit Communist positions around the western perimeter. As he worked, forces assembled for the upcoming rescue attempt.

Aboard *Coral Sea*, Willingham and the navy maintenance workers finished their repairs to Jolly Green 43. The aircraft was refueled and rearmed, and Purser and his crew launched at 1710. They joined Jolly Green 11 off Koh Tang ten minutes later. By 1730 they had been joined by Jolly Green 12 and Knife 51.[61] *Wilson's* gig was up on frequency and standing by off the east beach by 1753.[62] In the hours to come, the gig's crew was to exhibit an impressive blend of aggressiveness and discipline: laying in fire when appropriate, assisting the operation when they could, and keeping quiet and out of the way when they had nothing to contribute. Accurate .50-cal. fire from the gig significantly bolstered the available suppressive firepower, and the boat was on hand for rescue coverage should a helicopter go in the water.

More important still, the gig provided Undorf with an independent check on the situation. Heavily laced with experienced brown-water sailors, veterans of riverine combat in Vietnam, the gig's crew approached the campaign from its own distinct perspective, both physically and professionally. They could see and understand aspects of the tactical situation that other participants could not. Their competence, like Undorf's and like Cooper's and Keith's in Jolly Green 41 earlier in the day, was contagious. A telling detail of the ensuing action that stuck in the minds of many of the U.S. Air Force helicopter crewmen was the voice of the gig's radio speaker. Using the call sign Black Velvet 2— *Wilson* was Black Velvet—he transmitted in a deep, unhurried voice with a rich black-American accent, exuding competence, confidence, and calm. On occasion, the repetitive thud of the gig's .50-cal. machine gun could be heard in the background.[63]

Spectre 11, 21, and 22 launched for Koh Tang in sequence, apparently in response to a National Military Command Center order received by COMUSSAG/Seventh Air Force at 1455.[64] During the event, Spectre 22's guns were silenced by a fire control malfunction, but the other two AC-130s arrived over the island fully combat ready. Their intervention was to prove critical.

From this point, things moved quickly. A quick check back and forth between Lucas on the beach and *Wilson's* gig reconfirmed that helicopter extraction was the only practical solution. Spectre 11 arrived on scene at 1736 and began firing under Undorf's control at 1813.[65] Jolly Green 11, piloted by Don Backlund, would be the primary recovery helicopter.

At this point, Backlund and his crew had been in the air for fourteen hours. They had watched the operation unfold from the start, monitoring tactical radio frequencies with mounting frustration as plan after plan miscarried. Many of Backlund's crew were respected NCOs with extensive combat rescue experience. This was a vote of confidence for Backlund, since by Jolly Green custom the most combat-experienced flight mechanics and pararescuemen were allowed to pick their pilots when crews were formed for particularly dangerous or important missions. And, in fact, much of the 40th's combat experience resided in Jolly Green 11's flight mechanic, T.Sgt. Harry Cash, and in her two senior PJs, M.Sgt. John Eldridge and S.Sgt. Stu Stanaland. Although Backlund's first exposure to combat was in the Phnom Penh evacuation, he was on his third tour at Nakhon Phanom and had received his initial checkouts from men with recent combat experience. He and his crew knew what should have been happening and wasn't. Now, in Undorf, they perceived an instrument that just might make good the deficiency. Backlund made it clear to Undorf that time was rapidly running out. He urged him to bring in heavy ordnance—"hard stuff," as he put it— to suppress Communist positions around the east beach. The tone of voice in his radio transmissions reflected frustration, impatience, and insistence.[66]

Urged on by Backlund, Undorf launched final suppressive strikes. He then committed Jolly Green 11 to the eastern beach, supported by Jolly Green 12, Knife 51, and *Wilson's* gig with Jolly Green 43 and the two SH-3s providing backup rescue coverage.

Undorf cleared Jolly Green 11 in for the pickup shortly after Spectre opened fire. It was the moment of truth. The time was about a quarter past six in the evening. Backlund called for smoke from the survivors, got it, and landed his aircraft on the beach at 1820, drawing intense ground fire in the approach. The gig requested permission from Undorf to fire, got it, and began laying in fire just north of the survivors. As Backlund and his crew held their position, the air force crewmen and marines scrambled for the helicopter's open ramp. They conducted an orderly withdrawal, emptying their weapons at enemy positions as they ran. *Khmer Kraham* soldiers closed to within hand-grenade range of the helicopter as the marines loaded, only to be cut down by minigun fire from Jolly Green 11's door and window guns, manned by Cash and Eldridge. With no time to call in strikes, Undorf engaged Communist positions with his OV-10's .50-cal. machine guns. Knife 51, hovering close offshore, joined in with her miniguns, engaging charging enemy soldiers at Undorf's direction. Fisk and Cooper knocked out Knife 51's cabin windows with rifle butts to add fire from their GAU-5s—short-barreled versions of the M16—to the suppressive effort.

By prearrangement, Jolly Green 11's ramp gunner, Stu Stanaland, notified Backlund when the last marine had boarded, and the helicopter lifted off. Some three minutes had elapsed between touchdown and takeoff. During that period, Undorf made five to seven firing passes. On the run-out, Jolly Green 11 was attacked by a heavy machine gun inside the tree line north of the beach. Its position was marked with a line of waterspouts reaching out across the surface of the water for the big helicopter. Undorf rolled in on it, opened fire with his .50 calibers, and it stopped firing. Jolly Green 11 had sustained battle damage, but by 1823 it was off the island with all twenty-five survivors aboard and accounted for.[67]

As Jolly Green 11 pulled off, a C-130, acting on orders from COMUS-SAG/Seventh Air Force, dropped a fifteen-thousand-pound BLU-82 bomb on the center of the island.[68] The drop was not coordinated with the extraction procedures other than to avoid interfering with them.[69] *Wilson's* bridge crew and some of the marines inside the perimeter observed the drop without knowing what it was; the marines at first thought it was an off-target resupply drop.[70] A parachute pulled the bomb in its extraction cradle from the C-130's open ramp; then a second

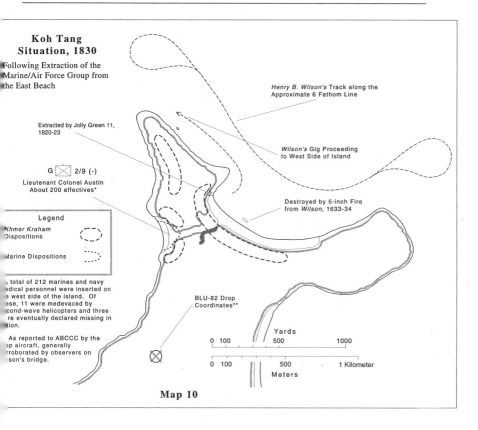

**Koh Tang
Situation, 1830**

Following Extraction of the
Marine/Air Force Group from
the East Beach

Henry B. Wilson's Track along the
Approximate 6 Fathom Line

Extracted by Jolly Green 11,
1820-23

Wilson's Gig Proceeding
to West Side of Island

G ⊠ 2/9 (-)

Lieutenant Colonel Austin
About 200 effectives*

Destroyed by 5-inch Fire
from Wilson, 1633-34

Legend

Khmer Kraham
Dispositions

Marine Dispositions

a total of 212 marines and navy
medical personnel were inserted on
the west side of the island. Of
these, 11 were medevaced by
second-wave helicopters and three
were eventually declared missing in
action.

BLU-82 Drop
Coordinates**

As reported to ABCCC by the
top aircraft, generally
corroborated by observers on
Wilson's bridge.

Yards
0 100   500   1000

0 100   500   1 Kilometer
Meters

Map 10

parachute attached to the bomb deployed, pulling the bomb free from
the cradle. The bomb descended toward the center of the island beneath
its parachute while the lighter cradle fell more slowly, drifting north
toward the marine perimeter. It was still in the air when the bomb
detonated.

The results were awe-inspiring. Shock waves arced out through the
humid tropical air, clearly visible from *Wilson's* bridge. Inside the marine perimeter, Keith had not seen the drop but heard and felt it: "All of
a sudden the world shook. I looked up expecting to see a mushroom
cloud." Both *Wilson's* bridge crew and the marines assumed that the
cradle was a second bomb. As it drifted toward the perimeter, marines
frantically clawed at the ground, trying to dig in before it hit.[71] The
cradle landed some forty meters outside the perimeter. As the day wore
on, Keith, now serving as the battalion operations officer, worried that
it might go off or that the Khymer Rouge might be able to detonate it.

The official U.S. Air Force history states that the enormous bomb was dropped "to apply maximum psychological pressure" on the enemy. Be that as it may, the blast and massive report, clearly audible from *Wilson's* bridge, no doubt affected Communist morale.[72] Undorf, the closest competent observer, noted a marked reduction in traffic along footpaths following the bomb's impact; the traffic may have been reinforcements moving toward the north end of the island.[73] Whatever additional effect the BLU-82 had is unclear. The stated reason for its use may represent only a part of the truth—a consideration that reopens the question of the *Khmer Kraham* order of battle.

It is possible that the BLU-82, whether by accident or design, disrupted the deployment of *Khmer Kraham* reserves. This may have happened either directly by destructive impact or indirectly through the impression that the clearing created by the bomb was a landing zone for the insertion of additional marines. These considerations notwithstanding, Communist pressure against the marine perimeter did not slack off. To the contrary, sniper fire increased as the day wore on.[74] But the number of enemy troops facing the marines does not seem to have increased, of which the best evidence—though indirect—is the fact that no general infantry assault was later mounted against the perimeter. This can be explained by three basic hypotheses, either individually or in combination: first, that the *Khmer Kraham* commander had already committed his reserves, in which case the DIA and IPAC estimates were essentially accurate; second, that he held back a reserve out of caution; and third, that the BLU-82 drop neutralized his reserves. The close correlation between the DIA and IPAC estimates of Communist strength on the island and Austin's after-the-fact appraisal of the forces actually committed against him is suggestive but in itself inconclusive.

A final bit of evidence, although inconclusive in itself, suggests a fuller appreciation and, in my view, a convincing one. A *Khmer Kraham* radio transmission from Koh Tang intercepted after the battle indicated that the island's defenders suffered 55 killed and 70 wounded, a total of 125 casualties.[75] If the numbers were even approximately correct, logic suggests that even the higher DIA estimate of enemy strength on the island was substantially short of the mark. The reason for this is straightforward: the behavior of Koh Tang's *Khmer Kraham* garrison during the afternoon and, as we shall see, into the evening did not resemble that of a force in the process of being annihilated. Casualties of 30 to 50 percent are generally held to render ground combat units ineffective, except, perhaps, for exceptionally good troops in static defense.[76]

As a rule, only extraordinarily tough, highly motivated, well-trained and well-led troops continue to function after suffering casualties of 80 percent or more, particularly if they are sustained during a relatively brief period, as was the case here.[77] That Koh Tang's defenders remained effective and reactive to the end suggests that the force on the island numbered two hundred fifty or so and that reserves were systematically committed as the day wore on. The belief that there were uncommitted Communist forces on the island is supported by the results of a strike on the south end of the island about a quarter past four in the afternoon by F-4s with Mk-84 bombs and 20-mm cannon fire, which produced secondary explosions.[78]

In the end, however, our analysis is tentative for lack of historical data. Like all combat forces, the *Khmer Kraham* possessed a distinctive fighting style or signature. But such signatures manifest themselves in ways that vary as a function of circumstances, not least among them the nature of the opposing force. The Koh Tang engagement represents the only occasion on which the *Khmer Kraham* engaged U.S. line infantry, or for that matter any first-class western-trained infantry, in a stand-up fight. One cannot extrapolate from a data base of one. What we have to say is thus speculation, but the evidence suggests that whatever local reserves the *Khmer Kraham* commander at first held back were committed against the marine perimeter along the western cove by mid-morning. Had there been a reserve force in the center of the island, it would probably have been sent in against Austin's command group as it worked its way north. We should not, however, draw premature conclusions.

Operational caution was a *Khmer Kraham* trademark: witness the slowness with which they tightened the noose around Phnom Penh. It is therefore unlikely that the southern beaches of the island were undefended to begin with or that they were completely denuded of defenders in the course of the day. As American objectives became more apparent, and especially as extraction operations began, reserves would have been moved north. To that extent, the BLU-82 drop and air strikes against the southern part of the island during the course of the day probably served a useful purpose.

The rescue of Cicere's platoon and the crew of Knife 23 on the east beach was balanced by a setback twenty minutes later. A communications mixup led to the commitment of Jolly Green 12 in an attempt to rescue either a marine or Lucas—which is unclear—erroneously believed to have taken refuge in the remains of Knife 23. Believing that the survivor was incapacitated and hiding inside the helicopter, Jolly Green 12's pilot, Capt. Barry Walls, hovered above the shattered fuselage and lowered the rescue hoist to the door. Knife 51 supported the attempt with minigun fire, hovering just offshore and shooting under Nail 68's direction.[79] The *Khmer Kraham* defending the east beach were fully aroused, and the hovering helicopter made a perfect target. Jolly Green

12 was hit hard—harder, in fact, than any other helicopter that survived the operation—and aborted when the flight mechanic, Sgt. Jesus DeJesus, was wounded and shot from the crew door. The helicopter made it to *Coral Sea,* out of commission for weeks to come.[80]

The resolution of matters on the east side of the island eliminated the most pressing tactical problem. But yet another helicopter had been struck from the friendly order of battle, and it was not clear what was to be done next. The marines in the western perimeter were clearly next on the agenda, and Undorf contacted Austin for guidance. Austin made it clear that the situation was critical. Dark was approaching, and the marines would have to be either reinforced or extracted. If the decision was to extract, the operation would have to be swiftly completed. The marines were still hard-pressed, and as their numbers diminished, those remaining would be increasingly vulnerable to being overrun by the *Khmer Kraham.* Once started, extractions can be reversed only with great difficulty if at all. A decision to extract would thus be irrevocable once made: the limited number of helicopters made that a given.

Unable to obtain orders or guidance from Cricket, Undorf took matters into his own hands: he contacted Austin and gave him a choice. Undorf thought he could arrange for reinforcements, but he wasn't sure; matters at U Tapao were beyond his control. He was certain, however, that as on-scene commander he could bring in the helicopters with which he was in radio contact to extract the marines. Undorf was also confident of his ability to orchestrate the air power on hand to effectively support them. This he communicated to Austin. Weighing the odds carefully—for neither alternative was attractive—Austin chose extraction.[81] Undorf and Austin had, in effect, made a national policy decision.

CHAPTER 7

Extraction

THE DECISION TO EXTRACT was one thing. Execution was another, for the forces available to pull it off were marginal, and daylight was rapidly fading. Few aphorisms have held true across the entire sweep of military history. One, mentioned earlier, concerns the benefits of surprise to assaulting infantry and the risks of depending on it. Another holds that to disengage from a skilled, aggressive, and determined foe is among the most difficult and dangerous of tactical evolutions. A third states that any operation or maneuver is infinitely more difficult in darkness than in daylight. The tiny American force on and above Koh Tang and in the waters offshore thus faced one of the most daunting tactical scenarios imaginable. It did so in isolation, both because there was no meaningful backup available and because the urgency of swift execution made the efforts of higher echelons of command irrelevant. A key tactical development helped to counterbalance these negative operational factors: the forces in contact had a clearly established chain of command. Nail 68 was in charge.

The extraction would have to be coordinated with a controlled marine withdrawal to the beach. That would not be easy, for *Khmer Kraham* resistance remained fierce and intelligent, reacting to changing circumstances quickly and efficiently. It is unlikely that the Communist defenders of Koh Tang had a great surplus of available manpower, but what they had they used well. By late afternoon, the *Khmer Kraham* had emplaced a significant proportion of their machine guns for antiaircraft use and employed them with characteristic discipline. They held their fire until the fighters and OV-10s were pulling out of their runs to avoid being spotted.[1] Against this was balanced the tactical air power overhead, waiting to strike at Undorf's request, and more limited but more precise firepower in the form of Spectre 11. With the AC-130 came low-light-level television (LLLTV), which Spectre systems operators could use to accurately trace the marine perimeter and even track individuals within it. This was one area where darkness would work to American advantage.

The problem was not a lack of firepower but a lack of helicopters. When Undorf and Austin decided to extract, both Jolly Green 11 and 12 had suffered battle damage and neither could be relied upon. Judging from the timing of the decision and the information available, Undorf could be certain of only two H-53s: Jolly Green 43 and Knife 51. *Wilson's* gig was insurance. *Holt* was prepared to put two boats in the water capable of taking off seven men at a time. The two SH-3s could handle fifteen men each[2]—if they could survive in the landing zone. But to rely on any of these fallbacks as the primary means of extraction would be desperate in the extreme.

If the American Marines were to get off clean, it would have to be by H-53. To compound the problem, the night would be starless and moonless: besides Communist fire, the helicopter crews would face potentially lethal problems of spatial disorientation and loss of control without clear visual references. Undorf's decision to recommend extraction was therefore bold in the extreme. It was also—as events would confirm—both timely and correct.

In addressing the interplay of objective and subjective factors in military calculations, Clausewitz stated that in the whole realm of human activities, war most closely resembles a game of cards.[3] The analogy aptly describes the situation that Undorf faced in proposing extraction to Austin. Some things he could predict and control with reasonable certainty, some things he could not—and time was of the essence. Here Clausewitz's analogy suggests a high-stakes poker game where the winning hand is not determined until the last card is turned, and hesitation in betting can fatally compromise a hand before it fills out.

Undorf bet on a weak hand and drew aces. The first was dealt by the 40th ARRS. At 1515, after an unscheduled stop at Korat to check a suspected flight control malfunction, the Jolly Green piloted by Lt. Col. McMonigle arrived at U Tapao.[4] While the aircraft was being serviced, McMonigle conferred with squadron aircrew members on the ramp. Apparently acting on his own initiative and authority, he turned the aircraft over to a crew commanded by 1st Lt. Robert Blough on the spot and sent them toward Koh Tang.[5] Blough launched at 1645, using the call sign Jolly Green 44.[6] Undorf's second ace was dealt by the navy: the Military Sealift Command volunteers had the *Mayaguez* operating under her own steam by midafternoon, and *Holt* was able to cast off her tow. After escorting the container ship well clear of land into international waters, *Holt* unloaded the last of the boarding party by boat and headed for Koh Tang. She would arrive only an hour before sunset. There would be no one to direct her fire in the waning moments of daylight, and her 5-inch gun would remain silent, but her intervention was to be critical.

It was apparent, at least to Undorf and the helicopter crews, that delay would only make things worse. Extraction began without further preliminaries. It is apparent from review of the chronology that Undorf initiated the extraction within minutes, perhaps seconds, of reaching agreement with Austin. Their discussion would have taken the better part of a minute, and notifying the helicopter pilots of the plan and determining the order in which they would go in required additional coordination. Yet the first extraction sortie followed Jolly Green 12's futile commitment on the east beach by less than ten minutes (map 11). An important subsidiary detail was the size of the LZ: it would hold only a single H-53. The battle would be resolved on a narrow margin. That margin would be rendered adequate by competent tactical leadership.

Learning of the decision to extract, Davis approached Austin. "You got the day shift," he said, "I'll take the night." He thus volunteered to take responsibility for the final phases of the operation. Austin agreed.[7] Davis and McNemar began pulling Golf back to a shorter defensive perimeter anchored on a low knoll facing the cleared strip. After setting in the new perimeter, they ordered a cease-fire to allow Echo to disengage and pass through and in front of Golf's lines in order to get back to the beach for extraction.[8] The *Khmer Kraham,* sensing what was transpiring, increased their fire. Echo successfully disengaged but in the process left behind a three-man M60 team. Whether they were dead or alive has never been determined.

The helicopters started cycling into the west beach shortly after 1840. Knife 51, low on fuel after sustained hovering while providing fire support for rescue operations on the east beach, was first. The sun had set some twenty minutes earlier; although the western horizon was still clearly visible, night was falling fast.[9] To the marines on the island, the big helicopter appeared abruptly, like a black silhouette looming against the rapidly darkening gray of the western sky.[10] Although the marines were preparing to evacuate, they had received no advance warning of its approach. Knife 51's appearance set off a general exchange of hand grenades around the perimeter and started a firefight joined by the helicopter's miniguns.[11] As the helicopter touched down, the *Khmer Kraham* illuminated the marine perimeter with mortar-launched flares. With time clearly critical, Brims held his position on the beach. The battalion medical officer shepherded his wounded out into the water to begin the evacuation.[12] Loading up swiftly, Knife 51 departed for *Coral Sea* to re-fuel and rearm with forty-one marines aboard.

Jolly Green 43 was next, landing at 1847. Purser and his crew took on fifty-four marines, the heaviest load of the day. Among them was First Lieutenant Keith, who was later to recall the intensity of the enemy fire. As the helicopter held its position on the beach for what seemed an interminable time, he could clearly hear mortar rounds exploding on the LZ.

As the marines were boarding, Undorf found the mortar position and set off a smoke rocket to mark it for a flight of A-7s. The fighters, however, were unable to see the mark in the darkness.[13] The A-7s had been doing good work with Mk-82 bombs and 20-mm fire and were not quite finished, but for the moment Undorf's hands were full.[14] Spectre offered to illuminate the area for the fighters with parachute flares, but things were happening too quickly to permit the necessary coordination. During this interval, *Wilson's* gig laid in suppressive fire north of the marine perimeter.

At this critical juncture Jolly Green 44, approaching in the dark and unable to see Jolly Green 43 blacked out on the beach below, began an approach to the occupied LZ. Jolly Green 43's copilot, 1st Lt. Robert Gradle, listening carefully to the confused radio traffic, recognized a familiar voice when Blough announced his intentions. Realizing what was happening, Gradle turned on the aircraft's searchlight, risking exposure to enemy fire to avoid a collision between the two helicopters.

Blough aborted his approach. Jolly Green 43 lifted off for *Coral Sea* at 1850 with battle damage, and Blough came back around for a second try. Driven off by ground fire on their second attempt, Blough's crew went in again, landing at 1854. As the marines boarded, *Wilson's* gig suppressed fire south of the perimeter, and Nail 68 rolled in with .50-cal. fire.[15] Jolly Green 44 was gone within three minutes with forty marines aboard.[16]

Some seventy-three marines remained on the island, and the enemy was pressing hard. Aside from *Wilson's* gig, the OV-10s' machine guns, and helicopter miniguns, Spectre 11 was now the only usable firepower available.[17]

Holt was standing by off the west beach. Blough and his crew, recognizing that time was critical, saved precious minutes by taking their marines to the frigate. Holding an H-53 over the cramped flight deck had been difficult enough in daylight. Now it was dark, and Blough's crew had never attempted the evolution before. To make things worse, Jolly Green 44's landing light and searchlight were both inoperative.[18]

But Jolly Green 44's flight mechanic, S.Sgt. Bobby Bounds, possessed exceptional night vision. Leaning outside the aircraft, he was able to guide his pilots in.[19] By 1908, Blough's crew had off-loaded and were on the way back to the island. Meanwhile Undorf and Roehrkasse, low on fuel, were transferring on-scene command to a replacement flight of OV-10s: Nail 69 and 51, flown by Capt. Seth Wilson and 1st Lt. Will Carroll, respectively.[20]

As the handoff got underway, the aircraft overhead lost radio contact with the marines inside the shrinking perimeter. Attempts by *Wilson's* gig to reestablish contact failed. Spectre 11 was running low on fuel and ammunition. A critical moment was at hand. Making a final low pass with his landing lights on to ensure that the marines had not been over-run, Undorf transferred on-scene control to Wilson. During that interval, the marines reestablished radio contact. By then Spectre 11 had departed, after a final sensor sweep of the shrinking perimeter. Spectre 21 was still fifteen miles out.[21]

Wilson and Carroll took over under less than ideal circumstances. Dividing the tasks at hand between them, they went quickly to work. Wilson delegated fire support to Carroll and concentrated on getting the helicopters in and out. Carroll briefed the new Spectre crew on the tactical situation. It took the gunship ten minutes to sight in its guns and prepare to fire.[22] *Wilson's* gig was down to a thousand rounds. At this point, Blough's crew in Jolly Green 44 started back in, helped in their approach by a strobe light that Davis had thrown up on the beach beyond the perimeter.[23] In the moonless, starless night both Blough and his copilot, 1st Lt. Henry Mason, experienced vertigo: again Bounds talked them back onto the approach path. They landed under fire at 1915 as Spectre 21 responded to hostile volleys around the shrinking perimeter, taking out a mortar position in the process. Under Davis's and McNemar's orders, the marines delivered prepared suppressive fire of two M16 magazines as the helicopter touched down.[24] Jolly Green 44 took repeated hits while loading and traded fire with an automatic weapons position on the way out, suppressing it with minigun fire. Loaded with thirty-four marines and having lost engine power to salt-water ingestion during the approach, Jolly Green 44 was unable to attempt the approach to *Holt* and recovered aboard *Coral Sea* at 1930.

There were now twenty-nine marines on the island. At 1926 they reported that they were in danger of being overrun; moreover, some of Davis's men were nonswimmers and had no flotation gear.[25] For the first time since the extraction started, there was no helicopter nearby or inbound. Davis turned to McNemar and said, "Gunny, I think we've had it." Although not prepared to concede defeat, McNemar was not inclined to argue the point, either.[26]

Harold E. Holt *from the cabin of Jolly Green 11 approaching to unload her marines about 6:00 A.M., 15 May. The transfer began simultaneously with the assault on Koh Tang . . . in broad daylight. Twilight is brief in the tropics, and whatever plans there may have been for a dawn assault had clearly gone by the boards. The structure forward of the flight deck is Holt's helicopter hanger; the square housing aft of the flight deck is a missile launcher. This photograph was taken by 1st Lt. Ronald L. "Rat" Rand, air force photographer and member of Jolly Green 11's crew. (USAF photo)*

Members of Golf Company, 2nd Battalion, 9th Marines, run from Knife 22 toward a waiting Jolly Green after their forced landing, shortly after 7:00 A.M., 15 May, several miles west of Trat, Thailand. The border runs close to the coastline and the mountains in the background are inside Khmer Rouge territory. (USAF photo)

Sometime after 7:00 A.M., 15 May, near Trat, Thailand: Pararescuemen T.Sgt. Wayne L. Fisk, center, and Sgt. Ronald L. Cooper, Jr., right, crew members of Knife 51, confer with an unidentified marine as the marines transfer to a waiting Jolly Green. Fisk, a veteran of the November 1970 Son Tay Raid, was on his fifth Southeast Asia combat tour. (USAF photo)

Lester A. McNamar, Golf Company's Gunnery Sergeant, prepares to fire into Knife 22's cockpit before departing for U Tapao. The site was insecure and the decision was made to disable the aircraft. (USAF photo)

Golf Company marines catch a short nap on the U Tapao ramp as preparations to launch the second wave approach completion. These men had had little sleep for the past two days. The rotors of the Jolly Green in the background are turning and marines are loading up. (USAF photo)

Marines on the west side of Koh Tang, afternoon of 15 May. The thatched hut is about sixty yards inland just north of a small footpath. (Courtesy James H. Davis)

*Center of the marine perimeter, looking north along Koh Tang's rocky western shoreline. The BLT 2/9 aid station is working out of a **Khmer Kraham** bunker overrun in the initial assault. (Courtesy James H. Davis)*

*Jolly Green 43 proceeding to USS **Coral Sea** on a single engine. The helicopter would return to Koh Tang after shipboard repairs to receive the largest load of the day—fifty-four marines in a single lift. (USAF photo)*

Shortly after 2:00 P.M.: The east beach is shrouded with a combination of tear gas, dispensed by A-7s to cover Jolly Green 43's rescue attempt, and smoke from Henry B. Wilson's *guns.* Wilson *is in the foreground. (USAF photo)*

Mid-afternoon, 15 May: Success! Under tow by Harold E. Holt, *the* SS Mayaguez *begins to get up steam. (USAF photo)*

Golf Company officers inspect the damage to Jolly Green 12 aboard Coral Sea *en route to Subic Bay after the action, 16 or 17 May. From left to right: Capt. James Davis, Company Commander; 1st Lt. James "Dick" Keith, executive officer; and 2d Lt. Michael Cicere, 3rd Platoon commander. (Courtesy James H. Davis)*

Reunion of the crew of Knife 51, the last helicopter off Koh Tang, at Nakhon Phanom Air Base, Thailand, 17 May. From left to right: 1st Lt. Dick Brims, aircraft commander, in cap and sunglasses; S.Sgt. Marion Riley, flight mechanic/gunner; and Pararescueman T.Sgt. Wayne Fisk, in camouflaged fatigues. (Courtesy Wayne L. Fisk)

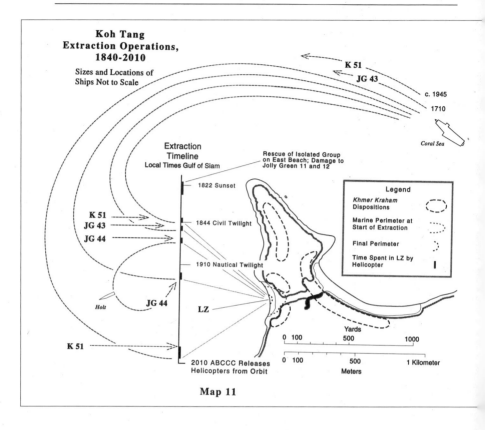

Koh Tang Extraction Operations, 1840-2010

Sizes and Locations of Ships Not to Scale

Map 11

Knife 51 lifted off from *Coral Sea* some twenty minutes later. Her minigun canisters were replenished with 7.62-mm rounds, testimony to the efficiency of the improvised H-53 servicing and maintenance procedures aboard the carrier. In the half-hour since Jolly Green 44 had left Koh Tang, flying conditions had deteriorated. In addition to the darkness, visibility was now hampered by haze and smoke. Spectre 21 dropped parachute flares to cut the darkness, but from the standpoint of the helicopter crews, the flares made things worse instead of better. The flares oscillated as they descended and bobbed in the water as they burned out, causing visual references to constantly shift. The combination created rich opportunities for confusion, spatial disorientation, and vertigo.

Wilson guided Brims in with UHF/DF (direction finder) steers and by intermittently turning on his OV-10's landing lights as he orbited the LZ at a thousand feet.[27] He was well within small-arms range of the Communist positions below. Each time Wilson turned his lights on he drew fire, which Spectre 21 suppressed. To a detached observer, it would no doubt have been an impressive pyrotechnical display. Making the approach blacked out, Brims, backed up by his copilot, 2d Lt. Dennis Danielson, brought Knife 51 to a hover above the LZ. As he rotated the aircraft to point the ramp toward the beach, he lost his hover references. Disoriented by the descending flares, Brims allowed the nose of the aircraft to pitch upward. Reacting to screamed abort calls on intercom, he pulled in power and began an instrument takeoff toward open sea as Knife 51 slid backward over the trees.

Brims tried again. Again he and Danielson lost their references in the collage of inky blackness, shifting shadows, and shimmering lights. Overcome by vertigo, they aborted the approach. On the third try, they put the helicopter in the water. It was a near thing.

Brims was keenly aware of the value of the perceptions and experience of his mixed Knife/Jolly Green crew. He had made it clear to the flight mechanics and pararescuemen at the outset that he valued their judgment and inputs. As Knife 51 lifted off the water, they talked things over on intercom. Brims suggested that they turn on at least one light to illuminate the LZ. The crew endorsed the idea.

On the fourth attempt, Knife 51 went in with all lights on—landing light, spotlight, hoist light, and hover light—a beacon for ground fire. As the helicopter neared the beach, the *Khmer Kraham*, plainly aware of what was happening, increased their fire. Spectre 21 replied with descending streams of 20-mm and 40-mm rounds. Brims's gunners responded with their miniguns. The intensity of the hostile fire was such that the marines tried to wave Knife 51 off, but Brims and his crew had had enough. They pressed in, landing on the now-flooded LZ, ramp toward the beach.

The marines had pulled back into a horseshoe perimeter ten to fifteen meters across with the anchor men in the water. From the perspective of Knife 51's crew, the position was marked by the muzzle flash and tracers of outgoing suppressive fire. The marines' attention was directed outward. They were settled into their positions, and it was hard to get them moving. Davis and McNemar addressed the problem in direct fashion. Moving along the perimeter, they shook and kicked their men and motioned them back to the helicopter.

Technical Sergeant Fisk requested permission to depart the helicopter to ensure that no one was left behind. His intercom was inoperative, so he used sign language to indicate his intent to the senior flight mechanic, S.Sgt. Marion Riley. He received Brims's permission the same way. Fisk deplaned and began motioning marines aboard. Davis and McNemar conducted an orderly withdrawal, directing the last marines aboard with Fisk behind them.[28]

Fisk remembered seeing the body of a marine near the tree line earlier in the day. He again requested and received permission to leave the helicopter. While he was doing so, something slammed into him from behind. It was two final marines charging up the ramp in the darkness.[29]

Fisk's first thought was that the Communists had rushed the aircraft. His heart in his mouth and adrenaline up, he spun around to bring his GAU-5 to bear—and saw two marines sprawled at his feet. His pulse returning to something approaching normal, Fisk again signaled to Riley to hold the helicopter on the LZ. He looked for Davis and found him by his captain's bars in the dim red glow of the cabin lights. Yelling into his ear to be heard above the rotor blast, engine noise, and gunfire, Fisk asked Davis if all his men were aboard. Davis yelled back that he thought they were. Fisk wanted to be certain. Again he went through the sign language exchange with Riley. Again he received a nod of approval. Again he departed the helicopter for a final check. As he left, McNemar stepped off the ramp to back him up. Knife 51 had been on the ground for nearly ten minutes.

Brims and Danielson looked out to sea into the dead black of the tropical night, monitored the aircraft systems, and waited.

As he made his way along the beach, Fisk was engaged by Communist fire from several positions. He responded with his GAU-5 and in so doing became the last U.S. ground combatant of the Vietnam War. Observing the exchange, Spectre 21 attacked Fisk's assailants with a descending wall of 40-mm and 20-mm rounds. Fisk circled the now-vacant perimeter and found nothing. As he started back for the helicopter, a green illuminating flare arced out of the jungle. His immediate reaction was that it was the signal for an enemy assault. Suddenly aware of the stark vulnerability of his position, Fisk headed for the helicopter on the run. Seeing him coming, McNemar jumped back aboard.

As Fisk hit the ramp, a crew member called the abort. Knife 51 lifted off. But the ramp had been placed in the "down" position to allow it to seek its own level on the rocky beach, and as the helicopter lifted off the ramp started down. Davis was watching. There was just enough light for him to see the expression on Fisk's face, and for a fleeting instant, he found the pararescueman's look of total disbelief amusing. Fisk fell on his back and began sliding out of the aircraft, throwing his arm backward for help. McNemar was closest to Fisk and grabbed for the first thing at hand. He got Fisk's microphone cord, thinking, "I hope this doesn't come unplugged." It did. He grabbed Fisk's leg. Fisk got a hand on McNemar's leg or belt. As the two slid backward, Davis grabbed McNemar's flak vest. Fisk's hand, thrown backward over his shoulder, connected with another in what he remembers as a "viselike" grip.

Hanging onto the sides of the helicopter, cargo tie-down rings in the cabin floor, and each other, the marines formed a human chain to drag the three men inside. The ramp went to the full down position. It was all they could do to hang on, but McNemar and Davis, at the end of the chain, pulled Fisk far enough forward to reach the ramp control. Fisk repositioned the control, leveling the ramp. As the ramp came up, the combined strength of the human chain, no longer fighting gravity, and Knife 51's acceleration catapulted Fisk into the cabin. He landed on top of Davis. They embraced. It was a fitting end to a very short war—and a very long war, for that night's events were the last act of America's military venture in Vietnam.[30]

Knife 51 lifted off shortly after eight o'clock with twenty-nine marines aboard. Brims and his crew had been on the ground for nearly ten minutes. As the helicopter climbed out, the LZ was still marked by the repetitive flashes of the strobe light Davis had thrown out from the perimeter. It would take time for the reality to sink in, but for all practical purposes the *Mayaguez* affair was over.

Jolly Green 44 had returned to Koh Tang some five minutes earlier and was orbiting close offshore. So was Jolly Green 11, which had arrived on station shortly after Knife 51. So were the two SH-3As from *Coral Sea*, marines at the ready with their M16s. They were not needed. At 2010 Cricket released the Jolly Greens to return to U Tapao. *Wilson's* gig departed the west beach and made a final check of the shattered remains of Knife 23 before rejoining the destroyer.

Later that night, using trucked-in parts and tools and specialists flown in by H-43, 40th maintenance finished temporary repairs to Jolly Green 13 sufficient to attempt a staging flight back to U Tapao. Jolly Green 13 made it, landing at 2325.[31] Knife 52 tried during the afternoon but experienced partial flight control hydraulic failure and made a second emergency landing.[32]

At three o'clock in the morning *Henry B. Wilson* came alongside *Coral Sea* to refuel. The Thai government was protesting the deployment of U.S. combat troops into Thailand without prior consultation or approval, and *Wilson* took over one hundred marines of BLT 2/9 aboard for transport to Subic Bay. The marines had returned from Koh Tang distributed more or less at random among *Wilson*, *Holt*, *Coral Sea*, and the U Tapao hospital. A head count was underway to determine how many were missing. Ultimately the total of those unaccounted for reached three: members of an Echo Company M60 team that had been pulled from the line shortly after the second wave touched down and were never seen again.

Although the story relies on a single source, there was apparently a postscript to the extraction. A fourteen-man platoon of SEAL Team One under Lt. (jg) R. T. Coulter was flown from Subic Bay to *Coral Sea* while the Koh Tang operation was in progress. After landing with his team on *Coral Sea* by carrier on-board delivery (COD) aircraft, Coulter was escorted into the cabin of Rear Admiral Coogan, commander of TF-73. Coogan wanted Coulter and his men to go into Koh Tang in open boats, unarmed and under a white flag of truce, to retrieve the bodies of marines and helicopter crewmen. Leaflets dropped in advance would advise the Khymer Rouge of their peaceful intentions. Coulter had talked briefly with marines just back from Koh Tang on his way to the admiral's cabin and had gained a clear impression of what the marines had faced on the island. He was not inclined to risk his team's survival on the basis of Communist literacy, let alone intentions. Coulter refused the order, recommending instead that his team swim ashore at night for a reconnaissance. The matter was dropped.[33]

During the early morning hours of the sixteenth, translators came out to *Wilson* by helicopter from U Tapao. Just before noon the destroyer made a final pass along the beaches looking for marines reported missing, announcing peaceful intent by loud hailer and asking for information in French and Khymer.[34]

The result was anticlimactic, for Khymer Rouge camouflage and fire discipline held to the end. From *Wilson's* bridge and railings, Koh Tang seemed devoid of life. There was neither friendly response nor hostile reaction.

CHAPTER 8

Aftermath: Analysis and Lessons

MEMORIES OF COMBAT fade quickly. The reactions of participants uttered immediately after the experience can capture reality in a way that later, fully staffed-out responses cannot. Clausewitz put it well, although incompletely, for he omitted from his list of the stresses of war the profound emotional relief that follows a close brush with disaster.

> If no one had the right to give his views on military operations except when he is frozen, or faint from heat and thirst or depressed from privation and fatigue, objective and accurate views would be even rarer than they are. *But they would at least be subjectively valid.*[1]

Two such subjectively valid reactions to the *Mayaguez*–Koh Tang affair made it into the official record. They were objectively valid as well. The first was in a teletypewriter message sent through channels to the 21st and 40th by Colonel Johnson. It was transmitted some thirty-six hours after the last of his marines came off Koh Tang. Navy communications channels remained saturated for some time after U.S. forces disengaged, and as a nontactical message, Johnson's missive had to wait its turn. It was therefore composed earlier, though how much earlier we can only guess. Most likely, the first draft began to form in Johnson's mind when he received word that Davis was off the island and had left no marines behind. It bears repeating:

SUBJECT: RECOGNITION AND APPRECIATION
1. TO US, "SEMPER FIDELIS" EXTREMELY MEANINGFUL. YOUR ACTIONS *MAYAGUEZ*/KOH TANG AFFAIR EPITOMIZED THAT MEANING.

2. WITH DEEPEST SINCERITY, TO THE "JOLLIES" AND "CHAR-LIES," WE'RE WITH YOU, ANYWHERE, ANYTIME, ANY MISSION. THANKS.[2]

The memo requires little explanation. *Semper Fidelis*, "always faithful" in Latin, is the Marine Corps motto. The reference to "Charlies" was to the *C* in the aircraft designation of the Knives' CH-53s.

The lessons embedded in Johnson's message are implicit but clear: the courage, determination, initiative, and improvisation of the Knives and Jolly Greens had meant the difference between success and failure, even—certainly from Johnson's standpoint—catastrophe. To the professional abilities and moral qualities of the air force helicopter crews that Johnson so generously praised we can add the operational capabilities of their H-53s. The big, powerful helicopters, more heavily armed and armored than their marine counterparts, had performed magnificently in a mission for which they were not designed and for which their crews were neither briefed nor trained. The irony is that the H-53 was designed in response to a Marine Corps requirement: it is all but certain that the air force on its own would never have procured so capable and tough a helicopter (Appendix B).

The H-53s had flown at far greater ranges than was usual in air assault operations, requiring commensurately greater fuel loads. Every helicopter in the final extraction had lifted from Koh Tang a significantly greater weight in living marines than its normal rated load. We can only speculate as to how many more helicopters might have been lost without the Knives' and Jolly Greens' self-provided fire support, but minigun fire clearly made an important contribution to survival. The big helicopters were able to absorb an impressive amount of battle damage and keep flying. This is true even taking into account the vulnerability of the CH-53s' external fuel tanks.

The extra equipment and capability of the HH-53s had made a crucial contribution. In the first instance, aerial refueling enabled the rescue helicopters to carry additional guns, armor, and marines to Koh Tang in place of fuel. The HH-53s put more marines on the beach per sortie than did their special operations counterparts and took proportionately fewer losses in so doing. In the second, HH-53s continued flying despite battle damage that would have destroyed a CH-53 and perhaps avoided some as well because of their extra firepower. How many HH-53s were preserved by their additional weapons and armor we cannot say, but it is clear that several were saved by the explosion-retardant foam in their external fuel tanks.[3] The most clear-cut and dramatic example is Jolly Green 13, an example worth reviewing in context.

Jolly Green 13 was hit while trying to pull marines off Koh Tang instead of put them in, so loss of the helicopter would not have changed the balance of forces on the island. Moreover, although 13 might have been available had the action continued past midnight, the helicopter received enough damage to put it out of the fight. Jolly Green 13 could not participate in the second-wave insertions or in the extraction, and one might therefore argue that its survival was irrelevant. But such an argument is inherently linear and war is not. It ignores the shock that would have reverberated up and down the chain of command—and laterally among the Knives, Jolly Greens, and fighter pilots—following the destruction of yet another helicopter on Koh Tang two and a half hours after the first assault. We have seen how the loss of Knife 23 and 31 on the east beach during the initial insert focused attention and tactical effort on what was, in fact, a subsidiary operation. We can only speculate concerning the impact of a second such distraction. It is unlikely to have been positive.

The second immediate reaction to the Koh Tang campaign to make it into the records was generated by *Henry B. Wilson's* skipper, Comdr. Mike Rodgers. Sent to the commander of the Seventh Fleet by teletype several weeks later (apparently to document an earlier informal report), it was retransmitted to the 56th SOW. Like Johnson's message, it is unlikely to have earned its author any points with his superiors.

The subject line says it all: SUPERLATIVE PERFORMANCE OF OV-10 A/C [aircraft].[4] A carefully phrased two-page assessment, Rodgers's message contains a concise analysis of the final stages of the Koh Tang operation. It makes one central point forcefully: that Undorf and Wilson imposed order on chaos and in so doing prevented serious loss to the American forces engaged. In praising the Nail FACs' performance, Rodgers pointedly emphasized the OV-10's limited radio equipment. The tactical and operational lesson that Rodgers clearly drew out of the operation is evident: all the communications in the world cannot replace a competent on-scene commander.

In the realm of policy, the *Mayaguez*–Koh Tang operation had been successful regarding President Ford's stated goals and was widely interpreted as such. Significantly, media and congressional critics accused the administration of using excessive force but not of failing to achieve its political objectives. Ford suffered some embarrassment from the findings of the General Accounting Office investigation—which singled out intelligence failures, specifically the nonuse of the DIA and IPAC estimates—when Democratic leaders in Congress had the report declassified just in time for his television debates with Governor Jimmy Carter, his Democratic opponent in the 1976 presidential election.[5] But in the end, Ford's undeniable success in recapturing the *Mayaguez* and obtaining the release of the crew with modest casualties took the sting out of the criticism. The GAO report had little impact.

But although we can judge the *Mayaguez* affair a clear success in policy terms, we are not concerned with policy in isolation. Indeed, we have proceeded on the premise that policy can never be considered by itself. Instead, we are interested in the interactions among policy, strategy, operations, and tactics and with the way in which uncertainty and risk transfer among them. As with our initial formulation of the problem, the lessons are most readily approached in question format: what were the operational and tactical risks? What strategic and policy risks did they entail? How effectively were those risks anticipated and dealt with? And finally, how did U.S. communications capabilities bear on the outcome? These questions can be summed up in Clausewitzian terms: how effective were American efforts to anticipate friction and deal with it?

First, it is clear that unexpected factors over which U.S. planners had little or no control played a major role in driving events, particularly in the early stages of the crisis. What if, for example, the Khymer authorities had taken the *Mayaguez* into Kompong Som on the thirteenth? U.S. forces were in no position to interfere, and the Khymer Rouge could have surrounded ship and crew with troops of enough strength to render a rescue mission impossible. The answer, so far as one can be given, is that the swift application—or threatened application—of force by the United States probably induced the Communist leaders to trim their sails, eventually abandoning the *Mayaguez* and relinquishing her crew.

This consideration does not reduce to window dressing the strenuous American attempts to quarantine the ship and prevent the removal of its crew to the mainland, for U.S. planners could not know with certainty what was afoot. Nor would the Communists have had any clear evidence of American resolve. Lieutenant General Burns applied force in accordance with presidential dictates and came as close to success as was possible without incurring self-defeating penalties through the inappropriate or excessive use of force. The decision to permit the fishing boat with the *Mayaguez's* crew aboard to proceed to Kompong Som is the prime example, with an important caveat: Secretary of Defense Schlesinger's stalling tactics had enabled Burns and his staff to use their discretion. Here, the system of command and control worked well, largely because of the excellence of electronic communications. In short, President Ford and his subordinates accurately assessed the salient risks during the preliminary operations and dealt with them effectively.

Similarly, the strength of the Khymer Rouge on Koh Tang was not subject to U.S. control. Most of the defenders were on the island when the *Mayaguez* was seized, the only likely addition being the crews of sunken or beached patrol boats. Their numbers and strength could have been reduced by preinvasion bombardment, but this was ruled out—legitimately, in my view—for fear of harming the crew. Still, the tactical effectiveness of the Khymer Rouge defenses on Koh Tang could have been minimized by realistic planning, starting with an estimate of enemy capabilities and intentions. The U.S. forces were well served in this regard, for accurate estimates were available. Their nonuse is a textbook example of friction at work. But it would be simplistic to attribute this intelligence failure to simple administrative oversight, the focus of the GAO investigation, for the origins of the problem ran much deeper. The core of the matter is that tactical planning under USSAG/Seventh Air Force aegis failed to address the enemy as a reactive opponent.

Which numbers were briefed is not the point. How enemy opposition was to be addressed and dealt with was, and it was here that the most serious planning failure occurred. The lack of an effective means of providing fire support on call to the helicopters when they went in to Koh Tang is at once the clearest evidence of failure and its most basic manifestation. There was, simply put, no workable plan to coordinate air and naval gunfire support with the assault. Even if BLT 2/9's forward air control team had made it onto the island with radios functioning, most of the same problems would have been encountered. The lessons of Dieppe, Tarawa, Normandy, Okinawa, the Pusan Perimeter, Inchon, and untold thousands of engagements in Vietnam were forgotten. For this, Lieutenant General Burns and his staff bear full responsibility. They do not, however, bear the entire blame. The reasons for the lack of effective coordination require closer examination.

ABCCC was the common point of contact for the forces involved and in principle an important means of reducing friction. But the Cricket controllers had not briefed with the assault force and had only the sketchiest notions of marine doctrine and tactical capabilities. Most damning, no one in the operational chain of command above Davis and McNemar, a captain and a gunnery sergeant, seems to have done a worst-case tactical assessment. Theirs became explicit only when they saw the aerial photographs of the *Khmer Kraham* beach defenses. This failure can be attributed to a lack of initiative on the part of the ABCCC deployment commander, but the ultimate responsibility falls, in no special order, on Burns and his staff and Baxter and Anders.

Whatever the reasons, the costs were real. When the helicopters began taking fire shortly after six o'clock on the morning of the fifteenth, there were A-7s overhead Koh Tang. But the fighters were not prepared to deliver supporting fire and, as analysis of their radio transmissions makes clear, had no clear idea of how to go about it. Tellingly, nearly forty minutes elapsed before the fighters established contact with the marines on the beach.[6] At bottom, this failure was one of planning and anticipation instead of one of hardware and procedures. It is all the more inexplicable because the A-7s were based at Korat, where current and accurate intelligence on Koh Tang was available—including the IPAC and DIA estimates and AC-130 reports of antiaircraft fire from the island the night before.[7]

But the inherent unpredictability of war is a double-edged sword that cuts both ways, and not all unexpected factors worked against U.S. forces. By all rights, *Henry B. Wilson* should not have been off Koh Tang at 0718 on 15 May, yet she was. To be there, her captain and crew had had to do everything exactly right for no less than sixty hours running. Not only was *Wilson* unpredictably in the right place at the right time, she performed unpredictably well once there. *Wilson's* accurate reaction to the dispatch of the Thai fishing vessel from Kompong Som was absolutely vital to policy success, and her contribution to the successful outcome of the operation went well beyond that. *Wilson's* role in achieving success, as much as any chain of events in the affair, clearly sustains my initial assertion about the unpredictability of outcomes in war.

My operational experience and reading of history suggest that unexpectedly good timing and unexpectedly good performance are more likely to be encountered in combination than in isolation: well-trained, well-led combatants tend to make their own luck. A line from the musical *Pippin,* about kings and war, puts it neatly: "It's smarter to be lucky than it's lucky to be smart." That reality was repeatedly demonstrated on, above, and in the waters surrounding Koh Tang.

This brings us to the Koh Tang invasion proper. This is the heart of our study, for it was on Koh Tang that the greatest risks were incurred. It was also on Koh Tang that U.S. forces approached the brink of tactical and operational disaster, with policy implications that can only be described as grim. Consider the newspaper headlines and network television lead stories that would have ensued had the marines been overrun. The American public was—and is—sensitive to the loss of life. Dead soldiers are bad, but the loss of an entire unit, however small, would have been far worse. For Communist Cambodia, a fourth-rate power by the most charitable estimate, to inflict an unequivocal military defeat on the United States would have entailed immense damage to American credibility and prestige. The only real historical precedent was the April 1961 Bay of Pigs debacle, but with two important differences. First, failure at the Bay of Pigs was arguably more one of intent and will than of capability; second, and most important, the units overrun were not American, and the men captured were not members of the United States military. President John F. Kennedy and his advisers could take comfort, cold though it must have been, in the thought that few doubted their ability to defeat Fidel Castro had they chosen to apply full force. But if the American Marines on Koh Tang had been overrun, there was no immediate way to reverse the situation.

Granted, forces capable of handling Koh Tang's garrison would have been available within twenty-four hours. *Hancock* was scheduled to arrive at 1700 on the sixteenth, with two companies of marines and eleven CH-53As embarked plus a full complement of heavy weapons and helicopter support, including four AH-1J gunships.[8] But to what effect? In itself Koh Tang had no strategic value at all, let alone policy significance. To have seized the place with overwhelming force in the aftermath of disaster would only have added to the embarrassment and the butcher's bill. Congressional critics, newspaper editorialists, and television news anchors would have invoked memories of Hamburger Hill and a thousand other meaningless geographic points in Vietnam soaked with American blood, but in a broader context—for the *Maya-guez* affair was more than just a battle. It was both a small war and the last battle of a larger one.

In summing up our analysis, we return to question format: how close did U.S. forces come to failure on Koh Tang? What risks were incurred, and how were they addressed? What were the uncertainties, and how were they dealt with?

Any such inquiry must begin with the enemy. There can be no question about the competence of the *Khmer Kraham*, for they accurately anticipated both the nature and direction of the American attack. Defenses around the northern beaches, the best helicopter landing zones, and the most likely ones in light of probable U.S. policy objectives were well sited and well dug in. The impression of Communist competence is reinforced by the fact that the defenses were improved just before the attack.[9]

The period of greatest danger to the marines was probably between the first assault and about nine-thirty to ten in the morning, when the immediate threat was relieved by Spectre 61's fire support and reinforcements brought in by Jolly Green 41. As to why the *Khmer Kraham* failed to mount a general counterattack during this interval we can only speculate. Part of the answer is obscured by the fog of war and likely to remain so. We can, however, reasonably speculate as to how the scenario played out. The most basic consideration is that the *Khmer Kraham* had no way of knowing with certainty how vulnerable the Americans were or when that vulnerability was greatest. More fundamentally, the *Khmer Kraham* commander on Koh Tang must have worried about the danger of exposing his troops to air power should they emerge from cover, and properly so. The ineffectiveness of the U.S. fighters, however, should have relieved him of any misapprehension on this score by 0700 at the latest. We will probably never know why he failed to press his counterattacks harder. Perhaps he was overruled by higher authorities. Perhaps he overestimated U.S. helicopter reserves.

Whatever the case, the shrewdness of his preparations and his aggressiveness in execution make ineptitude an unlikely hypothesis. The failure to press home an infantry attack against the small, isolated group of Americans off the east beach suggests a conscious decision to leave them in place, perhaps as bait for the strong and well-entrenched anti-helicopter defenses or perhaps simply to serve as a distraction. The failure of the *Khmer Kraham* to mount a more effective effort to overrun the marine position should not blind us to the fact that their defensive plan was sound and well executed. To criticize the Khymer Rouge commander for a presumed lack of aggressiveness smacks of mirror imaging, for we know neither what his orders were nor how many reserves he possessed. In the end, Communist forces on Koh Tang successfully defended the island. Their commander and his superiors might well have considered that a victory, and with good reason.

ABCCC's immediate diversion of the surviving first-wave helicopters to the west beach probably averted disaster, and the Cricket controllers get high marks on this score. The pilots and crews of the helicopters involved—Knife 32, Jolly Green 42 and 43—deserve similarly high marks. The indispensable ingredient for survival at this point was the unflinching persistence of the helicopter crews in making their insertions, and they made good. Without the intelligent and quickly made decisions by Lackey, Pacini, and Purser and their crews in the early minutes of the confrontation, the outcome would have been very different. The difference between unflinching and suicidal is vitally important, however fine the line between them may be. It is difficult to see how these helicopter crews could have drawn that line more finely. Conversely, Cricket's preoccupation with rescue operations—a familiar air force mission—diverted attention from reinforcement and support of the marines on the west beach. It also helped to foster a general impression that the main ground action was on the east side of the island.[10]

ABCCC's decision to divert Spectre 61 to U Tapao with instructions to refuel and return to the fight was critical. Although unrecognized as such at the time, Spectre 61's intervention in the ground battle between eight-thirty and ten o'clock was pivotal. So were Jolly Green 41's repeated and ultimately successful attempts to insert, not least of all because they brought Spectre into the fight. This series of actions—the only instance of close and effective air-ground coordination until the arrival of Undorf and Roehrkasse after four in the afternoon—was critical. The crew of Jolly Green 41 acted as the catalyst in this turn of events, and her pilots, First Lieutenant Cooper and First Lieutenant Keith, deserve special praise. Spectre 61, however, was running low on fuel and departed shortly after 1000. Her effectiveness, moreover, went unappreciated except by the marines within the western perimeter, and they were unable to communicate with their commander, Colonel Johnson, at U Tapao.[11] For unknown reasons, additional AC-130s were not dispatched until late afternoon, and then only in response to an order from the National Military Command Center.

The bedrock on which all rested was the ability of the marines on the ground to quickly organize themselves and respond to an unanticipated tactical situation. That the isolation of Austin's command group from the main body had no perceptible influence on the combat effectiveness of either speaks highly for the quality of 2/9's marines and for the abilities of their platoon commanders and squad leaders. This is all the more so because BLT 2/9 was a newly reconstituted unit. Keith, in command of the main perimeter in the early, critical hours, played a pivotal role and merits particular praise. It should be noted that the marines went in fully armed and equipped for the worst, despite the optimistic intelligence estimates.[12] This implementation of standard procedures in accordance with basic Marine Corps doctrine was decisive in containing the adverse effects of friction. The marine combat performance cannot be faulted. Davis and McNemar deserve plaudits for G Company's performance.

But combat performance could do only so much. Despite the repulse of *Khmer Kraham* counterattacks during the morning and the successful linkup shortly after noon, the marines still faced a grim situation. At their period of greatest strength, following the second-wave insertions, they barely outnumbered the well dug-in defenders according to the most optimistic of estimates. They would have been in serious danger if forced to spend the night without reinforcement. Fatigue and ammunition depletion would have been serious problems, and although ammunition could have been parachuted in by C-130, the only way to get fresh marines to the island was by helicopter.

The number of available helicopters would have been inadequate—indeed, might have dropped to zero—but for the independent actions of helicopter pilots and maintenance crews. Those responsible for bringing Knife 51 into action—Brims stands out—made a critical contribution. So did those responsible for bringing Jolly Green 44 into commission. It is worth noting in this regard that the decision to send Jolly Green 44 to Koh Tang, vital to the success of the extraction operations, was apparently made independently by the 40th Squadron commander, Lieutenant Colonel McMonigle, without reference to USSAG/Seventh

Air Force or any higher authority. As with *Wilson*, Jolly Green 44's arrival over Koh Tang at the critical moment was improbable, and her crew's performance once there was improbably good. Captain Blough's decision to take his first load of marines to *Holt*, made entirely on his own initiative, was pivotal.

All of this might well have gone for naught but for the belated arrival over Koh Tang of Nail 68 and 47. We have already outlined the circumstances that brought Major Undorf and Captain Roehrkasse to Koh Tang. The arrival of the OV-10s, like most of the other pivotal events, was driven at least in part by individual initiative acting outside of formal command channels. Extraction operations are notoriously difficult—indeed, disengagement under fire from an aggressive enemy is arguably *the* most difficult of military evolutions. If there was one indispensable ingredient to the success of the extraction, it was Undorf's success in imposing a degree of order on a chaotic situation. The potential for friction in the tactical situation he found was enormous. The fact that he and Austin were forced by a lack of direction from above to begin extraction procedures on their own speaks volumes. Undorf, ably seconded by Austin, overcame the effects of friction through keen tactical observation, critical analysis, and timely decisions. As a competent commander on scene, he did what ABCCC could not: he controlled the battle.

A final, crucial point of the battle came in the final stages of extraction as the number of marines on the beach diminished. It reached the danger point just as Spectre 11 was forced to depart and Undorf and Roehrkasse were running out of fuel. At this critical juncture, Undorf orchestrated an orderly turnover of on-scene command to Wilson and Carroll. They in turn deserve enormous credit for the speed and efficiency with which they sized up the situation and assumed effective control. That and the successful withdrawal of the marines back to their final perimeter along the beach—conducted in darkness broken only by muzzle flash, tracers, and the occasional flare—deserve praise. Davis and McNemar would have taken the blame had things gone wrong. Things did not go wrong, and the credit belongs to them. Brims's competence and determination and that of his crew were indispensable. Technical Sergeant Fisk, the last man off, deserves special praise.

The *Mayaguez* affair and the Koh Tang invasion in particular effectively demonstrate the manner in which uncertainty and risk can propagate upward from tactical to policy considerations in war. They demonstrate, moreover, how risks and uncertainties can feed synergistically on one another as they move from tactics to operations to strategy to policy and back, multiplying the potential for catastrophe at each level. The *Mayaguez*–Koh Tang affair also offers dramatic evidence of the way in which seemingly trivial precautions can have far-reaching effects in minimizing the adverse effects of fog and friction. Perhaps the most important lesson to emerge from our analysis is that the precautions of this kind that were beneficial emerged from the application of common sense based on combat experience, not from calculations of cost benefit effectiveness. The decision by the Aerospace Rescue and Recovery Service to install explosion-retardant foam in the 450-gallon auxiliary tanks of HH-53s probably saved the United States a humiliating defeat. The marines' insistence on going into what was advertised as a walkover fully armed and ready for battle probably had the same effect. The PACAF decision not to install explosion-retardant foam in the 650-gallon auxiliary tanks of CH-53s in the interests of cost containment very nearly reversed the outcome.

Risk and uncertainty, friction and fog have influenced war since time immemorial. Beyond underlining their enduring relevance, the *Mayaguez* operation graphically demonstrates how sophisticated, long-range communications can amplify their effects as well as damp them out. ABCCC's failure to relay messages from the marines on Koh Tang to their commander at U Tapao—owing at least in part to communication saturation—set up the U.S. forces for disaster. The National Military Command Center order to put AC-130s over Koh Tang helped to prevent that disaster from occurring. I invite you, the reader, to review the action and extract additional examples, for there are many.

CONCLUSIONS

All military operations are subject to risk and uncertainty, but from the American perspective, the *Mayaguez* crisis was particularly fraught with them. This was partly because of the policy constraints imposed on the Ford administration by political realities, manifested tactically as time constraints. Adding to the difficulties were the enormous distances involved, the unavoidably heterogeneous forces committed, and the contradictory operational objectives that inevitably emerged from the resultant matrix. Against these sources of friction weighed the unprecedented excellence of the communications facilities available to the president, the secretary of defense, and subordinate commanders. Never before in the history of warfare had a national commander been able to communicate with troops in combat so well, so quickly, so clearly, and across such great distances.

But these technical means of overcoming the effects of friction, while invaluable in certain critical instances, were as much a hindrance as a help. In the end, the president's commitment of U.S. forces, while carefully and competently weighed at the national level, nearly produced disaster. This was not because of poor policy decisions on the part of Ford or those in his inner circle. It was certainly not the result of inept execution by soldiers, sailors, and airmen fighting an armed enemy half a world away. Those close enough to the enemy to hear the report of his ordnance, see the tracers, feel the impact on their airframes, and witness the consequences on the flesh of their comrades did very well indeed. The culprit was information saturation at intermediate levels of the chain of command acting in synergistic combination with tactical and operational ignorance at those same levels.

Those running the show, competent as they may have been in policy, strategic, and operational terms, were tactical babes in the woods and, with few exceptions, utterly unaware of it. My reference is not entirely, or even particularly, to civilian policy makers. The salient example is the unfamiliarity with helicopter operations exhibited by senior Air Force commanders and staff members. This was a lethal combination, barely manageable in the planning stages and uncontrollable once battle was joined.

The very speed and clarity of radio communications from and between higher headquarters was not a solution to the problem but its principal cause. Many of those involved, especially in the higher echelons, equated quick and reliable electronic communications to command and control. Indeed, the notion was built implicitly into air force doctrine. The operative words for the third and fourth letters in the ABCCC acronym—command and control—make the point. But ABCCC's capabilities were at best a mixed blessing. They permitted direct communications between USSAG/Seventh Air Force and forces in combat on and near Koh Tang, but at the same time they prevented effective control of those same forces. In the aggregate, the remarkable communications capabilities available to higher-command echelons served mainly to amplify the effects of inadequate tactical knowledge and to perpetuate indecision. ABCCC lost control of the situation on and around Koh Tang during the first wave debacle and never fully regained it. (In fairness, however, we should note that ABCCC controllers' actions were instrumental in preventing total disaster in the first moments of battle.) The false impression of positive control conveyed by direct electronic communications to those in command only made things worse.

The problem was resolved and catastrophe averted not by superior high-level communications but in spite of them. It was done by subordinate commanders, junior officers, and NCOs acting on their own initiative in response to the demands of the tactical situation, employing a general awareness of strategic objectives and policy goals. They did what they had to do to ensure the survival of their fellows and the preservation of national honor. It was to them that success was due.

This is not to say that good communications are bad: they are, in fact, essential. A key lesson of the *Mayaguez* operation is the absolutely critical importance of clear and reliable short-range tactical communications. Without first-rate tactical radios, backed by sound aircrew, infantry, and ship communications procedures and discipline, the U.S. situation would have come unraveled. But communications must be used selectively to support command responsibilities carefully delegated in accordance with tactical, operational, and organizational realities. Instantaneous global communications may look like a security blanket viewed from the White House or National Military Command Center. They are not. Instead they are a swift and exceedingly sharp double-edged sword that, if misunderstood and misapplied, can cause lethal self-inflicted damage. No amount of communications can replace a competent and responsible commander on scene. To attempt to do so is to invite disaster.

All of this was evident to operationally sensitive analysts soon after the fact. But were the lessons learned? The evidence is mixed. The problems so clearly evident in the *Mayaguez* affair tragically reappeared in the April 1980 Iranian hostage rescue attempt. The smoking wreckage and abandoned helicopters at Desert One were symptomatic of more than bad luck and inadequate training. The episode suggests that command and control practices at the national level had actually degenerated since 1975. The isolation of tactically knowledgeable commanders from one another and from responsible operational planners, largely unavoidable in the *Mayaguez* affair, seems to have been deliberately fostered in the Iranian episode. Confused and divided lines of command and tactical micromanagement from Washington were very much in evidence.

A cursory review of the military aspects of the 1982–83 U.S. intervention in Lebanon suggests an endemic reluctance to come to grips with the problem of overcontrol and micromanagement. The retaliatory bombing by carrier-based navy aircraft of Syrian antiaircraft missile positions in the Bekaa Valley on 4 December 1983, in particular, provides a classic example of higher-command interference with basic tactical decision-making processes.

The results of the October 1983 invasion of Grenada, the closest operational analog to the *Mayaguez* incident since, seemingly present a more favorable picture. A closer look, however, supports a more guarded prognosis. The Grenada invasion was not characterized by direct operational control by the National Military Command Center and White

House or by higher-command echelon micromanagement. Nevertheless, it offers prominent examples of the same sort of inadequate preparation, interservice misperception, muddled communications, and tactical miscalculation that so nearly brought the Koh Tang operation to grief. Published accounts suggest that inadequate intelligence and the lack of adequate maps were—as with the *Mayaguez* affair—a major cause of embarrassment.[13]

The 20 December 1989 invasion of Panama would seem to offer encouragement; certainly, Operation Just Cause provided evidence of our ability to effectively plan and mount complex offensive operations. Moreover, the evident willingness of President Bush and his senior advisers to let military commanders run the show operationally was commendable. In the end, however, the Panamanian invasion was a systematically prepared operation where the planning process was able to turn full cycle.

The largest commitment of American military might since the *Mayaguez*-Koh Tang conflict was in Operation Desert Storm, our response to the August 1990 invasion of Kuwait by the forces of Baath Socialist Iraq. Given some five months to build up our troops in Saudi Arabia, our air forces struck the following January with overwhelming might, defeating the Iraqi air defense system in short order. They attacked a wide array of targets inside Iraq with spectacular—if not always uniform—precision and relentlessly hammered Iraqi ground forces in the Kuwaiti theater of operations in preparation for the ground offensive, which followed just over a month later. The result was the liberation of Kuwait and swift, if incomplete, victory over the Iraqi military. Desert Storm was a massive and complex operation and the returns are not yet all in; they are sure to be controversial, and indeed already are.

As evidence of the point, at the time of writing the air force was successfully blocking distribution of the Gulf War Air Power Survey, an exhaustive, albeit preliminary, study of the use of air power in the conflict commissioned by Dr. Donald Rice, the Bush administration's secretary of the air force. This action was taken presumably because the study contains well-documented and candid treatment of such matters as command and control arrangements, intelligence problems, and the equivocal results of the air campaign against mobile SCUD ballistic missile launchers. I should add that I participated in the Gulf War Air Power Survey as chief of the task force charged with examining weapons, tactics, and training.

The problems faced by U.S. forces in the Persian Gulf in 1990–91 were very different in scale and kind from those faced in the Gulf of Siam fifteen years earlier. Still, based on what has appeared in the public record and the *Gulf War Air Power Survey Summary Report*, which was released in 1993 (but which the air force has stopped distributing), a number of general observations are in order.[14] First, the United States and its allies had the leisure of some five months to deploy forces and develop plans in Operation Desert Shield, so Desert Storm was no real test of our ability to improvise and orchestrate military operations on short notice. Second, the U.S. participants in Desert Storm were the beneficiaries of a recent revolution in information processing and transmission technology: compact and reliable "scrambler" telephones were available in abundance, as were encrypted facsimile machines, high-quality color Xerox machines, and a host of lesser, but in the aggregate important, devices. Moreover, the tactical quality of the information transmitted was enhanced in many crucial instances by compact and highly accurate navigational devices, notably global positioning system (GPS) indicators. These enabled combatants to determine their location within tens of meters by means of electronic triangulation using satellite transmissions. Night viewing devices of various kinds—notably night vision goggles and infrared television systems—had come of age since the Vietnam War, enabling American forces to maneuver and fight in the dark with unprecedented success.

Although communications at and between the highest echelons of command seem to have worked much as they had six years earlier, the profusion of secure telephones and other transmission devices supported a mass of back-channel communications that provided a flood of information—some of it vital—without clogging primary command channels. Of at least equal importance, the proliferation of secure telephones and facsimile machines permitted unprecedentedly close lateral coordination among tactical units. This had an especially beneficial effect on air operations because participants in large multiunit strikes could work out coordination problems in detail well in advance without hindering the transmission of essential orders. Finally, and perhaps most impressively, communications among mobile ground forces and between ground maneuver elements and supporting air forces clearly played a major role in enabling U.S. and coalition troops to wage a ground campaign of unprecedented speed and lethality with amazingly few casualties.

All of this would seem to augur well for the future. But would the profusion of lateral communications have had an equally beneficial effect had we been forced to act swiftly, before our forces were fully deployed and our plans had matured? Conventional wisdom suggests that the abundance of communications would have helped. The lessons of the *Mayaguez*–Koh Tang crisis point to a different conclusion: that unless used with great competence and restraint, a multiplicity of electronic communications can be an instrument of confusion instead of clarification, a breeding ground for risk and uncertainty as much as an agent of suppression. During the Persian Gulf War, we had time to establish lines of authority and communications protocols before our forces were committed to combat, so the issue never arose. The question is whether our leaders were aware of the double-edged nature of the magnificent communications at their disposal. The answer to that question is unclear.

There was, however, a small but more accurate test of these kinds of capabilities and problems: Operation Eastern Exit, the evacuation of the American Embassy in Mogadishu, Somalia, on 5–6 January 1991, only ten days before the start of Desert Storm. Here, as with the *Mayaguez* affair, the crisis broke quickly, with the outbreak of full-scale civil war in the Somali capital on 30 December. The forces immediately available to deal with it were minimal. Beset by a swift and near-total breakdown of public order, the American ambassador to Somalia, the Honorable James K. Bishop, requested evacuation of the remaining Americans in Mogadishu, plus personnel from a number of other friendly diplomatic missions, on 2 January. Our military command responded by dispatching the assault carriers USS *Guam* and USS *Trenton* south from the Persian Gulf shortly before midnight that same day. The task force carried elements of 1st Battalion Second Marines and a SEAL team. *Guam's* air complement consisted of two CH-46 squadrons; *Trenton's* included a detachment of CH-53Es.

Although supported by Kenya-based air force AC-130s, the operation was at heart a navy-marine affair revolving around the capabilities of marine CH-53Es. By 1991, the Marine Corps had fitted the bulk of its H-53 fleet for air-to-air refueling. The first two CH-53Es launched from *Trenton* when the carrier was no less than 466 nautical miles from Mogadishu; they carried a ground security force of sixty marines and SEALs.[15] The H-53s reached Mogadishu at dawn on 6 January after two aerial refuelings from land-based marine KC-130s, inserted the marines and SEALs, and brought out the first 61 evacuees. *Guam* closed Mogadishu during the evening and launched two waves of CH-46s in the early morning hours of the sixth to pull out an additional 220 evacuees and the ground security force. All went smoothly, despite indications of radar activity from surface-to-air missiles.

As with Eagle Pull in the spring of 1975, American forces were blessed with a strong and decisive civilian leadership on the spot. Like Ambassador Dean in Phnom Penh, Ambassador Bishop clearly saw the portent in the unfolding situation. He reduced his staff to the minimum required early in the game and issued the warning order and request for evacuation in a timely fashion. There were familiar glitches. The most recent maps of Mogadishu available to the aircrews were printed in 1969, and the H-53 pilots had difficulty finding the embassy: the embassy staff lacked signal gear and was reduced to marking the landing zone with a strobe light and a hand- waved white flag.[16] Still, it worked.

The question is, How were risk and uncertainty dealt with? Specifically, what role did electronic communications play in helping planners to anticipate risk and minimize its adverse impact? Were we better able to control the potential for escalating risk inherent in a profusion of high-quality electronic communications in 1991 than in 1975? My verdict, at least, is inconclusive. Those who planned and executed Eastern Exit were helped by their shared navy-marine doctrine, training, and procedures. They were also helped—or so says the cynic—by the focus of high-level decision makers' attention on events elsewhere, for Desert Storm was about to begin.

Other, later examples of small-scale commitments of U.S. forces on short notice yield more equivocal lessons. Communications problems do not seem to have been a factor in the loss of eighteen Army Rangers, helicopter crew members, and mountain infantrymen in a 3 October 1993 raid against Somali warlord Muhammad Farah Aidid that went wrong. One lesson, however, emerges clearly from that tragic episode and the events that led up to it: small-scale operations against numerous and well-armed enemies far from friendly bases are apt to remain a staple of U.S. military campaigns for the foreseeable future.

The lessons of the SS *Mayaguez* incident—and the Koh Tang operation in particular—thus retain their validity. Whether they have been assimilated by the U.S. military services and national command structure remains to be seen.

APPENDIX A

Tactical Communications

THE TECHNICAL CHARACTERISTICS of electronic communications played a major role in establishing the parameters of the *Mayaguez*–Koh Tang operation. They also helped to determine the outcome and therefore merit a more detailed examination. My focus is on tactical, rather than strategic, communications. Even now, a comprehensive technical analysis of the strategic systems used in the *Mayaguez* affair would be ruled out by security restrictions. In the end, however, that is irrelevant because the very excellence of these systems renders such an analysis unnecessary. Understanding the central architecture of the command and control net, who was in it, and what kinds of information could be passed along its various branches provides most of the information needed for a basic analysis of the strategic and operational decision-making process. Figures 1 and 3 were prepared with this in mind. Little more is either possible or necessary. Tactical communications, however, are another matter. In contrast to strategic communications, there was not a superabundance of capacity, and clarity was an issue. In addition, the basic technical parameters are unclassified.

The main characteristics of the tactical radios to be discussed here can be understood by using straightforward and relatively simple technical criteria. Broadly speaking, maximum transmission range is proportional to wave length and inversely proportional to operating frequency. Wave length and frequency, in turn, are inversely related: the longer the wave length, the lower the frequency. All else being equal, clarity in voice transmissions is an inverse function of wave length and a positive function of frequency. An important secondary characteristic is that antenna length is a function of frequency as well: the higher the frequency, the shorter the antenna. Thus, voice radios that operate on higher frequencies generally offer greater clarity, require shorter antennas, and are more compact. They also have less range. The radios with which we are concerned here operated on one of four frequency bands: HF, or high frequency, 2.0–29.999 MHz (megahertz); VHF/FM, or very high frequency/frequency modulated, 30.0–75.95 MHz; VHF, or very high frequency, 116.0–151.95 MHz; and UHF, or ultrahigh frequency, 225.0–399.9 MHz.[1] The naval vessels involved carried tactical voice radios in all of these categories as part of an essentially complete communications suite, so we will omit them from further discussion.

HF voice radios, the basic means of long-range tactical command and control in the *Mayaguez*–Koh Tang operation, were carried in RF-4Cs, F-111s, rescue HC-130Ps, CH-53s, and HH-53s as well as the ABCCC EC-130s. HF transmissions follow the curvature of the earth, permitting extremely long transmission ranges. The corresponding penalty is susceptibility to electronic interference and lack of clarity.

The air force and navy had standardized on UHF for tactical aircraft interplane and air-to-ground voice communications and on a common emergency, or Guard, frequency in the UHF band. All aircraft engaged in the operation were so equipped. UHF radio communications offer excellent clarity and are line of sight; that is, transmissions do not follow the curvature of the earth. The Guard function is provided by a separate receiver tuned permanently to the Guard channel and normally left on. Air force and navy aircrew survival radios and parachute "beepers" in use at the time operated on Guard frequency, and the survival radios had three additional SAR (search and rescue)-dedicated UHF frequencies. A distressed aircraft or downed aviator could contact any and all air force, navy, or marine aircraft within range by transmitting on Guard. The corresponding disadvantage was that Guard transmissions blocked or interfered with reception on all UHF radios within range unless the Guard receiver was turned off, something that aviators are reluctant to do both by virtue of their training and because of the natural desire to monitor emergencies.

This factor placed a premium on radio discipline in SAR missions, particularly in the early days of the Southeast Asia air war when survival radios operated only on Guard. It speaks well for the aircrews of the Koh Tang operation that extraneous Guard transmissions were not a problem except, briefly and understandably, in the wake of the decimation of the first wave. Certain U.S. Air Force aircraft, including HH-53s and HC-130s, had a UHF and VHF/FM secure voice capability in the form of the KY-28 system. This scrambled and unscrambled voice transmissions by means of encoding instructions that were set using an instruction key that was changed daily. The KY-28 was awkward to use, and transmitting on any other radio while using it could damage the radios and the aircraft's electrical system. In addition, clarity was poor. Encrypted transmissions sounded like Donald Duck. I am not aware that the KY-28 was used in the *Mayaguez*–Koh Tang crisis.

While the navy and air force standardized on UHF, the army standardized on VHF for interplane communications. This was a natural choice because army aircraft usually flew at lower altitudes, and VHF transmissions follow the curvature of the earth—although not to the same degree as HF. Compared with UHF, VHF offers significant advantages in range—especially between stations on the ground or at low altitudes—although some quality is sacrificed. In order to communicate with army ground units and aircraft in Vietnam, air force FAC, special operations, and Rescue Service aircraft were equipped with VHF radios. To keep UHF clear for emergency transmissions and as a matter of convenience, King and Jolly Green crews generally used VHF for internal SARTF (Search and Rescue Task Force) communications. A number of VHF frequencies were assigned for this purpose. A FAC involved in a SAR mission would typically use one of these to coordinate his efforts with the rest of the SARTF through King while working strike flights on UHF.

VHF/FM frequency-modulated voice radios operating in the band just above HF were the standard means of tactical electronic communications for U.S. ground forces. Because of the technical characteristics of frequency modulation, range was short but clarity was excellent. FAC, rescue, and special operations aircraft were equipped with VHF/FM radios to permit contact with ground troops. The first dedicated air force "Sandy" RESCORT aircraft were special operations A-1Es. Jolly Green and Sandy pilots quickly adopted FM, or Fox Mike, for primary interplane coordination. This was partly because of the excellent short-range clarity and partly because, in the early days, no one else operating over North Vietnam and Laos had FM, and other agencies couldn't horn in. Clarity was almost invariably excellent with aircraft radios and somewhat less so with the less powerful, battery-operated, hand-held ground sets. The marine FM radios operated reasonably well in the Koh Tang operation, although power and clarity were problems on occasion.

A final point concerning tactical radio communications concerns what might be termed auditory span of control: how many channels a pilot or crew could monitor and work simultaneously. I know of no scholarly work on the subject. Personal observation and experience, however, suggest that the number varies as a function of the quality and fidelity of transmission, individual ability, personal preference, and the degree of stress under which the individual or crew is operating. The question of quality and fidelity requires additional comment. Unlike range, fidelity cannot be measured in hard, quantitative terms, but it can be vitally important tactically. The point is made by an example from combat aircrew recovery procedures during the Southeast Asia war. Higher headquarters and training organizations devoted much time and effort to the problem of authentication: ensuring that the object of the rescue mission—the survivor—was really who he said he was. The most common method was a card that was filled out by each aircrew member and kept on file in his unit's intelligence office. Recorded on the card were the answers to a series of a half-dozen or so personal questions. The questions and answers were brief and consisted of information that the survivor would be unlikely to forget under stress and that no one else would be likely to guess. Authentication was accomplished by relaying the correct responses to several of these questions from the unit to the Rescue Coordination Center and thence to the SARTF. These might require the downed aviator to name his favorite drink, his brand of cigarettes, or his wife's maiden name.

Although the system worked well, it was rarely used. The reason was simple: in most combat rescue missions, the downed aviator was capped (the verb *cap* derives from combat air patrol) by a wingman when he went down. He made initial contact using his survival radio, speaking to someone who knew him personally and recognized his voice. Short-range clarity was good with the UHF survival radios, and as on-scene command transferred from aircraft to aircraft, each successive on-scene commander learned to recognize the individual's voice. Usually survivors were asked to authenticate only when this chain of aural recognition was broken or when controlling agencies insisted upon it and there was time to accommodate their wishes.

The limiting case of auditory span of control from my own experience involves a Jolly Green crew making a combat pickup, a close parallel to the insertions and extractions in the Koh Tang operation. The most important voice communication channel was between the pilot and the flight mechanic who talked the aviator in to a hover or landing on intercom, looking out the door or window and working from visual references. In the final stages of the maneuver the flight mechanic transmitted on hot mike; that is, using an open microphone instead of keying his microphone for each transmission. While this was going on, the gunners kept the pilots informed of obstacle clearance laterally and to the rear, called out enemy activity, and announced intent to return fire. Obviously, an enormous amount of tactically critical information was passed on over the intercom system. The danger of information saturation was real, but well-trained, disciplined crews kept the number and length of transmissions down to the absolute minimum. It would be only a slight exaggeration to say that an HH-53 crew under these circumstances had a single, collective brain served by at least five sets of eyes and that intercom voice transmissions were the link between eyes and brain.

Next in importance to transmissions on intercom were communications between the survivor, the primary recovery helicopter, and Sandy RESCORT fighters on the downed aviator's UHF survival radio. This was invariably on the Guard channel in the early days; later on, the SARTF and survivor normally used one of the other three UHF survival radio frequencies once initial contact had been established on Guard. The Jolly Green pilot or copilot would generally coordinate air support with the Sandys on another radio, usually FM, and the copilot would maintain contact with the King HC-130 on VHF. The flight mechanic ordinarily monitored only the intercom and the survivor's radio frequency. Other crew members backed up the pilots by monitoring one or another of the other radios. Typically, the volume was turned down to prevent interference with tactically critical communications on the intercom, with the survivor, and with the Sandys. This was a useful technique, because the crewman could identify the radio on which a given transmission was received by its volume.

Meanwhile, the King pilots and navigator, in addition to coordinating supporting tactical fighters and their tanker support, monitored all relevant frequencies to back up the Sandys and Jolly Green crew (actually, two Jolly Green crews, since we committed in pairs with a "high bird" backing up the primary recovery helicopter). They also kept the Rescue Control Center informed of our actions and intentions and off our backs. Communication with the Rescue Control Center on HF was generally left to King.

Although admittedly impressionistic, the evidence suggests to me that this scenario pushed crews and their members very close to the limits of their ability to process and effectively use auditory information under the stress of combat. There was considerable variation among Jolly Green pilots and crews in the way in which they used the electronic communications available to them, and the variation itself supports the belief that we are dealing with a near approach to an inherent physiological and psychological limit. Some aircraft commanders preferred to turn off everything but the intercom and the primary UHF survival radio frequency used by the survivor and Sandys, delegating the rest to the copilot. Others would work the Sandys on FM at the same time to ensure immediate fire support on request and to be able to communicate with them independently of the survivor. The one point of common ground was that all implicitly recognized the vital importance of clear voice communication on tactically essential channels and organized their auditory monitoring hierarchy accordingly.

APPENDIX B

The H-53: An Air Force Pilot's Perspective

THE OPERATIONAL CHARACTERISTICS of the H-53s assigned to the 21st SOS and 40th ARRS were major determinants of the way in which the *Mayaguez*–Koh Tang operation was planned. Their flight and maintenance characteristics played a key role in determining the outcome—or rather in establishing the range of possible outcomes—for the battle hinged on a number of highly improbable events. If there was a single, unavoidable, critical path in planning and execution, it was the capabilities and limitations of the CH- and HH-53s that transported the American Marines to their objectives and got them back. Several factors combined to make that path as critical as it was, not all of them readily quantifiable.

The first of these was the small number of H-53s available, a straightforward numerical consideration. The second factor was maintainability and in-commission rates: of those available, how many could be brought into commission when they were needed, how quickly, and with what degree of assurance. Although less readily quantifiable than the first factor, this, too, can be addressed in numerical terms. Here we are concerned with the qualitative factors involved in keeping the H-53 in safe flying condition. The third factor was the basic performance parameters that determined what the aircraft could do operationally, parameters that owed much to the H-53's Marine Corps origins. We have addressed these in gross quantitative terms, but there is more to operational effectiveness than speed, payload, range, and the tradeoffs among them. Some key factors, like maneuverability, are not readily quantified—not least of all because they are dependent upon aircrew skill, motivation, and knowledge. Many of the critical determinants of aircraft performance affecting combat effectiveness are heavily dependent on human factors and shade off into the subjective. It is those we are primarily concerned with here. What was the H-53 like to fly? What was it like to maintain? How much confidence did the crews have in it?

I do not pretend that my assessment of the H-53 as procured, maintained, and operated by the U.S. Air Force during the Southeast Asia conflict is definitive and unbiased. What I have to say here reflects my reaction to the machine as a pilot. As such, it is based on personal opinion. But what I have to say also reflects the information available to the men who flew in the *Mayaguez*–Koh Tang operation. There are matters on which honest men can differ, and I have tried to point these out. One point should be made clear up front: I am not concerned with the H-53 as procured, maintained, and flown by the navy and Marine Corps. The air force H-53 was a very different kettle of fish.

The H-53 entered the air force inventory through a peculiar chain of circumstances that left an indelible imprint on the aircraft. Designed by Sikorsky Aircraft Company in response to a March 1961 Marine Corps request for proposal, the H-53 was a progressive development of the earlier piston-engined HR2S.[1] The HR2S originated from the findings of a 1946 Marine Corps requirements board that called for a helicopter with a five-thousand-pound payload to support amphibious assault operations. By the standards of the day, the payload requirement was enormous—in 1946 most helicopters could carry little more than a pilot and passenger—and the H-53's exceptional performance was a direct result of that far-sighted requirement.

By specifying their operational needs ambitiously but in general terms, the marines got a superior machine. There is, I believe, a lesson here, for the track record of U.S. military aircraft designed through tightly defined specifications rigorously justified by cost-benefit effectiveness has been less than sterling. The TFX/F-111 is the prime example, although the B-1B and a host of lesser programs might be cited as well.[2] It is worth observing in passing the situation with the V-22 Osprey tilt-rotor vertical takeoff and landing assault transport. This machine has encountered opposition, in no small measure because the ambitious Marine Corps requirement around which it was designed is difficult to justify through cost-benefit comparisons that are implicitly based on the performance of existing systems.

Defining the requirement for a heavy-lift helicopter was only the first step. In the fiscally austere post-World War II defense environment, action in response to the board's finding was slow. But in March 1951, Sikorsky was awarded a developmental contract, winning out over competing designs by Piasecki and McDonnell.[3] The HR2S was a capable machine, limited by the complexity of its twin R-2800 piston engine installation. It had the standard Sikorsky configuration, with a single lifting rotor and an antitorque tail rotor. The main rotor was fully articulated; that is, each blade moved independently in the vertical and horizontal planes and was controllable in pitch. The main rotor blade spars were monolithic aluminum extrusions. Except for the engines, it looked a lot like the H-53.

Nor was the resemblance coincidental. The H-53 owed a great deal to the HR2S. The power train was an evolutionary development of that of the HR2S: the main rotor had the same seventy-two-foot diameter, but with six blades instead of five; and the four-bladed tail rotor was of similar design and dimensions.[4] The key difference was the replacement of the HR2S's R-2800s with General Electric T-64 turbines. The adoption of turbine engines yielded enormous dividends, not only in speed and useful load but in mechanical simplicity and reliability.

The H-53 won a navy-marine design competition over a navalized version of the tandem-rotor Vertol CH-47 in the summer of 1962, and a production contract was let that September. Start-up, however, was delayed by fiscal strictures and by pressure from Secretary of Defense Robert McNamara to reconsider the Vertol proposal in the interests of interservice commonality. With Marine Corps encouragement, Sikorsky went back to the drawing board with a sharp pencil, cutting costs to the bone to win the contract. It is likely that the H-53's electrical system lost its battery at this point. Deliveries to operational units of the CH-53A, the first production version, did not begin until September 1966.[5] When the CH-53A entered service, it was the biggest, fastest, and most capable military helicopter in the free world. With the sole exception of its three-engined CH-53E derivative, the CH-53A's C-, D-, and J-model descendants remain so today.[6] The fact that the Marine Corps and our special operations forces are still dependent on so venerable an aircraft speaks volumes for the inadequacies of our defense procurement system.

Even before its birth as an independent service, the U.S. Air Force was ambivalent about helicopters. It is most unlikely that the air force would have procured high-performance rotary-wing aircraft had it not been for the demands of the air war against North Vietnam. The stimulus was the need to rescue airmen shot down deep within enemy territory.[7] When the Rolling Thunder campaign started in March 1965, the standard air force rescue helicopter was the Kaman HH-43B, designed as an aerial firefighting vehicle for noncombat local base rescue. The H-43's limited speed, range, and payload made it unsuitable for long-range combat missions, even in the later HH-43F version equipped with self-sealing fuel tanks and armor protection. Something more capable was needed quickly. Modified versions of the H-53 and the smaller H-3, an earlier Sikorsky product designed for the navy as an antisubmarine platform and procured by the air force in modified form as the CH-3C, were the obvious candidates.

The air force approached Sikorsky with the problem. The H-3 came first, helped along by the fact that Sikorsky was already producing the CH-3C for the air force. The CH-3C was modified by adding jettisonable external fuel tanks mounted on stub wings extending from the sponsons; limited quarter-inch titanium armor-plate protection; an external hydraulic rescue hoist; a Doppler radar navigation system; a full radio communications suite including HF, VHF, VHF/FM, and UHF radios; and more powerful engines to compensate for the added weight.[8] The result was the HH-3E, which began combat operations from bases in Thailand in October 1965. The HH-3E was an operational success, but the added weight stretched the design to its limits. The HH-3E was an interim solution that was still in service during Operation Desert Storm in the spring of 1991.

The HH-53 was to be the definitive long-range combat aircrew recovery helicopter. Procurement would take longer, however, because more extensive modifications were envisioned and because the air force would have to compete with the Marine Corps for space on the production line. Also, the air force had no preexisting contractual arrangements with Sikorsky for the H-53 design and procurement and was forced to deviate from normal procedures in the interest of time. In the meantime, air force engineers and test pilots at Wright-Patterson AFB, Ohio, demonstrated the feasibility of helicopter aerial refueling with the H-3. The HH-3E was retroactively fitted with a pneumatically extendible refueling probe, and by early 1967 operational crews were receiving air refueling training.[9] The HH-53 was intended to be air-refuelable from the beginning.

Like the HH-3E, the HH-53 was fitted with jettisonable external tanks mounted on stub wings extending from the sponsons, an external hydraulic rescue hoist, quarter-inch titanium armor-plate protection for critical components, a pneumatically extendible refueling probe, a Doppler radar navigation system, and a full radio communications suite. In addition, the HH-53's power margin permitted significant defensive armament. That chosen was three Gatling-type, electrically driven, six-barreled 7.62-mm miniguns mounted in the crew door, in the left forward cabin window, and on the cargo ramp. From the standpoint of firepower and weight, the electrically driven minigun was not an obvious choice. It was heavy, its mechanism was mechanically complex, and, for reasons discussed below, it required its own independent electrical system.

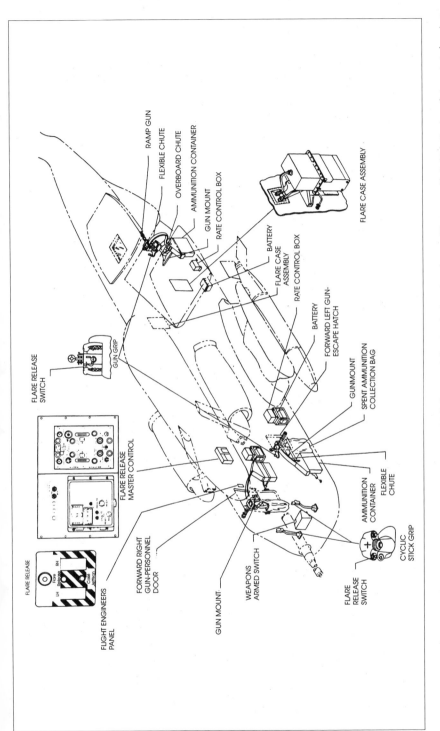

RAMP GUN

FLEXIBLE CHUTE

OVERBOARD CHUTE

AMMUNITION CONTAINER

GUN MOUNT

RATE CONTROL BOX

BATTERY

FLARE CASE ASSEMBLY

RATE CONTROL BOX

BATTERY

FLARE CASE ASSEMBLY

FORWARD LEFT GUN-ESCAPE HATCH

GUNMOUNT

SPENT AMMUNITION COLLECTION BAG

AMMUNITION CONTAINER

FLEXIBLE CHUTE

CYCLIC STICK GRIP

FLARE RELEASE SWITCH

WEAPONS ARMED SWITCH

GUN MOUNT

FORWARD RIGHT GUN-PERSONNEL DOOR

FLARE RELEASE MASTER CONTROL

FLARE RELEASE SWITCH

GUN GRIP

FLIGHT ENGINEERS PANEL

FLARE RELEASE

FIGURE 4. *Armor Plate Installation. Cutaway drawing adapted from the H-53 flight manual showing the location of armor. The quarter-inch thick titanium plate protected against small-arms fire, but was easily penetrated by .50 cal./12.7-mm rounds at ranges out to several hundred yards. Additional armor not shown in the diagram included plates in the fuselage side and crew door to protect forward minigun positions, as well as an armored "tub" used as a mounting for the ramp minigun on rescue H-53s.*

Presumably, the choice was influenced by the minigun's successful use on the air force AC-47 gunship and the existence of contractual relationships with the manufacturer, General Electric. A .30-cal./7.62-mm weapon with a high rate of fire was clearly preferable to a slower-firing weapon in the .50-cal./12.7-mm category for suppressive use. But the minigun's maximum rate of four thousand rounds per minute was more than was needed. Crews almost always used the slower two-thousand-round rate of fire to conserve ammunition and reduce the probability of jams. There were much lighter and simpler gas- and recoil-operated infantry machine guns extant with rates of fire exceeding twelve hundred rounds per minute, but they were apparently not considered—perhaps because they were not of American design.[10]

The first version was the HH-53B, an interim design with the external fuel tanks supported by struts pending redesign of the sponson. From the aircrew perspective, the HH-53B and HH-53C were virtually identical. The first two HH-53Bs reached Udorn in August 1967, and six more were delivered before the arrival of the first HH-53C in September 1969.[11] Like the HH-3E, the HH-53 was a success, sharing most of its predecessor's operational virtues and few of its vices. Tactical Air Command subsequently procured the H-53 for special operations but without aerial refueling or a ramp minigun.

The haste with which the American Air Force procured the H-53, though a remarkable achievement, created problems. All air force vehicles were required to have an independent, battery-driven backup electrical system to provide essential cockpit lighting and emergency instrumentation for instrument flight, typically a turn-and-slip indicator. The H-53 had no such system; in fact, outside of the minigun system it had no battery at all. The aircraft was started with a charge of compressed air that fired the APP (auxiliary power plant), a compact gas turbine mounted in the "dog house" above the cockpit and forward of the rotor head. The APP drove the generators, which provided electrical power for systems checkout and engine start. Once the engines were started, they drove the generators, and the APP was turned off. The arrangement may have made sense in achieving autonomy in the field, but if both generators failed under instrument conditions and you couldn't reset one of them immediately, you were a statistic. Like all single-rotor helicopters, the H-53 was inherently unstable.

Another apparent casualty of the irregular procurement program was the basic flight manual, or "dash one."[12] The air force customarily purchased aircraft technical data from the manufacturer, but in the case of the H-53, the relevant manuals were written by civil service technical writers at Warner-Robins Air Material Center, Georgia. The official reason was presumably to save money. The real reason was apparently to

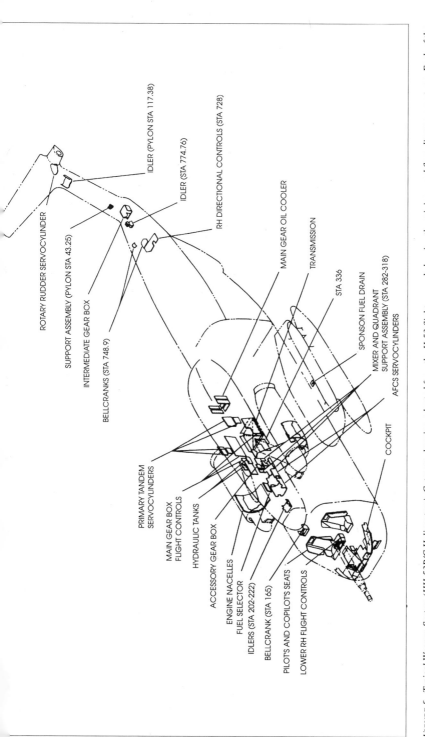

ROTARY RUDDER SERVOCYLINDER

SUPPORT ASSEMBLY (PYLON STA 43.25)

INTERMEDIATE GEAR BOX

BELLCRANKS (STA 748.9)

IDLER (PYLON STA 117.38)

IDLER (STA 774.76)

RH DIRECTIONAL CONTROLS (STA 728)

MAIN GEAR OIL COOLER

TRANSMISSION

STA 336

SPONSON FUEL DRAIN

MIXER AND QUADRANT
SUPPORT ASSEMBLY (STA 282-318)

AFCS SERVOCYLINDERS

COCKPIT

PRIMARY TANDEM
SERVOCYLINDERS

MAIN GEAR BOX
FLIGHT CONTROLS

HYDRAULIC TANKS

ACCESSORY GEAR BOX

ENGINE NACELLES

FUEL SELECTOR

IDLERS (STA 202-222)

BELLCRANK (STA 165)

PILOT'S AND COPILOT'S SEATS

LOWER RH FLIGHT CONTROLS

FIGURE 5. *Typical Weapon System (HH-53B/C Helicopters). Cutaway drawing adapted from the H-53 flight manual showing the minigun and flare dispenser systems. Each of the six-barreled 7.62mm miniguns was provided with its own battery. Only rescue H-53s were equipped with a third minigun on the cargo ramp. The flare cases dispensed AN/ALE-20 flares to decoy infra-red missiles.*

preserve civil service jobs. The one thing certain was that the flight manual was poorly written. When I joined the H-53 community in 1974, much of the manual was written in language that was anything but clear. Many key passages were self-contradictory or simply wrong. Standardization submitted change request after change request, and over the years things gradually got better, but the pace was glacial. The problems were not fully ironed out until 1980–81.[13]

Probably the tech data that inspired the most complaints was that required for maintenance check flights, or functional check flights (FCFs), as they were called. Obtuse writing wasn't the only problem. Ordinarily, FCF checklists are expanded versions of the normal operations checklist, with the requisite maintenance checks superimposed on the normal checks. That way, there is only one checklist to run. In addition, FCF dash ones normally contain both the normal operating limits and the data needed to make the checks; for example, exhaust gas temperature as a function of density altitude and free air temperature for engine topping. With this setup, one crew member could run the FCF checklist and refer to the FCF dash one while the other two flew the airplane.

Not so with the H-53. The FCF checklist contained only the maintenance checks, so it was necessary to run the normal operations checklist and the FCF checklist together. That required two sets of eyes. Also, the FCF flight manual did not contain normal operating limits, so many checks required reference to the normal dash one as well as the FCF manual. I have less-than-fond memories of FCFs for flight control rigging with the flight mechanic reading the FCF checklist, the copilot reading the normal operations checklist, the FCF dash one open in the copilot's lap, and the normal dash one open in my lap. Not only did the open flight manuals potentially impede flight control travel, but a good deal of self-discipline and attention were required to ensure that at least one crew member was looking outside at all times.

To make things even more interesting, certain FCF procedures were decidedly sporty. My favorites were the rigging checks for forward and aft cyclic control stick travel. These were made with the helicopter loaded to the maximum allowable longitudinal cg (center of gravity) limit, forward or aft depending on the check. To verify adequate aft stick travel, you loaded the helicopter to the maximum forward cg and hovered laterally to the right at the greatest allowable sideways speed of thirty-five knots (how you were supposed to know was unclear because there was no lateral airspeed indicator). The aircraft was therefore pushed to the limit in two performance criteria at once. Under those conditions, the nose of the aircraft would begin to tuck under. If you had enough aft stick travel to recover, the helicopter passed the check.

What you were supposed to do if you did *not*, the FCF flight manual did not say. Vern Sheffield and I talked it over one day and decided that the best move would be to apply right rudder so you'd at least hit the ground going straight ahead.

The check for adequate forward stick travel was almost as bad: you loaded the helicopter to the aft cg limit and flew it to the maximum allowable forward speed in level flight. If you still had forward stick travel, the aircraft passed the check. At least you knew what your airspeed was, and if you ran out of stick travel, you could presumably recover by reducing power before the machine went out of control. H-53 units had special calibrated lead bars to load the aircraft to the cg limits. Lead is very dense, and by putting the bars at the extreme end of the cabin, you could get the desired cg with the minimum added weight. But if you got caught with a cyclic travel FCF away from home station, the only ready solution was to drive a flight-line tug into the cabin, park it, and tie it down in the appropriate position. That was less than ideal because flight-line tugs are extremely heavy, and the weight cut into your power margin. On one occasion, at Nellis AFB, Nevada, in the summer of 1978, I found myself facing not only the extreme airspeed and cg limits but maximum allowable gross weight for hovering under the prevailing conditions. If we had lost an engine during either check, we'd have had our hands full.

At bottom, the H-53 was an early 1960s upgrade of a 1950s design, and it showed its age in a number of areas. One was the vacuum-tube avionics, which were prone to unreliability until they warmed up, particularly under humid conditions. Another was the hundreds of fiber seals in the hydraulic system. Under pressure they would retain their integrity indefinitely, but when the aircraft was shut down, they cooled and shrank. When you cranked up again, there was a good chance that at least one seal would fail to reseat. When that happened, you had to find it, disconnect the line, replace it, and then reservice and bleed the affected system.

Hydraulics deserve particular attention, and the contrast between fixed-wing aircraft and helicopters is instructive. With fixed-wing aircraft, lift, thrust, and control of the aircraft in pitch, roll, and yaw are provided by essentially independent systems. If the engines fail, the ability of the wings to produce lift is not affected; similarly, a flight control malfunction affects thrust not at all and lift only indirectly.[14] With a single-rotor helicopter, thrust, lift, and control are all provided by the main rotor, which controls the aircraft not only in pitch and roll but in speed and altitude as well. Without proper control inputs to the main rotor system, a helicopter is immediately and catastrophically unflyable. The nature and magnitude of the forces involved dictate that control by means of direct mechanical linkages is possible only with relatively small helicopters. The problem is compounded by the single lifting rotor/tail rotor configuration, which is inherently unstable about all three axes. This makes flight control fatiguing even with hydraulic boost. Gyroscopic stabilization systems that substitute electronic impulses for aerodynamic stability effectively solved the problem, but these, too, were dependent on hydraulics.

The H-53 had no fewer than three separate hydraulic systems, four counting the cargo winch system: the first- and second-stage flight control systems and the utility system, each with its own pumps, accumulators, and reservoirs. The design was conservative, and there were backups within backups—a Sikorsky hallmark—but they were complicated and not easily learned. The point is made by tracing the path of flight control inputs through the system. Two reference gyros provided attitude information for the pilot's and copilot's attitude indicators and for the two AFCS (automatic flight control stabilization) systems, 1 and 2. Either of the two AFCS systems was capable of providing stabilization in pitch and roll independently, but normally they worked in parallel, combining and averaging their outputs. The AFCS units combined cyclic stick-control inputs with attitude information from the reference gyros to produce discrete signals in pitch and roll for the corresponding AFCS servos.

Control inputs from the collective pitch lever, rudder pedals, and a lateral accelerometer drove the altitude and yaw AFCS servos. Outputs from the four AFCS servos went into a mechanical mixing unit that translated discrete pitch, roll, yaw, and collective signals into commands to the three primary flight control servos and the tail rotor servo. The primary flight control servos provided control in pitch, roll, power, and rotor RPM by changing the angular orientation and vertical position of a stationary swashplate beneath the main rotor head. This swashplate was set inside a rotating swashplate, which controlled the cyclic and collective pitch of the main rotor blades by means of pitch links that transmitted control inputs to the blades. The tail rotor servo provided control in yaw by changing the collective pitch of the tail rotor by means of a stationary and rotating swashplate and pitch link assembly. If all of this sounds complicated, make no mistake: it was.

After the above preamble, it will come as no surprise that many crew members found the H-53's flight control system complex and difficult to understand. Many were uncomfortable with it. The essentials were as follows: the primary flight control and the tail rotor servos were two-stage units, designed to maintain control with either stage should the other suffer hydraulic failure or internal mechanical failure or be shut down. The same was true of the pitch and roll AFCS servos. The first

stages of the primary flight control and tail rotor servos were driven by
the first-stage hydraulic system, which performed no other function.
The second-stage hydraulic system drove the second stages of the primary flight control servos and provided pressure for AFCS 1; that is, for
the first stages of the AFCS pitch and roll servos and for the AFCS yaw
and altitude servos. The utility hydraulic system drove the second stage
of the tail rotor servo and provided pressure for AFCS 2; that is, for the
second stages of the AFCS pitch and roll servos. The first-stage hydraulic pump was driven by the main rotor system, providing for flight control hydraulic pressure in autorotation in the event of complete power
failure. The second- stage and utility pumps were driven either by the
engines or by the APP.

You could maintain flight control with first-stage hydraulics alone,
but without the AFCS you flew the aircraft by brute force. This was
extremely fatiguing and took more than the normal quotient of skill,
especially on instruments. AFCS-out flight was taught and practiced as
an emergency procedure only. You could lose either second-stage or utility hydraulics and still fly normally, but if you lost first-stage and then
lost either second-stage or utility, you were dead meat. The end would
come immediately and catastrophically if you lost first- and second-
stage. It would come more gradually, if not more gracefully, if you lost
first-stage and utility. Either way you were a goner. It is only fair to
add that I know of no verifiable instance in which these circumstances
actually happened. I do know of a case where most of a Jolly Green
crew bailed out needlessly because they *thought* they had lost flight
control hydraulics.

There is, or used to be, an aphorism among air force pilots that no
matter how much power the designer builds into the machine, headquarters will find a way add enough "essential" equipment to make it
overloaded and underpowered. All other helicopters I flew during my
air force career shared that problem; it was the only real flaw of the HH-
3E, the HH-53's predecessor in rescue service and a real pilot's machine
that I loved dearly. The H-53 was different. It was actually *over*powered,
the only military helicopter I was aware of that could merit such a
claim. During the summer of 1993, I spoke to Lt. Col. Rich Comer,
commander of the 20th SOS during Operations Desert Shield and Desert Storm and Barry Walls's copilot as a young second lieutenant in the
Koh Tang operation. He told me that the categorization still applied to
the MH-53J, despite the addition of terrain avoidance radar and FLIR
(forward-looking infrared). Once in a while we get something right.

Add the armor, add the drop tanks, add the miniguns and ammunition, add the refueling probe and internal plumbing, add an extra crew
member or two for insurance, and those big, beautiful General Electric

T-64 engines just kept on trucking. Under any conditions but the most extreme—100°F (38°C)—plus on an August afternoon in the high Nevada desert—you hit the main gearbox torque limits before you ran out of power.

Like all single-lifting rotor helicopters, the H-53's hover performance tailed off sharply at density altitudes above eight thousand feet or so. In any serious situation I ever encountered, however, the gearbox was the limiting factor. If you got into real trouble, you just kept pulling collective until you hit the transient torque limits or the problem went away. You might exceed the transient exhaust gas turbine temperature limits if you weren't smooth, but normally the problem went away first. Finesse helped: you *could* get into power settling, but that's another matter. In addition, the H-53 was astonishingly maneuverable, although the young pilots I flew with in 1974–75 were not trained to exploit that maneuverability. It was not as smooth on the controls as the H-3, nor was it as good an instrument platform. But once you learned its ways, the H-53 did whatever you asked it to do with little complaint. From the pilot's standpoint, the only inherent problems with the basic configuration were cockpit visibility—which was no more than adequate—and limited ground clearance for the tail rotor and rear fuselage when landing and in a hover.

The cockpit visibility problem was partly caused by the small size of the side cockpit windows. This had further adverse consequences because the side windows also served as the pilots' primary emergency exit. For a broad-shouldered man wearing a backpack parachute—which we did—it was a tight fit. Emergency egress from the cockpit was not the best, and a word on parachutes is in order as well. To the best of my knowledge, Jolly Greens and Knives were the only helicopter crews to routinely wear parachutes. We began doing so in 1965 because our penetration tactics involved overflying small-arms and heavy automatic weapons fire at altitudes of eight thousand feet or more. When necessary, we would also cut through the top of the engagement envelope of 37-mm antiaircraft guns at ten to eleven thousand feet, despite the lack of oxygen equipment.[15]

The combat helicopter pilot's normal response to heavy battle damage is to autorotate: descend with the engines disengaged from the rotor system to land as quickly as possible. But if you were hit by antiaircraft artillery at such altitudes, odds were that the aircraft would explode, disintegrate, or burn before you reached the ground—hence the parachutes. By regulation, chutes were required for flight exceeding eight thousand feet above ground level and when aerial refueling. The flight mechanics and pararescuemen normally removed them at other times, but cockpit clearances were tight, and taking off your chute in the cockpit was a real chore. Some pilots slipped out of their harnesses before descent (the parachute was your back cushion), but even that involved a lot of thrashing around near the flight controls. Most of us just left it on.

In reality, parachutes were of marginal utility to H-53 drivers. On several occasions, pararescuemen and flight mechanics successfully parachuted from a stricken Jolly Green while the pilots did not. I know of no case where the converse was true. If the pilots made it, everybody made it. In a grim way, our parachutes were a badge of honor.

The rear fuselage and tail rotor clearance problem resulted from the need to make the helicopter sufficiently compact to fit on a carrier hangar deck. The landing gear was short. If you touched down on level ground with a nose-up attitude of more than 9.5°, the tail skid beneath the tail would hit before the wheels of the main landing gear. The H-53 was rigged for minimum drag at optimum cruise speed; that is, with the main rotor tilted forward to produce thrust for cruise flight, the fuselage was level. As a result, the H-53 hovered in a left-wing-low, nose-high attitude. Consequently, landings from a hover were singularly ungraceful: left main, right main, nose gear; wham, wham, bam! Tail clearance was a problem even in normal operations on level ground and runways, let alone over trees and in rough terrain. The tail rotor itself was vulnerable at flare angles that were normal in other helicopters—that was the reason for the skid—and you had to be especially careful maneuvering close to the ground. You learned to live with these problems.

In the fall of 1973, when I learned I was going into the H-53, I called my old buddy Barry Kamhoot and asked him about it. Barry had checked me out in HH-3Es at Udorn in 1966 and was a good, thinking pilot with lots of experience in a wide range of helicopters, including the '53. He responded that the H-53 wasn't as nice to fly as the H-3 but that it was tough, had plenty of power, and was a typical Sikorsky product with lots of reserve. Barry hit the nail on the head. It *was* tough, as the Koh Tang operation documented all too well. And if it was not as light on the controls or as good an instrument platform as the H-3, it was highly maneuverable. This was a point that Sikorsky and the marines made by rolling and looping one, filming the exercise, and circulating the film among H-53 units. Admittedly, the demonstration used a lightly loaded aircraft, but the H-53 really *was* maneuverable, as we discovered when we relearned the value of tactical approaches and got into air-to-air training with fighters in 1977–78. It turned out to be a considerably more difficult target for an attacking fighter than either the Huey or the H-3, and power was a key ingredient. Besides having a highly competitive roll rate, an H-53 could accelerate from 90 to 170

knots in little more time than it takes to tell about it. That complicated
the fighter pilot's lead problem and reduced the number of firing passes
he could make in a given time.

The H-53's power and maneuverability significantly reduced the adverse effects of most of the undesirable flight characteristics that helicopter pilots worry about. Power limitations were rarely a factor. In
contrast to most other helicopters, you didn't constantly worry about
conserving RPM during an approach. The main exceptions resulted
from the H-53's high disk loading; that is, high gross weight as a function of the main rotor disk area. The high disk loading translated into
high rotor downwash velocities. The downwash in a hover was capable
of picking up sizable objects—rocks, branches, and debris—and throwing them up into the rotor system. With reasonable care, however, the
problem was not particularly serious. This was so partly because the
extruded aluminum rotor blade spars, which included the leading edge,
were tough and partly because the engine intakes were protected by
efficient engine air-particle separators, or EAPS. Designed to protect engine compressor and turbine blades from the abrasive effects of sand and
grit, the EAPS provided perfect protection against foreign object damage
(FOD). The performance penalty was a trivial 150-lb. weight and a 3
percent loss in engine power. We and the Knives always flew with
EAPS installed.

The high disk loading also entailed high descent rates in autorotation, and the H-53 autorotated like a greased safe. The optimum glide
ratio—distance covered in unpowered flight divided by altitude lost—
was only 4.5:1.[16] That is pretty steep, and it looked even steeper because
visibility from the cockpit straight ahead and down was poor. It *was*
steeper when you turned because you had to keep the nose down to
prevent rotor RPM from bleeding off. Close-in turning autorotations
could get you into some interesting attitudes, and practice autorotations required a fair amount of attention and finesse. They weren't
particularly difficult, though, once you got the hang of it, and were excellent confidence-builders. Because of the poor cockpit visibility, you
had to initiate your flare at the bottom based mainly on radar altimeter
readings. Because of landing gear structural limitations and the tail rotor clearance problem, practice autorotations ended with a power recovery at 150 feet. In 1975, practice autorotations had been banned by
Rescue Service on the twin premises that the chances of simultaneously losing both engines in normal operations were remote and that
practice autorotations entailed appreciable risk. The logic was sound as
far as it went, but—characteristically—excluded the risks of combat
and the benefits of aircrew confidence.

Another problem where the H-53's power didn't help was power settling, a condition analogous to getting behind the power curve in a fixed-wing aircraft. You knew you were in power settling when you pulled up on the collective pitch lever—the stick in your left hand that controls power and vertical movement—and instead of slowing its rate of descent, the helicopter dropped out from under you. Power settling is a real heart-stopper, and those who have experienced it remember it vividly. In 1975, the experts hadn't decided what power settling was. To the best of my knowledge, they still haven't. There were at least three possibilities: the main rotor becoming imbedded in a self-created ring vortex; the main rotor blades thrashing through the air in a stalled condition, producing little or no lift in a manner analogous to cavitation; and a condition in which a rapid application of collective increases the demand for power more rapidly than the engines can accelerate to produce it.[17]

Power settling was fluky and unpredictable. It generally happened at low airspeeds, particularly during downwind approaches, and when hovering out of ground effect (the "ground cushion" encountered at altitudes equal to or less than the main rotor diameter). You got out of power settling by lowering collective to recover RPM or by pushing the nose down to gain airspeed. H-53 pilots got into power settling on occasion but usually managed to recover without serious incident. In 1975 we were well aware of the phenomenon and were concerned about it, mostly because we didn't understand it. The conventional wisdom was that you prevented power settling by avoiding low airspeed descents and downwind approaches out of ground effect. It seemed to work.

The H-53 tended to wallow in a hover if you didn't stay on top of it. Compared to the H-3, the controls were sloppy and took getting used to. But as far as sheer maneuverability—the capacity to make rapid and precisely controlled excursions in airspeed, pitch, roll, and yaw—it beat anything else I have ever flown.[18] This was especially true with tactical approaches, low-altitude maneuvers designed to get the helicopter from high-speed flight to a hover or landing as quickly as possible. Tactical approaches pushed to the limit are maximum performance maneuvers, testing the capabilities of both helicopter and pilot. A brief discussion of them is a good way to illustrate the H-53's characteristics and capabilities. Also, the air force's handling of tactical approaches reveals the philosophy behind the training that its helicopter crews received.

Tactical approaches were a bone of contention between those in the air force who believed in the importance of realistic, combat-oriented training and those who believed that the avoidance of accidents was the crux of our existence. Tactical approaches were formally incorporated into the Rescue Combat Crew Training School curriculum in the summer of 1966, and for several years thereafter students received thorough training in them. In 1966–67 we devoted a minimum of three or four training sorties of an hour and a half each almost entirely to tactical approaches and rescue hoist operations. That enabled the good-to-average student to become proficient, at least to the point of knowing his own limitations. But in time, as successive wing and squadron commanders had to brief rescue and MAC safety officers on the measures they were taking to prevent accidents, the emphasis on tactical approaches diminished. By the time I went through H-53 upgrade in the spring of 1974, we were down to a single demonstration sortie. The student himself wasn't even required to attempt a tactical approach. My instructor on that sortie, a fine officer and an exceptionally competent pilot in every other regard, was distinctly uncomfortable with tactical approaches. He made the requisite approach with jaw clenched and white knuckles (or so I surmise, for we were wearing gloves). I found to my horror that I was a living repository of forgotten knowledge.

There were several kinds of tactical approach. They were all, however, based on the common-sense dictum that you want to spend as little time as possible at low altitude and airspeed on a combat insert or extraction. That is where you are most vulnerable to enemy fire; getting in and out quickly is a good way to extend your life expectancy. Under most circumstances you go in low in the final stages of the approach, taking advantage of whatever cover and concealment the terrain offers. You avoid gaining altitude, because that makes you visible over a wider area. You have to come to a stop, so the trick is to slow down as quickly as possible. The most basic tactical approach, and in my opinion the best, involves trading off airspeed for g forces in a tight turn. There are other ways to do it: notably, a side flare approach in which you throw the helicopter into uncoordinated flight, using the drag produced by driving the fuselage laterally through the air to slow down. That works, and the technique was used by at least some of the Knives and Jolly Greens going into Koh Tang. Personally, however, I have never been comfortable with deliberately putting a helicopter into an extreme uncoordinated flight condition. The instruments don't tell you what you're doing, and the aircraft isn't designed to fly that way.

To understand how a turning tactical approach works, begin with an imaginary helicopter approaching its desired landing or hover spot at high speed. The normal way to begin an approach to a landing or hover is to flare: pulling the nose up while reducing collective pitch (that is, lowering the collective pitch lever to reduce power and the net, or collective, pitch on the main rotor blades). But if you flare while flying straight ahead at high speed, one of three things happens: you overspeed the rotor, you climb, or both—all tactically undesirable. The solution is to flare in a turn. Instead of climbing, you use the g forces generated by the turn to absorb the additional collective pitch needed to keep the rotor from overspeeding. You could pull up to 3.5 gs in the H-53 without exceeding the airframe limits, so you had plenty to work with.

From the H-53 pilot's standpoint, a typical tactical approach begins with a high-speed pass (120 knots indicated airspeed was typical for training, but it could be faster, up to the red-line speed of 170 knots) over the landing or hover point. This allows the flight mechanic to look down and confirm that there really *is* a survivor on the ground or that the LZ is clear. On receiving confirmation, you roll into a level turn, typically of 60° bank or more, initially reducing collective pitch slightly to prevent the onset of g forces from bleeding off RPM. You will have worked out in advance the amount and direction of turn depending on topography, wind, and tactical considerations. If possible, the final approach will be into the wind to save time and maximize tail rotor clearance. Any combination can work; the only essential ingredient is a coordinated turn to reduce airspeed.

In my experience, the fastest approach involved a quartering downwind pass over your spot followed by a buttonhook turn of 235° or so into the wind. That was best only by a narrow margin: 270° turns, or even 360°s, begun before you overflew your spot or with a short extension on downwind, worked fine. Once you had mastered the basic skills, tactical approaches were a very flexible and adaptable device. Note, too, that they were dependent on crew coordination as well as piloting skill, particularly in combat. Almost without exception, you were talked in on the final approach by the flight mechanic leaning out of the crew door. Clearances were frequently tight over rough terrain and trees; door, window, and ramp scanners served as your eyes.

Once established in the turn, you smoothly but aggressively apply back pressure on the cyclic. That raises the nose and, as in a straight-ahead flare, forces airflow up through the main rotor system, increasing RPM. You counter the rise in RPM by increasing collective pitch, at the same time maintaining back pressure on the cyclic to keep the nose coming up. By the time you have turned 90° or so, your application of cyclic will have tilted the main rotor far enough back that the thrust vector is pointed ahead of the helicopter's vertical axis. From that point, increasing collective pitch and power dramatically slows the helicopter and tightens the turn: more power makes you go slower, not faster. Shortly thereafter, your landing or hover point will appear off the nose, although you may not be able to see it at first because of poor downward cockpit visibility and will have to rely on a crew member to talk you in. You align yourself on short final, reducing collective as you roll out of the turn, then increasing it as the airspeed approaches zero. By now you're about thirty to fifty yards out, and the rest is just like any other approach. To put things in perspective, you could overfly your spot at 120 knots, do a 360° turn, be in a hover above it within about fifteen seconds, and do it all within a radius of two hundred yards.

The H-53 had one peculiarity in tactical approaches: maintaining a tight level turn to the right required a nose-down attitude of 5° or so. That doesn't sound like much, and it isn't. But it looks like a lot more at 60° or 70° of bank with the treetops whistling by just outside the cockpit. It took some getting used to. Tactical approaches were demanding to fly, but with practice they became more or less automatic and encompassed everything from a full-dress approach as described above to a quick, gentle, 180° buttonhook to a touchdown. With a delicate touch on the cyclic and smooth, aggressive applications of collective to slow you down, tactical approaches could be a thing of beauty and happened with deceptive speed, seemingly in slow motion.

The H-53 was enormously capable, but there was a darker side to the story, for the air force versions had a hidden lethal flaw. The U.S. Navy, the Marine Corps, the Luftwaffe, and the Israeli *Heyl Ha'Avir* lost H-53s to enemy action, to pilot error, to maintenance oversight, and to sheer boneheadedness. They didn't lose all that many, but they did lose some. And there were survivors. Air force H-53s went out of control, terminally and without warning, or they just didn't return. There were no survivors. More precisely, there were exactly two survivors: a pair of young pararescuemen who were sitting on the open ramp of an HH-53 with their parachutes on when it went out of control over the Tonle Sap in Cambodia in June 1973.[19] The last thing they heard on intercom was a final "Oh my God!" from the aircraft commander as the cyclic slammed back into his hand. When his body was recovered, the right thumb was torn from the socket.[20] By 15 May 1975, a total of four air force H-53s had been lost under similar circumstances, two Knives and two Jolly Greens. The total air force H-53 fleet numbered forty-three or forty-four at the time of the *Mayaguez* affair, so the loss rate for unknown causes was approaching 10 percent (the Tonle Sap crash went on the books as a combat loss to keep Rescue's safety record clean, but nobody who was familiar with the circumstances believed it).

In the spring of 1975, most thinking H-53 people considered the flight control system the prime culprit in the cause-unknown fatal accidents. What little we knew pointed to the primary flight control servos, the three large hydraulic actuators that transferred flight control inputs to the main rotor head. The most direct evidence was from the January 1975 crash. It had occurred in daylight not far from Nakhon Phanom, witnessed by a Thai schoolteacher who had watched the helicopter go out of control and explode in flight. His description of the helicopter's final moments suggested an extreme coupled control input; that is, one that combined pitch, roll, and collective components.[21] That eliminated the AFCS hydraulic servos as a cause, and the AFCS electrical system was incapable of producing forces that the pilot could not override. More conclusively, the Warner-Robins representative on the accident investigation board found a primary flight control servo retaining bolt in the wreckage that was scorched where the retaining nut should have been. That indicated that the nut, and presumably the primary servo, had parted company with the bolt *before* the aircraft exploded.

It was a good start, and with full benefit of hindsight that was exactly what had happened. But having made a sound deduction, Warner-Robins dropped the ball: the corrective action was to place a self-locking feature on the nut, assuming that vibration had caused it to rotate and back off the bolt. In fact, the nut had almost certainly shattered as a result of hydrogen embrittlement. Adding a self-locking feature did no good because the self-locking nuts were made by the same manufacturer using the same flawed process. The problem eluded accurate diagnosis for three more years, and at least one more H-53 was lost with no survivors.

The culprit was Warner-Robins's fixation on air refueling. Believing that aerial refueling put additional stress on the rotor head and associated components, early in the program Warner-Robins had directed the installation of extra-tough nuts to secure the primary flight control servos. This led to the procurement of the nuts, which turned out to be hydrogen-embrittled.[22] Just how many of the unexplained fatal crashes were attributable to the defective nuts is uncertain, but ironically the 13 May crash was not (see also chapter 4). The accident board traced its cause firmly to a defective sleeve-and-spindle assembly, the mechanism that holds the main rotor blade to the hub and permits it to rotate in pitch. The assembly had been improperly refurbished by the Naval Rework Facility, NAS North Island, and failed in flight, allowing the main rotor blade to depart the rotor hub.[23] The ensuing vibration quickly destroyed the aircraft.

The training of the Knife and Jolly Green crews that flew in the *Mayaguez*–Koh Tang operation differed only in detail. The 40th placed considerable emphasis on training in aerial refueling, and a number of 40th helicopters were equipped with the LNRS (limited night recovery system). This system, when everything was working (which it rarely did), permitted blacked-out approaches to a hover by means of a Doppler radar hover coupler and LLLTV (low-light-level television) setup. Select crews were required to maintain LNRS currency, although as it happened, it was of no value in either Frequent Wind or the Koh Tang affair.

It is also worth noting that the LNRS system was notoriously unreliable and drove maintenance up the wall.

Pilots in both squadrons received their initial H-53 qualification training at the Air Force Helicopter School, run by the 1550th Advanced Tactical Training Wing at Hill AFB, Ogden, Utah. Currency training for both units was event-oriented: it was based on the accomplishment of specific tasks. So many precision and nonprecision instrument approaches, so many simulated day and night hoist pickups, normal approaches, steep approaches, shallow approaches, and other maneuvers were required per quarter and semiannual period. As with all air force flying units, the aircrew training cycle revolved around annual proficiency checks and pilots' yearly instrument checks. Traditionally, the proficiency and instrument checks were scheduled according to the individual's birthdate and were administered six months apart. But Rescue Service threw the 40th a curve by following MAC's lead and adopting the "hard crew" concept in imitation of SAC. This concept meant assigning crew members permanently to a crew that always flew together with only limited substitutions. Each crew was assigned an artificial reference date for proficiency and instrument checks and took its check rides as a unit.

The hard crew concept worked for SAC in the 1950s and early '60s. Almost all SAC flying at the time was in training flights, deployments, and check rides. Everything could be scheduled well in advance, and crews stayed together for years. But it didn't work worth a flip for Rescue Service in Southeast Asia in the mid-1970s. As a result of the constant turnover created by one-year tours, the system started breaking down as soon as it was implemented. Personnel turbulence required frequent crew changes, and the reference date changed every time; that alone created a mountain of useless paperwork. To make matters worse, giving every member of a crew a full proficiency check on a single flight required some six or seven hours, and the stakes were high. The check rides tested endurance as much as proficiency. A bust by one crew member failed the entire crew, which then had to go through an exhaustive requalification program before it could fly operational missions or pull alert.

The headquarters-imposed rescue slogan current at the time was "Total Compliance!" We tried hard to comply, but how closely the paperwork correlated with reality was anybody's guess. In a perverse way, the slogan was totally appropriate—for a fraternal order of sadomasochists. If our currency and standardization program wasn't masochistic, I don't know what the term means.

In both squadrons, the accomplishment of required training events was closely monitored, by and large conscientiously so. The fundamental problem was that training requirements were driven by the demands of check flight criteria and revolved around stereotyped noncombat maneuvers. Given the preemptive air force emphasis on flight safety—or rather avoidance of training accidents—that which was not explicitly required was effectively prohibited. Tactical approaches were the primary victim. The normal, steep and shallow approaches that were part of every check ride began in straight and level flight at five hundred feet AGL (above ground level) and proceeded to the hover or touchdown point on a constant heading. Outside of a demonstration or two at Hill, they were the only kind of approach most of the young pilots had ever seen.

Although the training and evaluation system kept basic flight skills honed to a fine edge in such essential areas as systems knowledge, instrument flying, hoist operations, and aerial refueling, it let us down in gunnery, formation procedures, and tactics in general. How we trained and how we intended to fight diverged sharply, even on paper: in a classic display of institutional schizophrenia, Rescue Service regulations prohibited formation flying except in combat. The wonder is that we retained as much flexibility as we did.

The above account may make flying the H-53 for Uncle Sam's air force in the spring of 1975 sound like grim business, and in a way it was. A comment by a fellow Jolly Green pilot made shortly after the Koh Tang operation makes the point: "We ought to get air medals just for taking that sonofabitch off the ground." The implied reference was to the unexplained fatal accidents. Emotionally, I agreed with him. The H-53 was inherently dangerous in a way other air force vehicles were not, but it had its good side, too. The men who flew it in the spring of 1975 responded with a rare combination of dedication, good humor, and fatalism. I picked up a saying somewhere along the way that neatly summed it up. Flying the H-53 was like a passionate love affair with a beautiful nymphomaniac with a nasty temper and a black belt in karate: there were times when it was lots of fun, and there were times when it scared the hell out of you, but it always had your full attention.

Notes

PREFACE

1. Marshall was a flamboyant and controversial character, who inspired extreme positions concerning him, his work, and his methods. For a balanced appraisal see Maj. F. D. G. Williams, *SLAM: The Influence of S. L. A. Marshall on the United States Army.*
2. The seminal works are S. L. A. Marshall, *Men against Fire* (New York: William Morrow and Company, 1947) and Edward A. Shils and Morris Janowitz, "Cohesion and Disintegration in the Wehrmacht in World War II," *Public Opinion Quarterly* (Summer 1948): 280–315.

INTRODUCTION

1. Christopher Jon Lamb, *Belief Systems and Decision Making in the Mayaguez Crisis,* p. 165. Lamb offers a definitive account of policy and strategic decision making at the highest levels of the U.S. government.
2. Walter J. Wood, "'Mayday' for the *Mayaguez:* The Company Commander," *U.S. Naval Institute Proceedings* 102, no. 11 (November 1976). Contemporary press coverage and earlier published accounts did not address operational aspects of the incident in meaningful depth. The official air force account was released in 1977.

CHAPTER 1

1. *CINCPAC Command History, 1975* (henceforth *CINCPAC History*), app. 6, *The SS* Mayaguez *Incident,* pp. 1–3.
2. *CINCPAC History, 1975,* app. 1, *Eagle Pull,* p. 3; George R. Dunham and David A. Quinlan, *U.S. Marines in Vietnam: The Bitter End, 1973–1975,* pp. 102–104. *CINCPAC History* has the offensive starting on New Year's Day.
3. *CINCPAC History,* app. 1, pp. 7, 10.

4. There was no U.S.—Thai status of forces agreement: sovereign authority over U.S. bases in Thailand resided with the Thai crown, and the Thai and American flags flew side by side above the bases. Although in practice American commanders ran their bases much as they would have anywhere else, each base had a Thai commander in whom ultimate authority resided.

5. Lt. Gen. John J. Burns, interview with Hugh N. Ahmann, 5–8 June 1984, January 1986, p. viii.

6. Col. Sydney A. Batchelder, Jr., and Maj. D. A. Quinlan, "Operation Eagle Pull," *Marine Corps Gazette* (May 1976): 47–60. For Cambodia's military collapse, see Clark Dougan, David Fulghum, and the editors of Boston Publishing, *The Fall of the South* (Boston: Boston Publishing, 1985), pp. 31–45, 108–12, 121–25.

7. Batchelder and Quinlan, "Eagle Pull," p. 54. For a cogent analysis of the operational impact of seasonal weather patterns, see Lt. Gen. Philip B. Davidson, USA (Ret.), *Vietnam at War: The History, 1946–1975,* p. 38.

8. Batchelder and Quinlan, "Eagle Pull," pp. 52–53.

9. Besides the two H-53 squadrons at Nakhon Phanom, there was a rescue squadron in England, a special operations squadron in Germany, a partial rescue squadron in Florida, and a special operations detachment in Texas. These, plus a training squadron and a small Systems Command detachment at Hill AFB, Utah, comprised the entire operational air force H-53 strength. Thus, four of the six squadron equivalents were deployed overseas, and two of those were in Thailand. In fact, the personnel imbalance was even worse than this rough calculation suggests because the squadrons in Thailand were kept at full strength and those in the United States drawn down. In addition, the cadre at Hill AFB was composed entirely of experienced personnel: captains, technical sergeants, and above.

10. Captains and lieutenants are considered company grade and majors through colonels field grade. Junior field grade means newly promoted captains and lieutenants. Thirty H-53 pilots saw combat in the operation: one lieutenant colonel, one major, five captains, seventeen first lieutenants, and six second lieutenants. See Capt. Thomas D. Des Brisay, "Fourteen Hours at Koh Tang," in *The Vietnamese Air Force, 1951–1975: An Analysis of Its Role in Combat, and Fourteen Hours at Koh Tang,* pp. 152–54.

11. Only about a half-dozen of the sixty or so pilots assigned to the two squadrons had seen combat before Eagle Pull; author's recollection.

12. Chief Master Sgt. William Warren, USAF (Ret.), telephone conversation with author, 15 October 1990. In 1975, then-Senior Master Sergeant Warren was HQ ARRS senior standardization H-53 flight mechanic and, as such, monitored flight mechanic assignments. Fully qualified individuals hold a skill level of five or more on a scale of one to nine, a three being awarded upon successful completion of technical training school.

13. Author's recollection; Chief Master Sgt. Wayne L. Fisk, telephone conversation with author, 9 October 1990.

14. Author's recollection for the 40th; Capt. Geoffrey W. Trune, Capt. Richard L. Brasher, and Sgt. David T. Turley, *History of the 56th Special Operations Wing, 1 April—30 June 1975* (henceforth *History of 56th SOW*), vol. 1, narrative (29 September 1975), USAF Historical Research Center (USAFHRC), Maxwell AFB, Alabama (April—June 1975), p. 17, for the 21st.

15. Losses to MiGs over North Vietnam prompted a partial reversal of the trend, marked by the commissioning of the first aggressor squadron at Nellis AFB, Nevada, in June 1973, but this affected only fighter pilots. Realistic combat training for helicopter crews was reinstated in 1976 in conjunction with the Red Flag tactical exercises at Nellis. The navy was ahead of the air force in taking action to reverse the erosion of combat skills: the Naval Fighter Weapons School graduated its first Top Gun class in March 1969. Comdr. John B. Nichols, USN (Ret.), and Barrett Tillman, *On Yankee Station: The Naval Air War over Vietnam* (Annapolis, Md.: Naval Institute Press, 1987), p. 79.

16. See Appendix B.

17. *History of 56th SOW (U), 1 January—31 March 1975,* vol. 2, *Unit Historical Reports* (11 July 1975), p. 5.

18. Raynor L. Buckley, interview with author, 28 May 1987. During Frequent Wind, two of the three guns on the author's aircraft jammed to the point of inoperability on the first round.

19. *History of 56th SOW* (January—March 1975), p. 2; ibid. (April—June 1975), p. 17.

20. Ibid. (April—June 1975), p. viii. The C-118's final destination was bitterly apt: the Davis-Monthan AFB, Arizona, "boneyard."

21. Nakhon Phanom was tentatively scheduled for closure in July 1975; Burns interview, p. 361. It actually closed in September.

22. Personal recollection. In-commission rates were under high-level scrutiny in all flying units, and maintenance was under constant pressure to keep them up. This was a fertile source of disputes between flight crews and maintenance supervisors concerning aircraft status. With the 40th, all parties involved worked for the squadron commander, a lieutenant colonel and H-53 pilot who was responsible for both flying safety and the in-commission rate. In the case of the 21st, maintenance worked for the 56th SOW deputy commander for maintenance, a full colonel who reported to the wing commander and was responsible only for maintenance.

23. To cite two relevant specifics: on 20 April the 40th provided two airborne spares to replace out-of-commission 21st aircraft in the Frequent Wind deployment from U Tapao (Trune et al., *History of 56th SOW* [April—June 1975], pp. 20–21). The 40th was significantly faster in generating and launching aircraft in the initial *Mayaguez* deployment of 13 May.

24. Buckley interview. In the spring of 1975 Buckley, then a first lieutenant, was assistant maintenance officer of the 40th. He was the officer in charge of deployed 40th maintenance personnel aboard USS *Midway*

during Frequent Wind and at U Tapao Royal Thai Naval Base during the *Mayaguez* operation.

25. The first was lost 8 October 1969, the second 14 June 1973; author's notes of ARRS/MAC H-53 briefing, 2 December 1977, Scott AFB, Illinois, of all air force H-53 accidents, prepared and given by an ARRS/MAC standardization-evaluation team.

26. Author's opinion, based on a navy-marine H-53 accident summary received from the Air Force Safety Center, Norton AFB, California, March 1975; author's journal; see Appendix B.

27. Author's journal and author's conclusion; see Appendix B.

28. Burns interview, pp. 367–74. Between 21 March and 11 April the list of potential evacuees in Cambodia diminished from 1,191 to 590. *CINCPAC History,* app. 1, p. 10. This probably represents only a fraction of those evacuated: the list lengthened as the likelihood of Communist victory increased, and many who left were not listed.

29. Burns interview, pp. 365–68, 380.

30. Author's journal; 21st SOS and 40th ARRS aircrews were briefed on marine hand signals used to direct helicopters and ground-based visual approach aids.

31. Kenneth K. Kawanami, *History of the 3rd Tactical Fighter Wing, April—June 1975,* p. 47.

32. Batchelder and Quinlan, "Eagle Pull," p. 57. See Burns interview, pp. 374–75, for airlift operations. Pochentong was under intermittent rocket fire, and the fixed-wing evacuation was conducted by civilian contract aircraft operated by Bird Air and World Airways under COMUSSAG/Seventh Air Force control.

33. Batchelder and Quinlan, "Eagle Pull," p. 57.

34. *CINCPAC History,* app. 1, p. 14. Dean was thoroughly conversant with the military situation and closely coordinated his decisions with the military authorities.

35. Ibid., pp. 19–22.

36. Dougan et al., *The Fall of the South,* p. 122; Burns interview, pp. 380–81.

37. Kawanami, *History of 3rd Tactical Fighter Wing,* p. 48.

38. *CINCPAC History,* app. 1, pp. 22, 26; Batchelder and Quinlan, "Eagle Pull," p. 216. There were 84 American evacuees, 173 Cambodians, and 30 third-country nationals.

39. Lt. Col. Thomas G. Tobin, Lt. Col. Arthur E. Laehr, and Lt. Col. John F. Hilgenberger, USAF; Lt. Col. David R. Mets, ed., *Last Flight from Saigon,* USAF Southeast Asia Monograph Series, vol. 4, monograph 6 (Washington, D.C.: U.S. Government Printing Office 1978), pp. 8–10.

40. Burns interview, p. 391; see David Butler, *The Fall of Saigon,* pp. 143–49, for a balanced and generally sympathetic profile of Martin that substantiates this characterization.

41. From the beginning Martin prohibited contact with the press by military embassy staff without his explicit permission. Maj. Stuart A.

Herrington, USAF, *The Third Indochina War 1973–1975: A Personal Perspective*, pp. 101–102.

42. For the ARVN collapse, see Lt. Gen. Phillip B. Davidson, USA (Ret.), *Vietnam at War: The History, 1946–1975*, pp. 767–94; General Cao Van Vien, *The Final Collapse*, for the South Vietnamese perspective; and Colonel General Tran Van Tra, *History of the Bulwark B2 Theatre*, vol. 5, *Concluding the Thirty Years' War* (2 February 1983), for a North Vietnamese view.

43. A point made explicitly by Martin to Admiral Gayler and Lieutenant General Burns; Burns interview, p. 391.

44. Mets, *Last Flight*, pp. 24–27; Herrington, *Personal Perspective*, pp. 254–55.

45. Mets, *Last Flight*, p. 13; *CINCPAC History*, app. 1, p. 23.

46. Mets, *Last Flight*, p. 22.

47. Ibid., p. 24; Herrington, *Personal Perspective*, pp. 256–57. "Babylift" was a nickname given the operation in a USAIS news release.

48. Brig. Gen. Richard E. Carey and Maj. D. A. Quinlan, "Frequent Wind: Part Two, Planning," *Marine Corps Gazette* (March 1976): 44.

49. Herrington, *Personal Perspective*, pp. 256–57.

50. Mets, *Last Flight*, p. 43.

51. Ibid., p. 46.

52. Ibid., p. 46; Burns interview, pp. 390–91. Even then, implementation was slow. Not until the twenty-second did the flow increase significantly, from three hundred to five hundred evacuees per day to three thousand plus. Mets, *Last Flight*, p. 45.

53. Carey and Quinlan, "Frequent Wind: Part Two, Planning," pp. 36–37. The following narrative outlines the military response to a complex and rapidly developing situation only as it affected Option IV of Frequent Wind. To Gayler, Burns, and Steele, Option IV was only one contingency among many and not necessarily the most difficult. Option V, considered as late as 13–15 April, envisioned moving 130,000 evacuees by highway to Vung Tau under escort by elite ARVN units for evacuation by sea. Burns interview, pp. 388–92, esp. 389; Col. Robert A. Reed, End of Tour Report, 1 July 1974–30 June 1975, p. 3. Reed was USSAG/Seventh Air Force deputy chief, Operations Plans Division.

54. Brig. Gen. Richard M. Baughn, interview with Hugh N. Ahmann, 20–21 March 1979, p. 232; Burns interview, pp. 402–403. Certain DAO functions fell directly under COMUSSAG and CINCPAC: Baughn's circumvention of Martin was technically correct beyond being justified by the moral imperatives of the situation.

55. Dunham and Quinlan, *The Bitter End*, p. 157; Baughn interview, p. 232.

56. Mets, *Last Flight*, p. 46.

57. Carey and Quinlan, "Frequent Wind: Part Two, Planning," pp. 35–40. The figures are based on seating provisions for fully equipped troops and serve only to give an idea of the relative capacities of the two aircraft. Lt. Col. William R. Fails, *Marines and Helicopters, 1962–1973*, pp. 230–36.

With troop seats removed and evacuees seated on the floor, considerably larger numbers could be carried, particularly with the H-53, which was not power limited. With baggage left behind and a high proportion of diminutive Asian women and children among the passengers, the numbers could be staggering: the author's HH-53C carried over one hundred evacuees out of Saigon on one lift.

58. Author's journal; *Spectrum* 1, no. 3 (n.d., ca. 30 May 1975). The initial contingent was four HH-53s and six CH-53s; the 21st flew out two more CH-53s the next day, and two 40th aircraft returned.

59. Carey and Quinlan, "Frequent Wind: Part Two, Planning," p. 40.

60. Herrington, *Personal Perspective*, p. 321.

61. Dougan et al., *The Fall of the South*, p. 160.

62. Herrington, *Personal Perspective*, p. 335; interview, David Hume Kennerly, ABC "Good Morning America." I am indebted to William H. Masters, field producer—director, ABC-TV, for transcripts of interviews conducted for the 30 April 1985 "Good Morning America" program on the tenth anniversary of the fall of Saigon. White House photographer Kennerly was eyewitness to the activities of the presidential staff.

63. Mets, *Last Flight*, p. 90; Butler, *Fall of Saigon*, pp. 390–91.

64. Trune et al., *History of 56th SOW* (April—June 1975), p. 21.

65. Mets, *Last Flight*, p. 88; Butler, *Fall of Saigon*, p. 387.

66. Mets, *Last Flight*, p. 89.

67. Ibid., pp. 88, 93. To put this in perspective, a Huey's normal load is eight passengers. The Air America helicopters hauled an average of some fifty persons each in less than five hours, although several had to be abandoned because of battle damage and some refueled aboard TF-76 ships, requiring a round trip of at least 1+30 hours. The figure of one thousand is suspiciously round: the actual number may have been considerably larger.

68. U.S. Naval Observatory, *The Nautical Almanac for the Year 1975*, p. 89; sunset was 1906, civil twilight 1928, and nautical twilight 1953. At civil twilight, with good visibility and no overcast or illumination other than the sun, the horizon is clearly defined, and only the brightest stars can be seen. At nautical twilight the horizon can no longer be seen, and there is insufficient light for observations with a marine sextant (ibid., p. 258).

69. Mets, *Last Flight*, pp. 91, 97.

70. Burns interview, p. 420; author's journal. This was the only expenditure of ordnance by U.S. tactical air power apart from defensive machinegun fire by helicopters. A 37-mm battery was active southwest of Tan Son Nhut but could not depress its trajectory enough to effectively engage helicopters descending toward Alamo from the east. The VNAF was not so restrained. An AC-119K gunship took off from Tan Son Nhut following the initial rocket barrage and suppressed fire around the field throughout the night, only to be shot down by an SA-7 at about 0700. A-1Hs from Can Tho attacked the Communist rocket batteries, apparently under the direction of Air Marshal Nguyen Cao Ky, who con-

trolled the strike from his personal UH-1, and were still active around Tan Son Nhut at dawn. Butler, *Fall of Saigon*, p. 381; Mets, *Last Flight*, p. 82.

71. RHAW (Radar Homing and Warning) indications over the DAO Compound showed three SA-2 sites within range to the north and northeast; author's journal.

72. Mets, *Last Flight*, p. 93.

73. Reasoning that the danger of midair collision was greater than the SA-7 threat, Lt. Col. James L. Boulton, commander of HMH-462, ordered his crews to leave their lights on, a courageous and sound decision (information to the author). I ordered my element of two HH-53Cs and one CH-53C to extinguish navigation lights and lower anticollision beacons, leaving upper anticollision beacons illuminated. In the first quarter-mile of our final climb out from Alamo, my crew and I barely missed two H-53s that came at us out of the darkness with all lights extinguished.

74. Trune et al., *History of 56th SOW* (April—June 1975), p. 21; author's journal.

75. Mets, *Last Flight* , p. 106.

76. See Herrington, *Personal Perspective*, pp. 336–44, for a graphic eyewitness account.

77. Carey and Quinlan, "Frequent Wind: Part Three, Execution," *Marine Corps Gazette* (April 1976): 42. Three "Sparrowhawk" platoons were put into the embassy by CH-46 between 1700 and 2100.

78. Dunham and Quinlan, *The Bitter End*, p. 199; Mets, *Last Flight*, p. 106.

79. Herrington, *Personal Perspective*, p. 350. Herrington established radio contact with Alamo shortly after dark, but contact remained intermittent.

80. Lt. Gen. Richard E. Carey, USMC (Ret.), lecture, Ohio State University, 25 May 1988. The confrontation is alluded to in Carey and Quinlan, "Frequent Wind: Part Two, Planning," p. 43.

81. David Hume Kennerly interview. Kennerly has Martin refusing Kissinger's order to evacuate, then yielding to a direct presidential order. The former exchange probably took place by satellite telephone link.

82. Kawanami, *History of 3rd Tactical Fighter Wing*, p. 53.

83. Carey and Quinlan, "Frequent Wind, Part Three, Execution," p. 44.

84. Herrington, *Personal Perspective*, pp. 358–60. Herrington departed after the ambassador.

85. Mets, *Last Flight*, p. 108.

86. J. Michael Rodgers, interview with author, 10–11 June 1987. This was confirmed by the testimony of one of the author's students at Ohio State University, Mr. Vo Tri, who was aboard one of the barges.

87. Ray L. Bowers, *Tactical Airlift*, pp. 644, 644 n. 31, gives a total of 6,442 non-American and 1,373 American evacuees brought out by marine, air force, and Air America helicopter, not counting the 850 GSF marines. Carey and Quinlan, "Frequent Wind: Part Three, Execution," pp. 44, 45, give 1,373 Americans and 5,595 others, of whom 978 Americans and

1,120 others came from the embassy. Mets, *Last Flight*, p. 122, is in general agreement with Carey and Quinlan. The eight 21st SOS H-53s brought out no fewer than 1,831 evacuees and 249 GSF marines (Trune et al., *History of 56th SOW* [April—June 1975], p. 22).

88. A chilling incident that brings the point home involved a refugee-filled 21st SOS helicopter that experienced complete electrical failure over the South China Sea in darkness. The night was moonless and overcast. With neither cockpit lighting nor the electrically driven automatic flight control system (AFCS) for stability (see Appendix B), disaster was seconds away when a quick-thinking flight mechanic and copilot managed to reset a generator. Information to the author; Trune et al., *History of 56th SOW* (April-June 1975), p. 21.

89. James H. Davis, interview with author, 14 September 1991; Dunham and Quinlan, *The Bitter End*, p. 251n.

CHAPTER 2

1. Roy Rowan, *The Four Days of Mayaguez*, pp. 16–43. Thailand, Cambodia, and the Gulf of Siam are in the +7 time zone. Washington, D.C., is in the —5 time zone but was on eastern daylight time (EDT), making the local difference from Greenwich mean (Z) time —4. See Department of Transportation circular, "Observance of Daylight Saving Time in the United States" (1987). The time difference between the Gulf of Siam and Washington was therefore —11 hours. Where exact times are significant I have used twenty-four-hour notation.

2. Rowan, *Four Days*, p. 66.

3. The earliest evidence of transmission I have found was the message time-date group AmEmb Djakarta 120903Z May, cited in Urey W. Patrick, *The* Mayaguez *Operation*, p. 100, A-2; there were no doubt earlier informal contacts. The time-date groups on U.S. government messages begin with the originator—in this case the American Embassy, Djakarta—followed by a seven-unit time-date designator, the month, and the year. The first two digits of the time-date indicator give the day of the month, and the next four give the time of transmission; the letter indicates the reference time zone, in this case Z, or Greenwich mean time. I have deleted the year, since all were 1975.

4. Christopher Lamb, *Belief Systems and Decision Making in the* Mayaguez *Crisis*, p. 79; unpublished Georgetown University dissertation, same title (1985), p. 133.

5. Lamb, *Belief Systems*, p. 80. All times are local unless stated otherwise. Where the time zone is not clear from the context, I have specified eastern daylight time for Washington, D.C., and local time in the Gulf of Siam, designated by *G* in endnotes. Note that from 1300 until midnight Washington time, the local date in the Gulf of Siam was a day ahead.

6. Dr. James R. Schlesinger, telephone interview with author, 29 August 1994.

7. Lamb, *Belief Systems*, p. 57.

8. Ibid., p. 81.

9. Since *koh* is the Khymer word for island, the proper name of the place is Koh Tang or Tang Island. Koh Tang Island is a redundancy.

10. Walter J. Wood, "'Mayday' for the *Mayaguez:* The Company Commander," *U.S. Naval Institute Proceedings* 102, no. 11 (November 1976): 101.

11. For American combat personnel losses, see Lamb, *Belief Systems*, pp. 31–32; for losses in the preinvasion helicopter crash, see Trune et al., *History of 56th SOW* (April—June 1975), vol. 1, p. 26. The estimate of Cambodian casualties is my own, based on the sources cited.

12. This law was pointed out to me by Rear Adm. W. J. Holland, Jr., USN (Ret.).

13. Lamb, *Belief Systems*, pp. 31–32.

CHAPTER 3

1. Carl von Clausewitz, *On War*, trans. Michael Howard and Peter Paret (Princeton: Princeton University Press, 1976), p. 119.

2. Ibid.

3. Ibid., p. 183.

4. Sir Edward Creasy, *Fifteen Decisive Battles of the World*, appeared in no less than thirty-eight editions between 1851 and 1894 (John Keegan, *The Face of Battle* [London: Viking Press 1976], p. 57), far exceeding the popularity of more recent works in the same genre. For example, see John F. C. Fuller's *Decisive Battles: Their Influence Upon History and Civilization* (New York: Scribners Sons, 1940) and *Decisive Battles of the United States* (New York: Beechhurst Press, 1953) and Fletcher Pratt's *Battles That Changed History* (Garden City, N.Y.: Hanover House, 1956).

5. See Alan Beyerchen, "Clausewitz, Nonlinearity, and the Unpredictability of War," *International Security* 17, no. 3 (Winter 1992–93): 59–90, for a penetrating analysis of the relationships in question.

6. I owe the concept of cumulative risk to Col. Thomas A. Fabyanic, USAF (Ret.), who developed it in his USAF Air War College lectures on U.S. Army Air Force unescorted precision daylight bombardment operations in World War II.

7. Beyerchen, "Clausewitz," whom I am in part paraphrasing here, argues that war is an inherently nonlinear phenomenon with pockets of linearity embedded in it, that Clausewitz implicitly understood the relationships in question, and that few subsequent analysts have. As Beyerchen puts it, "The variables in war cannot be isolated from the parameters constituting the political context. And that environment itself evolves

dynamically in response to the course of a war, *with the changed context feeding back into the conduct of hostilities*" (p. 90) (my emphasis).

8. The only works I am aware of that address the problem of escalating uncertainty in these terms are Edward J. Drea, *Nomonhan: Japanese-Soviet Tactical Combat, 1939,* and Barry D. Watts, *Foundations of U.S. Air Doctrine: The Problem of Friction in War.*

9. Vietnamese government sources later dated the first of these raids to May 1975. They culminated in deep incursions into the border provinces in strength in the autumn of 1977 and spring of 1978 (Nyan Chanda, "The Bloody Border," *Far Eastern Economic Review* 100, no. 16 [April 2, 1978]: 17–19; and Chanda, "Clash of Steel among Comrades" and "Anatomy of a Conflict," *Far Eastern Economic Review* 99, no. 2 [January 13, 1978]: 10–12). Hanoi responded with the 25 December 1978 invasion of Cambodia and overthrow of the Khymer Rouge government. For Khymer Rouge designs on the Mekong border provinces from a Cambodian perspective, see David P. Chandler, *The Land and People of Cambodia* (New York, 1991), pp. 144–46.

10. *Khmer Kraham* is a contraction of *Yothear Khmer Kraham* (Khymer Rouge armed forces). The term was applied to Khymer Rouge forces in U.S. intelligence summaries.

11. David R. Mets, *Land-based Air Power In Third World Crises,* p. 38.

12. The question was raised by White House photographer David Hume Kennerly at the end of the fourth and final National Security Council meeting during the crisis, convened at 1352 EST on the fourteenth. Lamb, *Belief Systems,* pp. 91–92. The B-52s were based on Guam (see *CINCPAC History,* p. 24).

13. Lamb, *Belief Systems,* pp. 83, 177. Nor was Scowcroft alone: New York Assemblywoman Elizabeth Connelly, for example, telegraphed the White House, "We must not permit another *Pueblo* incident" (Lamb, *Belief Systems,* p. 159).

14. *CINCPAC History,* p. 11; John J. Lane, Jr., *Command and Control and Communications Structures in Southeast Asia (The Air War in Indochina),* p. 221.

15. Harold M. Hyman, *Quiet Past and Stormy Present? War Powers in American History,* p. 53. For Ford's awareness of the issues involved and concern to stay within the letter of the law, see Lamb, *Belief Systems,* pp. 160–62.

16. Lamb, unpublished dissertation, p. 146. Hyman, *Quiet Past,* p. 55, asserts that Ford violated the War Powers Act by not consulting with Congress. I disagree, although Hyman has a point on technical grounds.

17. Lamb, *Belief Systems,* p. 162.

18. Ibid., pp. 61, 122.

19. Ibid., p. 3. Lamb's analysis of the national decision-making process is comprehensive, penetrating, and persuasive; I have followed it throughout.

20. Ibid., p. 167.

21. Ibid., p. 164.

22. Patrick, *The Mayaguez Operation*, p. 29. SH-3s are embarked on attack carriers mainly to rescue downed aviators at sea.

23. Trune et al., *History of 56th SOW* (April—June 1975), p. 17; 1st Lt. Norman D. Norman, *History of the Fortieth Aerospace Rescue and Recovery Squadron, 1 January—30 June 1975*, p. 16.

24. Although USAF H-53s were occasionally used in South Vietnam, they were procured for the air war over Laos and North Vietnam. The 21st and 40th inherited their respective traditions in that arena. For rescue, see Earl H. Tilford, *Search and Rescue in Southeast Asia, 1961–1975*. USAF special operations helicopter units have not received monographic treatment, but Ray L. Bowers, *Tactical Airlift*, includes some coverage.

25. The Jolly Greens' "ass painting" was by no means the only manifestation of unit esprit to emerge from the Southeast Asia air war that would have seemed bizarre in more settled circumstances. In the early days of Nakhon Phanom's existence as an American base in 1965–66, newly assigned officers and visitors to the officers' club were expected to down an "afterburner." This was a shot glass of neat liquor set on fire and drunk while burning by the initiates in an elaborate ceremony their first night on base.

26. T.O. 1H-53(H)B-1 (1 November 1973), 1–22. JP-4 jet fuel weighs about 6.5 lb./gal. under normal ambient temperatures, and an H-53's two T-64 turbine engines consume some 2,200–1,700 lb./hr. in cruise flight at normal gross weights.

27. Dunham and Quinlan, *The Bitter End*, p. 245n.

28. By comparison, the cyclic rate of fire of the 7.62-mm M60, the standard U.S. infantry machine gun, is 550 rounds per minute, and the M16 rifle has a cyclic rate of 650–850 rounds per minute.

29. Patrick, *The Mayaguez Operation*, p. 50.

30. Burns interview, pp. 412, 437.

31. As PACAF assets, Sandy-designated fighters had been used for conventional attack duties under different call signs during 1965–73. But RESCORT was their primary mission, and for that they fell under rescue control. The procedures sketched out above cover only the basics, and variations were common. Where a fighter crew was downed while working with an airborne FAC, for example, King might designate the FAC on-scene commander pending the arrival of Sandys. If enemy opposition was strong, Sandy lead would assume the FAC role, controlling suppressive strikes by flights of tactical fighters obtained, coordinated, and cycled in by King. Tilford, *Search and Rescue in Southeast Asia*, is the basic source.

32. See figure 1, based on the diagram in *CINCPAC History*, p. 11.

33. Walter H. Baxter III interview and R. B. Janca interview, enclosures to *CINCPAC/IG Inquiry into Availability of Intelligence during Mayaguez*, Col. Duane E. Vandenberg (USAFHRC), henceforth *CINCPAC/IG Inquiry*). This document records the CINCPAC inspector general's investigation of GAO (General Accounting Office) questions about the

adequacy of intelligence provided to the Koh Tang assault force. It also contains detailed and apparently candid information about command and control relationships.

34. Memo with enclosures, Brig. Gen. James H. Johnson, USAF (PACAF/IG) to Adm. Noel Gayler, "SS *Mayaguez* Seizure." The enclosures to this document cover much of the same ground as those to the CINCPAC/IG inquiry but often from significantly different perspectives. The memo itself contains a detailed chronology. Janca clearly enjoyed Baxter's confidence and was plainly reassigned on short notice to take charge of a crucial function at a critical time. But his new command was part of the 307th Strategic Wing, a SAC unit, and SAC and PACAF regulations, methods, and procedures differed appreciably. It is hard to imagine how Janca could have developed a useful working knowledge of his command on such short notice.

35. *CINCPAC/IG Inquiry.*

36. Johnson to Gayler memo.

37. Rodgers interview, 10–11 June 1987. A destroyer burns fuel nearly four times faster at maximum sustained speed of thirty-one knots (nautical miles per hour) than at normal cruising speed of fifteen to seventeen knots. By going to maximum speed, *Wilson* cut her range by two-thirds (Donald P. Roane, telephone conversation with author, 5 January 1989).

38. Roane telephone conversation, 5 January 1989.

39. CINCPACFLT 121812Z May, cited by Patrick, *The* Mayaguez *Operation*, A-2.

40. Patrick, *The* Mayaguez *Operation*, p. 29.

41. Ibid., pp. 27, A-13.

42. Trune et al., *History of 56th SOW* (April—June 1975), p. 5, have the deployment order issued at 1800. 1st Lt. Calvin Wachs, *21st SOS Unit History Working Draft*, has the 21st alerted at 1830 and the first launch at 2030, a time verifiable by other sources. The author's journal refers to a 1730 deployment notification. See 40th ARRS Daily Flying Log, 13–18 May 1975, for 40th launch times. The 40th kept two HH-53s at Korat on immediate rescue alert. On the evening of the thirteenth, a third HH-53 was there for alert aircraft change-off and crew rotation the next morning.

43. This was done by means of dummy weight and balance forms for sequential deployment loads filled in with the requisite cargo and seats for maintenance personnel, identified by AFSC, the four-digit code indicating the individual's specialty and qualification level. Aircraft tail numbers and weight and balance data were left blank because weights and centers of gravity vary from aircraft to aircraft. Identical copies were kept on file in squadron operations and maintenance. On receipt of deployment orders, maintenance told operations which aircraft were in commission and assigned loads against them. Operations and maintenance then filled in the corresponding forms with the same tail numbers. The aircraft were loaded while preflight inspections were underway, and maintenance workers were matched with the requisite

AFSCs. Once specific aircraft were matched against loads, flight mechanics could begin weight and balance calculations. The final step was to weigh maintenance personnel and their baggage and tool kits on a gymnasium scale before boarding. The system was fast and efficient and was validated in the Eagle Pull and Frequent Wind deployments (author's observation).

44. Author's observation, based on visits to the office in question.
45. The H-43 detachments were attached to the 40th ARRS (Norman, *History of 40th ARRS* [January—June 1975], p. 3).
46. Col. William D. Mol, "End of Tour Report"; Col. Roger L. Sprague, "End of Tour Report"; Trune et al., *History of 56th SOW* (April—June 1975); Norman, *History of 40th ARRS* (January—June 1975). Udorn strengths are estimates.
47. For the genesis of the side-firing gunship concept and the AC-130, see Jack S. Ballard, *Development and Employment of Fixed-Wing Gunships, 1969–72.* The AC-130 gunship was preceded by the AC-47 gunship, called Spooky, and followed by gunship modifications of the C-119, called Stinger.
48. See Henry Zeybel, "Truck Count," *Air University Review* 34, no. 2 (January—February 1983): 36–45.
49. AC-130s graphically demonstrated their effectiveness in this role during the 1972 North Vietnamese Easter offensive, notably in the defense of Kontum and An Loc (Ballard, *Fixed-Wing Gunships,* pp. 235–47, esp. 243).
50. This barely touches on a complex tactical calculus. The AC-130 could not climb above the engagement envelopes of Soviet 85-mm and 57-mm antiaircraft guns. In order to effectively engage targets, it had to descend to about ten thousand feet above ground level, within the upper fringe of the 37-mm engagement "bubble." The gunship attack profile entailed flying in a circle around the target, so prolongued exposure to hostile fire while attacking a defended target was a given. At the same time, however, gunships proved effective at engaging and neutralizing antiaircraft batteries. With some seven thousand pounds of armor and fuel tanks protected by explosion-resistant polyurethane foam, the AC-130 was remarkably resistant to battle damage. All of the antiaircraft guns cited above, however, were capable of inflicting lethal damage. At night, the risk was manageable: Communist gunners fired under radar control, and the fire control radar emissions could be intercepted by the AC-130's passive ECM (electronic countermeasures) equipment. But to complicate matters, radar fire control increased effective slant ranges by 5 percent or so (see Ballard, *Fixed-Wing Gunships,* pp. 120–21). The chances of a first-shot kill were acceptably low; because shell bursts are highly visible at night, Spectre crews had time to evade or return fire. In addition, flak-suppression fighter escorts were provided. In daylight, the tactical calculus was radically different: camouflaged antiaircraft batteries firing under optical control could engage suddenly and without warning, posing unacceptably high risks.

The matter never became an issue during 1969–72 because trucks along the Ho Chi Minh Trail—the primary gunship target—moved almost entirely by night, obviating the need to commit gunships in daylight. In critical operational situations, gunship crews could and did descend to low altitudes to engage targets heavily defended by guns of lesser caliber. This, too, tended to be almost exclusively at night, when gunships were the only means of engaging targets close to friendly forces. The appearance of the SA-7 in the spring of 1972 posed a significant threat. But infrared decoy flares brought the problem under control, and AC-130s continued to operate in the upper fringes of the SA-7 envelope. The one threat that the AC-130 had no effective countermeasure against was the radar-guided SA-2, but this was not a factor in the *Mayaguez* operation.

51. The unreliability of the A-model's three-bladed propellers was another significant difference (information to the author, David R. Mets, Lt. Col. USAF [Ret.], 20 July 1990). A combat-experienced AC-130 pilot, Mets was operations officer of the 16th SOS during the *Mayaguez* affair.

52. Author's sense of the agreement among experienced air force H-53 pilots, flight mechanics, and maintenance personnel circa 1974–79. The H-53 had one of the lowest in-commission percentages among air force aircraft, and figures as low as 60 percent were not unheard of (see Appendix B).

53. Wachs, *Working Draft;* author's notes.

54. Dunham and Quinlan, *The Bitter End,* p. 24; Austin interview, *CINCPAC/IG Inquiry;* Wood, "The Company Commander," and J. B. Hendricks, "The Battalion Operations Officer," in "'Mayday' for the *Mayaguez*," pp. 100–10.

55. Dunham and Quinlan, *The Bitter End,* p. 241; Patrick, *The* Mayaguez *Operation,* p. 31; Wood, "The Company Commander," and Hendricks, "The Battalion Operations Officer," pp. 100–101, 104; Austin interview, *CINCPAC/IG Inquiry.* There is some dispute concerning the arrival of the final marines in the Koh Tang assault force at U Tapao. Patrick has them arriving at 1330 on the fourteenth; air force observers have told the author of watching marines proceed directly from C-141s to the assault helicopters shortly before takeoff on the fifteenth.

56. Davis interview.

57. Patrick, *The* Mayaguez *Operation,* fig. IV-3, "Command and Control," p. 50.

CHAPTER 4

1. The official published account is Thomas D. Des Brisay, "Fourteen Hours," in *The Vietnamese Air Force, 1951–1975: An Analysis of Its Role in Combat, and Fourteen Hours at Koh Tang.* This was derived from *Assault on Koh Tang* (DCS Plans and Operations, HQ PACAF), 23 June 1975 (SECRET, declassified 31 December 83).

2. J. A. Messegee, "'Mayday' for the *Mayaguez:* The Patrol Squadron Skipper," *U.S. Naval Institute Proceedings* 102, no. 11 (November 1976): 94.

3. Messegee, "The Patrol Squadron Skipper," p. 95.

4. Ibid.

5. Ibid., pp. 95–96. The aviators expected the *Mayaguez* to reach Kompong Som in six hours; she was therefore making about ten knots (nautical miles per hour) and would have reached Koh Tang at about 1045.

6. Burns interview, pp. 427–28. The operational authority granted Burns in support of Frequent Wind had been withdrawn several days earlier, and CINCPAC approval was required.

7. Des Brisay, "Fourteen Hours," p. 95; Burns interview, pp. 427–28. Messegee (p. 96) does not report seeing air force fighter-bombers off the island until "approximately 1500."

8. *CINCPAC History,* p. 16; Messegee, "The Patrol Squadron Skipper," p. 96.

9. *CINCPAC History,* p. 16. The two observations were reported to COMUSSAG/Seventh Air Force at 1733 and 1815G, respectively.

10. *CINCPAC History,* p. 18.

11. Ibid., p. 5; Burns interview, p. 383.

12. Schlesinger telephone interview, 29 August 1994.

13. Ibid.

14. *CINCPAC History,* p. 17.

15. Ibid., pp. 21–23.

16. Ibid., pp. 21, 23; Johnson to Gayler memo. A total of 125 security police were to be used. Before Eagle Pull, Lt. Col. Sydney A. Batchelder, Jr., USMC, the Phnom Penh ground element commander, had given infantry training to a number of security policemen at Nakhon Phanom. Although most of them had rotated back to the United States, some were among Huebusch's volunteers. Burns interview, p. 384.

17. Dunham and Quinlan, *The Bitter End,* p. 241.

18. Lamb, *Belief Systems,* p. 164, citing Robert Hartman, *Palace Politics: An Inside Account of the Ford Years* (New York: 1980), p. 32, and *CINCPAC History,* p. 24, outlines the logic behind the rejection of a helicopter assault.

19. Wachs, *Working Draft.* The precise time of arrival is uncertain.

20. By happenstance the 40th had three HH-53s at Korat on the evening of the twelfth, two on alert and one to rotate crews. The third aircraft had launched for U Tapao earlier.

21. Author's journal. I was in the JRCC and witnessed McMonigle's repeated, and ultimately successful, efforts to have the two helicopters diverted to U Tapao.

22. Henry M. Mason, interview with author, 28 May 1987. Mason, then a second lieutenant, was copilot of one of the aircraft.

23. Wachs, *Working Draft;* information to the author.

24. Schlesinger telephone interview. *CINCPAC History,* p. 18, reports that a highly classified intelligence source indicated Khymer Rouge intent to take the crew to Koh Tang.

25. *CINCPAC/IG Inquiry,* Austin interview, 4 November 1975; JCS planning guidance (JCS 140645Z), summarized in Patrick, *The* Mayaguez *Operation,* p. 6.

26. Cited in Lamb, *Belief Systems,* pp. 105–107, 107 n. 12. Transmission time was 2203Z 14 May/0503G 15 May.

27. U.S. Naval Observatory, *The Nautical Almanac for the Year 1975,* pp. 99, 258. Civil twilight, when the brightest stars are still visible but the horizon is clearly defined, was 0524G; nautical twilight, when the horizon is not yet well enough defined for observations with a marine sextant, was 0458G.

28. IPAC Report 13/2144Z May 75, cited in *CINCPAC/IG Inquiry;* Lamb, *Belief Systems,* p. 129. At this point *Khmer Kraham* battalions were about 200–220 strong (Burns interview, p. 439). The nominal strength of an infantry battalion in most armies is 500 to 700 men.

29. Austin interview, *CINCPAC/IG Inquiry;* Patrick, *The* Mayaguez *Operation,* p. 8. For Austin's experience in Vietnam, refer to remarks by Maj. Gen. Kenneth J. Houghton, USMC, commander, 3rd Marine Division, at a 19 May press conference at Subic Bay (CINCPAC 191902Z message [USAFHRC]).

30. 40th ARRS Draft Recommendations for Decorations for Heroism, Jolly Green 13 and 21 (14 May); information to the author, Joseph N. Gilbert. Captain Gilbert was the aircraft commander of one of the two helicopters.

31. Information to the author, David R. Mets telephone conversation, 20 July 1990.

32. I am aware of no credible evidence that antiaircraft artillery proper was firing from Koh Tang on 15 May. *Henry B. Wilson* spent over eight hours off Koh Tang close in-shore, and her captain's recollections are particularly persuasive. Rodgers heard a constant crackle of small arms, and some of those with him on the bridge reported hearing mortars (Rodgers interview). These men were familiar with small arms and naval ordnance, and aural evidence in this context is more conclusive than sightings of tracers, which can be deceptive, particularly at night. The 40th ARRS battle damage reports, cited below, provide abundant evidence of .50-cal./12.7-mm weapons and do not exclude the possibility of 14.5-mm ones.

33. The caveat covers the possible presence of 14.5-mm heavy machine guns on Koh Tang. The Soviet-designed 14.5-mm KPV heavy antiaircraft machine gun was used extensively by Communist forces in Laos and North Vietnam on fully traversing two- and four-barreled ZPU-2 and ZPU-4 mounts and appeared occasionally in South Vietnam in single-barrel form with antiaircraft tripod mount. Gunnery Sergeant McNemar was familiar with the weapon's report and does not rule out the possibility that one or more were in action on the east side of Koh Tang (Lester A. McNemar, interview with author, 23 December 1991).

34. The H-53 was capable of 170 knots but could sustain such speeds only when perfectly rigged and lightly loaded. When heavily loaded, cruise

was generally limited to 135–40 knots by vibration levels that increased with speed. See Patrick, *The* Mayaguez *Operation*, pp. 40, 62; and Appendix B.

35. Adapted from figure IV-1, Patrick, *The* Mayaguez *Operation*.
36. Fuel constituted about a quarter of the weight of an operationally capable, fully loaded CH- or HH-53. The rate of fuel consumption was roughly 30 percent greater with full tanks than at minimum fuel (T.O. 1H-53[H]B-1, 1–26, A-36).
37. This is a rule-of-thumb figure based on normal mission profiles. A lightly loaded H-53 cruising at optimum speed could stretch the figure. Conversely, hovering consumes fuel rapidly, particularly at high gross weights, and cuts swiftly into endurance.
38. Tides in the Gulf of Siam are diurnal. At 0530 on the fifteenth the tide was 1.64 feet and going out; previous high water was 3.71 feet at 1854G on the fourteenth; on the fifteenth low water was 1.24 feet at 0812G, and high water was at 1943G (U.S. Department of Commerce, *Tide Tables: High and Low Water Predictions, 1975, Central and Western Pacific Ocean and Indian Ocean* [Rockville, Md: 1974], pp. 322, 104). I am obligated to Lt. Jeffrey P. Tilbury and QMC Dalton H. Carter, USN, for the computations.
39. Austin interview; Johnson to Gayler memo.
40. J. M. Johnson, Jr., R. W. Austin, and D. A. Quinlan, "Individual Heroism Overcame Awkward Command Relationships, Confusion, and Bad Information off the Cambodian Coast," *Marine Corps Gazette* 61, no. 10 (October 1977): 31.
41. *CINCPAC History*, pp. 18–19.
42. Ibid., p. 19. On 1:240,000 nautical charts and 1:250,000 Joint Operations Graphics (Air) charts, the only maps available, the island is about an inch long.
43. Janca interview, *CINCPAC/IG Inquiry*.
44. Information from Captain Bob Watts, USN. To make precise heading changes, a single-screw vessel must have sufficient headway for rudder effectiveness. A double-screw vessel can change heading while dead in the water by going ahead on one propeller while reversing the other.
45. Several of the crew members involved had landed on navy ships in Frequent Wind but mostly on aircraft carriers—a far cry from the constricted flight deck of a destroyer escort, considered too small for an H-53 by navy-marine standards.
46. Baxter interview, *CINCPAC/IG Inquiry*.
47. Davis interview.
48. Austin interview, *CINCPAC/IG Inquiry*; Johnson, Austin, and Quinlan, "Individual Heroism," p. 28; Davis interview.
49. Davis interview; McNemar interview; Dunham and Quinlan, *The Bitter End*, pp. 243–44. Some sources imply that Baxter obtained an air force camera for McGowin, but this does not seem to have been the case.
50. Author's observation, evening of 15 May.

51. Austin interview, Johnson to Gayler memo.
52. Lt. Col. Randall Austin, USMC (Ret.), telephone interview with author, 23 December 1991.
53. McNemar interview.
54. Davis interview; McNemar interview.
55. Patrick, *The* Mayaguez *Operation*, p. 10.
56. Johnson, Austin, and Quinlan, "Individual Heroism," p. 28. The BLU-82 ("bluey eighty-two") was made from a commercial butane tank filled with a high-yield slurry explosive. Detonated by a contact fuse mounted on a four-foot extender rod for low-level air burst, it was extracted from the open ramp of a C-130 by parachute and descended the same way. Impressive accuracy was possible with AWADS-trained crews. Used in Vietnam to clear helicopter LZs in dense jungle, the BLU-82 was used against Communist troops with considerable effect by the VNAF in 1975.
57. Sketch of the map of the northern peninsula posted on a wall in U Tapao base operations, made by the author during the evening of 15–16 May; author's journal. Davis remembers designating three LZs on the east and four on the west (Davis interview), so this may represent a change to the original plan.
58. The RESCORT mission was performed by piston-engined A-1s from 1964–65 until replaced by the A-7 beginning in 1972. The A-7 saw limited combat action in that role. In 1975, while recognizing the A-7 as the best jet for the job, most combat-experienced Jolly Green pilots considered it a poor substitute for the A-1. The A-7's greater speed and turning radius not only made the job more difficult but required more aircraft: four A-1s could effectively cap a hovering helicopter, delivering suppressive firepower on call to any quadrant within seconds. To achieve similar results, six A-7s were needed. Experience in Red Flag tactical training exercises in 1977–79 convinced me that A-7 Sandys could be effective in the RESCORT role, but only after intensive and realistic training with Jolly Greens.
59. Patrick, *The* Mayaguez *Operation*, pp. 88, 91 (figure VI-2, "Reconstruction of Turnovers in 'SAR On-Scene' and 'On-Scene' Commander at Koh Tang as Reported in OPREP-4 Messages for 15 May").
60. 29FTW Craig AFB, AL 051915 November 75 message, Loyd J. Anders to D. E. Vandenberg, encl. to *CINCPAC/IG Inquiry.* Dunham and Quinlan, *The Bitter End*, p. 245, and the Johnson to Gayler memo chronology incorrectly have Anders present. The marines (see Johnson, Austin, and Quinlan, "Individual Heroism," p. 28) assumed that one of the participants, probably Baxter, was the 56th SOW commander.
61. Patrick, *The* Mayaguez *Operation*, p. 9.
62. Johnson, Austin, and Quinlan, "Individual Heroism," p. 28.
63. Patrick, *The* Mayaguez *Operation*, p. A-12. The 177 total includes ten navy medical corpsmen and a surgeon.
64. Johnson, Austin, and Quinlan, "Individual Heroism," p. 29.
65. Johnson To Gayler memo.

66. Crew rest rules were complex but were based on the requirement for eight hours of uninterrupted rest before reporting for flight. The air force took crew rest seriously as a means of reducing fatigue-related accidents. Crew rest could be waived, but adherence to the rules was deeply ingrained. The practical result was to isolate the helicopter crews from the planning process.

67. Author's recollection; Lt. Col. Vernon L. Sheffield, interview with author, 1, 2, and 3 June 1978. The author was performing a similar function at Nakhon Phanom.

68. Kawanami, *History of 3rd Tactical Fighter Wing*, pp. 54–55.

69. Ibid., pp. 55–57.

70. The IPAC estimate was transmitted at 0342G on the thirteenth; at 1535 on the fourteenth, USSAG intelligence sent a message revising its estimate of enemy strength on Koh Tang downward from a battalion of 300 to coincide with the IPAC estimate. 307th intelligence received both of these messages (see Merrill interview, *CINCPAC/IG Inquiry*).

71. Baxter interview, *CINCPAC/IG Inquiry*. Baxter's preoccupation stemmed partly from concern with the situation in Vientiane, Laos, where the American diplomatic mission was at risk in the wake of the recent Communist takeover. The helicopters committed to the *Mayaguez* operation were also tasked to evacuate Vientiane, and Baxter was involved in contingency planning for the situation.

72. Capt. Alan B. Geer interview, Hopkins interview, *CINCPAC/IG Inquiry*.

73. Porter interview, Huebusch 26 November 75 message, *CINCPAC/IG Inquiry*. Tellingly, Huebusch received the IPAC estimate through the intervention of friends at Udorn who had the message retransmitted to him by name.

74. Wachs, *Working Draft*.

75. Ibid., Patrick, *The* Mayaguez *Operation*, p. 54.

76. Davis interview.

CHAPTER 5

1. Anders 281645Z November message, *CINCPAC/IG Inquiry*; Wachs, *Working Draft*.

2. Charles D. Brown, interview with author, 28 May 1978; Sheffield interview; Terry D. Ohlemeier, interview with author, 1, 2, and 3 June 1978. First Lieutenant Brown and Captain Sheffield were 40th ARRS pilots, and Sheffield was the squadron assistant operations officer. Ohlemeier, then a first lieutenant, was a 21st SOS pilot. All were present.

3. Author's journal; Denham conducted no formation briefing before the Saigon evacuation. The standard air force formation was a flight of four divided into two two-ship elements. Set procedures prescribed the transfer of flight lead in case of aborts, the assignment of radio call signs, and so on. Most of the Knife and Jolly Green pilots had received their basic flight training in the army-run undergraduate helicopter

training program and were not fully trained in air force formation procedures.

4. Dunham and Quinlan, *The Bitter End*, p. 248n; Philip M. Pacini, interview with author, 29 May, 1 and 3 June 1987.

5. Anders message, Pannell 032030Z November 1975 message, *CINCPAC/IG Inquiry*; Sheffield interview; Brown interview.

6. Dunham and Quinlan, *The Bitter End*, p. 248n, say eighteen to twenty, quoting the BLT 2/9 FAC, 1st Lt. Terry Tonkin. Participants variously remember the upper limit of enemy strength briefed as twenty, thirty, or forty; all remember the lower limit as eighteen. The intensity of emotion among the helicopter crews about the underestimation of enemy strength is reflected in the following saying that made the rounds among the Knives and Jolly Greens afterward. "*Sure* there were eighteen guys on the island. They were all nine-level gunners [nine being the highest rating on the air force skill-level scale], down from Hanoi on an antiaircraft headquarters IG [inspector general] visit. They were all seven feet tall, could bench-press 350 pounds, and had their own personal .50 calibers with them!"

7. Information to the author, Sheffield interview. There is some debate on this point, but it was consistent with 21st SOS practice to strip the helicopters of armor to maximize lift capacity. During preparations for Eagle Pull, the 21st took extensive measures to lighten its aircraft while the 40th resisted pressure to do so.

8. In the absence of heavy or bulky equipment, each Jolly Green carried twenty-seven assault personnel and each Knife carried twenty (the average was nineteen), although there were exceptions: Jolly Green 43 carried twenty-nine, including the 81-mm mortar section (U Tapao Status Board; *Assault on Koh Tang*, 23 June 1975 [the official PACAF history, originally SECRET and later declassified, henceforth *Assault on Koh Tang*], chart A: insertion). See also n. 15, below.

9. The EC-130 in question landed at U Tapao about 2200 the previous evening after a flight from Clark and a six-hour orbit; this aircraft and staff remained on orbit until 1530, when they were relieved by an EC-130 and battle staff that apparently landed at U Tapao around 1800 on the fourteenth (Kawanami, *History of 3rd Tactical Fighter Wing*, p. 55–57; see n. 68 and 69, chapter 4, above.

10. Wachs, *Working Draft*. This is the only reference to the planned takeoff time I have found. Assuming a 120-knot ground speed, a realistic planning factor for the heavily loaded helicopters and the one commonly used, the assault force would have been over Koh Tang and the *Mayaguez* at 0542 with a one- to two- minute cushion.

11. McNemar interview; Davis interview.

12. Davis interview; McNemar interview.

13. McNemar interview.

14. Davis interview.

15. U Tapao Status Board, official air force photograph (Detachment 12, 601st Photo Squadron [AAVS] [MAC]) of the helicopter status board

used by Anders, Pannell et al. at U Tapao, taken sometime after 2215 on the fifteenth (henceforth U Tapao Status Board).

16. Information to author; Wachs, *Working Draft*; 40th ARRS Draft Recommendations, Jolly Green 11: one of a series of draft recommendations for decorations prepared under the author's supervision immediately following the events in question. These were research documents from which the actual submissions were prepared and contain details not found elsewhere.

17. Davis interview.

18. "Chronological Listing of Events," attachment to Des Brisay notes, henceforth Des Brisay Chronology; transcription of ABCCC tape of voice radio traffic, 15 May, by Des Brisay, henceforth ABCCC Voice Transcripts (USAFHRC), in this case of traffic on UHF helicopter control frequency; and 1st Lt. Norman D. Norman and 2d Lt. James E. Newland Time Line, henceforth Norman-Newland Time Line, giving locations and activities of 40ARRS helicopters on 15 May, to the minute where possible (author's collection). Compiled shortly after the fact by two 40th officers from aircraft flight records and postaction interviews, this document is based on information not used in other accounts and is an invaluable check for them. There is a systematic discrepancy between times on the Norman-Newland Time Line and those on the ABCCC Voice Transcripts (UHF), the latter giving progressively later times for the same events with the difference increasing to about twenty-two minutes by 0700. This was probably because the ABCCC tapes had stretched from repeated playing by the time Des Brisay reviewed them. Times on the Norman-Newland Time Line generally agree closely with those given by other sources, and I have used it as a baseline, adjusting ABCCC Voice Transcript times accordingly.

19. Denham announced loss of an engine seconds earlier but made no mention of hostile fire (ABCCC Voice Transcripts [UHF]).

20. McNemar interview; Davis interview.

21. ABCCC Voice Transcripts (FM).

22. Information to the author, fall 1975, supported by ABCCC Voice Transcripts.

23. ABCCC Voice Transcripts (FM). The ABCCC controllers knew their contacts only by radio call sign, and the marines' call sign—Bingo Shoes 01, 02, 09, etc., quickly corrupted to Bingo Foot—had no particular significance. I have referred to them by name for simplicity. The marines maintained excellent communications security throughout, refusing to pass tactically sensitive information such as troop strength in the clear.

24. Patrick, *The* Mayaguez *Operation*, p. 88.

25. Dunham and Quinlan, *The Bitter End*, p. 248.

26. FBI Special Agent James Dixon (Dick) Keith narrative, 28 August 1994, supplemented by 24 August telephone interview. Keith, then a first lieutenant, was Golf Company's executive officer.

27. Several helicopter and OV-10 pilots were given access to the ABCCC

voice tapes in preparation for USSAG and PACAF briefings, and the story originated with them. I believe it to be true in its essentials.

28. DCS Plans and Operations, HQ PACAF, in *Assault on Koh Tang,* p. 12.

29. ABCCC Voice Transcripts (FM).

30. Pacini interview.

31. Keith interview, 24 August 1994.

32. Keith narrative.

33. 40th ARRS Draft Recommendations, Jolly Green 41.

34. Knife 21 put in twenty-one marines: G Company's 1st Platoon under 2d Lt. James McDaniel plus Keith. Knife 32 carried fifteen and inserted thirteen (a marine was wounded while hovering, and an army linguist refused to deplane), and Jolly Green 42 put in twenty-seven (Patrick, *The* Mayaguez *Operation,* p. 56, table V-1; U Tapao Status Board). There were casualties by this point, and the exact number is uncertain: Patrick has sixty marines in the western perimeter as do Johnson, Austin, and Quinlan, "Individual Heroism," p. 30. The U Tapao Status Board suggests fifty-eight.

35. Johnson, Austin, and Quinlan, "Individual Heroism," p. 30; Des Brisay Chronology; Pacini interview; Patrick, *The* Mayaguez *Operation,* p. 12, fig. II-3, "The Situation about 0630," p. 56. The minimum distance is my own estimate based on the Pacini interview and map study: the maximum is from Johnson, Austin, and Quinlan, "Individual Heroism."

36. Des Brisay, "Fourteen Hours," and *Assault on Koh Tang* reflect this orientation in treating the extraction of the survivors of Knife 23 as a discrete SAR mission.

37. Norman-Newland Time Line.

38. The earliest mention of contact with the Knife 23 survivors in the Des Brisay Chronology is 0930; this, however, is based on the ABCCC tapes. The actual time may have been as much as thirty minutes earlier (see note 18, above).

39. Keith interview.

40. *CINCPAC History,* p. 26.

41. Davis interview.

42. There is no doubt on this point; cf. *Assault on Koh Tang,* 17, 19n, 21n. The latter two citations are based on Des Brisay's transcription of tactical voice tapes.

43. Patrick, *The* Mayaguez *Operation,* p. 91, fig. VI-2, "Reconstruction of Turnovers in 'SAR On-Scene' and 'On-Scene Commander' at Koh Tang."

44. Johnson, Austin, and Quinlan, "Individual Heroism," p. 32; and ABCCC Voice Transcripts (FM), in this case of transmissions on marine ground-force VHF/FM frequency. I have followed the latter where there was a conflict in times.

45. Keith narrative.

46. Ibid.

47. Johnson, Austin, and Quinlan, "Individual Heroism," pp. 30–31. The precise chronology is uncertain.

48. Keith narrative.
49. Patrick, *The* Mayaguez *Operation,* p. B-9. One source has Knife 22 landing at 0737 and another at 0750, probably reflecting "stretching" of time on the ABCCC Voice Transcripts (see note 18, above).
50. Wachs, *Working Draft;* U Tapao Status Board.
51. U Tapao Status Board; 1st Lt. Ronald Rand photographs and audiovisual caption information, AFAV-75-KOP-DC-1149-ST/MAC. These events were poorly documented at the time, and the memories of the participants I was able to contact were unclear—understandably so, since it was an undramatic interlude in a long and frenetic day. Lt. Col. Martin Nickerson, Jolly Green 12's copilot, remembered the marines returning to U Tapao aboard his aircraft. Rand's photographs place Jolly Green 11 and Knife 51 crew members S. Sgt. Stu Stanaland and T. Sgt. Wayne Fisk at Knife 22's landing site.
52. Patrick, *The* Mayaguez *Operation,* p. B-18.
53. Norman-Newland Time Line.
54. Wachs, *Working Draft.*
55. U Tapao Status Board.
56. Author's recollection and ex post facto estimate. Maintenance personnel assigned to the phase dock were almost without exception senior NCOs, typically technical sergeants and above, extremely well qualified and highly regarded.
57. 40th ARRS Daily Flying Log.
58. Des Brisay Chronology; Roger A. Peterson, "'Mayday' for the *Mayaguez:* The Destroyer Escort's Skipper," *U.S. Naval Institute Proceedings* 102, no. 11 (November 1976): 95.
59. Des Brisay Chronology.
60. Patrick, *The* Mayaguez *Operation,* pp. 97–98.
61. Rodgers interview; ABCCC Voice Transcripts (UHF).
62. Norman-Newland Time Line; Rodgers interview; ABCCC Voice Transcripts (UHF).
63. Keith narrative.
64. 40th ARRS Draft Recommendations, Jolly Green 41.
65. Rodgers interview.
66. There is irony in the recurrent concern for the presence of Caucasians reflected in the message traffic: much of the *Mayaguez's* crew was Asian.
67. Patrick, *The* Mayaguez *Operation,* p. 63.
68. Published in *Newsweek,* May 26, 1975, p. 6.
69. The first strike, on the Kompong Som oil storage complex, was ordered for 0745 but was rescinded by JCS order just before target time: the aircraft jettisoned their bombs into the sea. The second and third strikes, against the Kompong Som oil complex and the Ream airfield and naval base, attacked in close succession beginning at 0905. The mission of the fourth strike, beginning at 1130, was changed from a further attack on Kompong Som to close air support. The navy wisely declined this mission, because the carrier-based A-7Es and A-6s were

not equipped with radios capable of communicating with the marines on the beach.

70. Davis interview; McNemar interview; Keith interview.

71. Davis interview; McNemar interview. The *Khymer Kraham* seem to have been supplied exclusively with captured American grenades, suggesting that they were an elite force. McNemar was familiar with the sound of the Chinese grenades and heard none on Koh Tang.

72. Johnson, Austin, and Quinlan, "Individual Heroism," pp. 30–31.

73. Des Brisay Chronology, giving target coordinates just south of the west beach; Patrick, *The* Mayaguez *Operation*, table VI-3: "USAF TACAIR Flown (OPREP-4 Data)," pp. 78–80.

74. Norman-Newland Time Line.

75. Brown interview.

76. Videotapes of this imagery incorporated into a PACAF film show the helicopter seemingly enveloped in a ball of fire, actually superheated gases from the burning flare case that were translucent to the AC-130's infrared sensors, ingested in the helicopter's main rotor vortex. Then, in slow motion, the refueling probe emerges from the fireball, followed by the leading edge of the main rotor, the cockpit, and finally the fuselage as the aircraft picks up speed. The clip is reminiscent of classic Japanese science-fiction movies in which some imaginary prehistoric monster plods on about its business unperturbed, shrugging off cannon, napalm, and rocket fire.

77. 40th ARRS Draft Recommendations, Jolly Green 41.

78. Patrick, *The* Mayaguez *Operation*, p. 83 (for identification of the A-7s); ABCCC Voice Transcripts (FM).

79. ABCCC Voice Transcripts (UHF).

80. ABCCC Voice Transcripts (FM); Johnson, Austin, and Quinlan, "Individual Heroism," pp. 32–33; Keith narrative.

81. Keith interview.

82. ABCCC Voice Transcripts (FM). Johnson, Austin, and Quinlan, "Individual Heroism," p. 31, note an increase in the effectiveness of air support at "approximately 0900" but make no mention of Spectre. They also have Jolly Green 41 inserting at the same time, an hour earlier than was the case. The time at which Keith began to receive effective air support—a matter of prime concern to Austin that *did* take place at about 0900—probably stuck in Austin's mind.

83. Only two marines, Keith and Cassidy, were working air force aircraft at the time, and Keith says it was not him (Keith telephone interview).

84. Information to the author from Spectre crews, summer 1975, supported by ABCCC Voice Transcripts (FM). To the 16th SOS crew members who related the above account to me, it was simply a humorous anecdote. Its connection with events on the ground became evident only after careful analysis of times and events.

85. *Assault on Koh Tang*, p. 20n, confirmed by a sketch map of the marine perimeter given me by Sgt. Maj. McNemar (McNemar interview).

86. *Assault on Koh Tang*, p. 18n; Patrick, *The* Mayaguez *Operation*, p. 91.

Figure VI-2 shows Spectre 61 holding on-scene command for twenty to twenty-five minutes beginning at about 0950, the only time a Spectre held this command.

87. Des Brisay Chronology; Norman-Newland Time Line.

88. For the hole in the belly, see photographs in Des Brisay, "Fourteen Hours," pp. 128–29. For the rest, see Battle Damage Reports, HH-53C 69–5795 (Jolly Green 41), henceforth Battle Damage Reports. These were internal 40th ARRS documents detailing each hit sustained, followed by the appropriate call sign (author's collection). The size of the holes suggests that most of the damage was inflicted by .50-cal./12.7-mm. fire.

89. Patrick, *The* Mayaguez *Operation,* p. 91.

90. Keith interview.

91. Ibid.

92. *Assault on Koh Tang,* pp. 18–19; information to the author from Dick Keith.

CHAPTER 6

1. Sheffield interview.

2. Ibid.

3. Ibid.

4. U Tapao Status Board; Norman-Newland Time Line.

5. U Tapao Status Board.

6. 150455Z (1155G) JCS to CINCPAC message, chronological listing of significant message traffic, 150001Z—151315Z, Des Brisay Notes (USAFHRC), henceforth Chronological Message List. This source lists no earlier order to disengage, but the 1155G message was surely preceded by less formal orders. Patrick, *The* Mayaguez *Operation,* p. 62, maintains that the initial disengagement order was issued at about 1030–1045, despite a COMUSSAG/Seventh Air Force situation report to the contrary. I agree with Patrick.

7. *CINCPAC History,* p. 8.

8. Kawanami, *History of 3rd Tactical Fighter Wing,* vol. 6, Supporting Document 91, Cricket 02 [ABCCC] Mission Log, henceforth Kawanami, ABCCC Mission Log.

9. *CINCPAC History,* p. 9.

10. Ibid., p. 20.

11. Ibid., p. 9. USSAG/Seventh Air Force 161500Z May 1975 message to CINCPACAF, Supporting Document 95, in Kawanami, *History of 3rd Tactical Fighter Wing,* vol. 6, a compilation of after-action reports, lists twelve separate entities on the HF COMUSSAG/Seventh Air Force command net. These include OV-10 and HC-130 aircraft, presumably as on-scene commander, plus four additional HF nets, including the JRCC rescue net.

12. Cf. Burns interview, p. 437.

13. Sheffield interview.

14. Chronological Message List; Johnson's call was at 0945. In response to the GAO inquiry, Burns later stated that he had heard Hunt, whom he described as experienced in airmobile combat helicopter operations, discussing the Koh Tang intelligence summary with Johnson (Burns to W. H. Sheley, Jr., director, General Accounting Office International Division, Honolulu, Hawaii, 6 November 1975; Burns interview, *CINCPAC/IG Inquiry*). The discussion in question presumably took place at this time.

15. Author's journal, 25 May 1975 interview. It is worth noting that neither Cooper nor Keith had a boisterous, outgoing personality.

16. Patrick, *The Mayaguez Operation*, p. 63. According to Patrick, both overheard orders for the second wave to return to U Tapao, and both "objected . . . on the grounds that reinforcements were needed now and also to assist in the extraction. The order to insert the second wave was given a few minutes thereafter, apparently by the JCS" (p. 63).

17. The second-wave helicopters launched thirty-eight minutes apart and began their insertions twenty-five minutes apart in a different order, a circumstance clearly suggesting differing responses to changing orders (Patrick, *The Mayaguez Operation*, pp. 60, 62; Norman-Newland Time Line).

18. Chronological Message List.

19. At 0910; ABCCC Voice Transcripts (HF).

20. Trune et al., *History of 56th SOW* (April—June 1975), p. 15, states that the 23rd TASS was ordered to prepare "for immediate deployment" to U Tapao at 0920L.

21. U Tapao is 350 nautical miles from Nakhon Phanom. The cruise speed of the OV-10 varies depending on gross weight and the external stores carried, but rough calculations based on the elapsed time between their subsequent launch from U Tapao and arrival over Koh Tang suggest a cruise speed for the four aircraft of just over 145 knots. That would have put them on the ground at U Tapao shortly after 1200.

22. 40th ARRS Daily Flying Log. The actual time was 1150.

23. Spectre 61 was aware as early as 1005 that there were two distinct groups of marines on the west side of the island attempting to link up (ABCCC Voice Transcripts [HF]).

24. Dunham and Quinlan, *The Bitter End*, p. 255.

25. Johnson, Austin, and Quinlan, "Individual Heroism," p. 32; Keith interview.

26. Keith interview. Air force after-action reports list no expenditure of aerial ordnance near the main perimeter from 1030 to 1345 at the earliest (Patrick, *The Mayaguez Operation*, pp. 83, 86, table VI-5: "USAF Weapon Delivery Data" and table VI-6: "Distribution of Attacks by Hour").

27. Johnson, Austin, and Quinlan, "Individual Heroism," pp. 32–33; Keith narrative.

28. Johnson, Austin, and Quinlan, "Individual Heroism," p. 33.
29. Norman-Newland Time Line; Patrick, *The* Mayaguez *Operation*, pp. B-3, B-17.
30. Patrick, *The* Mayaguez *Operation*, p. B-18. The insertions were made between 1205 and 1215.
31. Ibid., p. 13.
32. Hendricks, "The Battalion Operations Officer," p. 105.
33. ABCCC announced the linkup at 1212 (ABCCC Voice Transcripts [HF]). Dunham and Quinlan, *The Bitter End*, p. 245, say 1245, citing 2/9's after-action report.
34. Keith narrative.
35. ABCCC Voice Transcripts (HF); Patrick, *The* Mayaguez *Operation*, p. 91, fig. VI-2.
36. ABCCC Voice Transcripts (HF).
37. Davis interview; Keith interview. Gunnery Sergeant McNemar considered Tutele "an excellent leader and an outstanding marine" (McNemar interview).
38. Keith narrative.
39. McNemar interview.
40. Davis interview; McNemar interview.
41. McNemar interview; Davis interview.
42. The H-53 had no aircrew oxygen system. For protection against CS and other incapacitating gases, crews were provided with ordinary troop-issue gas masks with a microphone placed inside the mask. The eyepieces severely restricted peripheral vision, the plastic lenses were far short of optical clarity, and the improvised microphone installation garbled radio and intercom transmissions. It is difficult to understand how they could have been approved for aircrew use.
43. Des Brisay Chronology; information to the author.
44. 1st Lt. Ronald Rand captured the moment in a photograph from Jolly Green 11. The photograph is blurred, but the streamer of fuel shows up clearly.
45. Patrick, *The* Mayaguez *Operation*, pp. 98–99.
46. Rodgers interview.
47. Patrick, *The* Mayaguez *Operation*, p. 99, for coordinates of two targets engaged with fifty-eight rounds; Rodgers interview.
48. Chronological Message List.
49. Des Brisay, "Fourteen Hours," p. 137.
50. Information to the author.
51. 40th ARRS Daily Flying Log.
52. Chronological Message List. The amount of time spent on the ground at U Tapao is an estimate (see n. 21, above).
53. Des Brisay Chronology; Des Brisay notes from a recording of voice transmissions made by Undorf as Nail 68, henceforth Nail Tapes.
54. Nail Tapes. The extreme professional competence of all parties to this discussion is apparent from Des Brisay's working notes (USAFHRC).

The amount of tactically relevant information per word transmitted was clearly exceptionally high.

55. Norman-Newland Time Line.

56. Wachs, *Working Draft.*

57. Battle Damage Reports, Jolly Green 13 and Jolly Green 43. Both aircraft took multiple .50-cal. hits on both sides. Both made their approaches on an east-west heading, and the Swift boat was the only likely source of .50-cal. fire from the south. Conversely, Jolly Green 12, committed to an abortive rescue attempt on the wreckage of Knife 31 after the destruction of the Swift boat (see below), although heavily damaged, sustained fuselage hits only on the bottom and right, or landward, side (Battle Damage Reports, HH-53C 69–5793).

58. This was at 1603 (Des Brisay Chronology).

59. Des Brisay Chronology.

60. Nail Tapes. Backlund was 40th ARRS standardization-evaluation flight examiner, a position of unusual responsibility for so junior an officer.

61. Patrick, *The* Mayaguez *Operation,* pp. B-17, 18; Norman-Newland Time Line.

62. Des Brisay Chronology.

63. Information to the author soon after the fact. I later heard portions of a voice tape that included the transmissions in question.

64. Orders from the NMCC to "put Spectres up and keep them up" were received by the USSAG/Seventh Air Force command post at 1455G (see ABCCC Voice Transcripts; Patrick, *The* Mayaguez *Operation,* p. 88).

65. Patrick, *The* Mayaguez *Operation,* pp. 86, 88. When Spectre 61 left is uncertain, but Patrick reports no AC-130 fire between 61's last engagement at 1015 and 11's first engagement at 1816. Spectre 21 was overhead Koh Tang during the extraction and prepared to drop flares in support but was unable to shoot because of a fire control malfunction.

66. Author's recollection from listening to ABCCC tapes shortly after the event.

67. Nail Tapes; 40th ARRS Draft Recommendations, Jolly Green 11; Wachs, *Working Draft.* Times from Norman-Newland Time Line are supported by Des Brisay Chronology.

68. Kawanami, ABCCC Mission Log, says the drop was at 1819, but times in this document have been "cleaned up." It states, for example, that the first wave touched down at the specified assault time of 0542, which we know not to have been the case. Des Brisay, who had access to sources that remain classified, gives no drop time but implies that it was shortly after Jolly Green 11 lifted off (Des Brisay, "Fourteen Hours," p. 144). Patrick, *The* Mayaguez *Operation,* p. 80, table VI-3: "USAF TACAIR Flown (OPREP-4 Data)," states that a flight of three C-130s dropped a single BLU-82 at 1823 under ABCCC control. *Wilson's* bridge crew and some of the marines mistook the BLU-82's parachute extraction cradle for a second bomb that failed to detonate.

69. Kawanami, ABCCC Mission Log; Patrick, *The* Mayaguez *Operation,* p. 108; Hendricks, "The Battalion Operations Officer," p. 107. Burns to

Sheley, 6 November 1975, attachment to *CINCPAC/IG Inquiry*, states that the bomb was dropped on orders from above "for its diversionary and inhibiting effect."

70. Rodgers interview; Hendricks, "The Battalion Operations Officer," p. 107.

71. Rodgers interview; Keith interview.

72. Des Brisay, "Fourteen Hours," pp. 144–45; Rodgers interview.

73. Undorf telephone interview, by author, Des Brisay working notes (USAFHRC).

74. Hendricks, "The Battalion Operations Officer," p. 107.

75. Burns interview, pp. 457–58.

76. The German defenders of Saint Lo and Monte Cassino and the Japanese defenders of Tarawa and Okinawa are relevant examples from World War II.

77. From the eighteenth century through the American Civil War, elite infantry units could sometimes continue to function as effective maneuver formations after sustaining casualties of 75 percent or more in a single engagement, although this was rare. The ability to withstand such casualties was also linked to the psychological support offered by tightly massed battlefield formations. The physical dispersal and psychological isolation imposed by modern firepower has made performance of this kind uncommon. The most extreme documented example I know of was a Japanese infantry battalion that suffered casualties of about 86 percent in mobile operations during the Nomonhan incident of July—August 1939, yet remained cohesive and combat effective. Other Japanese infantry units that took proportionately fewer casualties in the same battle (the average was 70 percent) showed a marked decline in effectiveness (Drea, *Nomonhan*, pp. 89, 99).

78. Kawanami, *History of 3rd Tactical Fighter Wing*, vol. 6, Supporting Document 95.

79. ABCCC Voice Transcripts (FM).

80. The aircraft took fifty-three hits, of which perhaps a dozen were .50-cal./12.7-mm, including multiple hits in the right external tank and damage to two main rotor blades and the main rotor shaft (Battle Damage Reports, Jolly Green 12).

81. Information to the author from air force participants in the Koh Tang operation, 15, 16, and 17 May 1975, considered in light of the sources cited. The account of the Austin-Undorf exchange in Des Brisay, "Fourteen Hours," p. 146, agrees with this interpretation in its essentials and strongly supports it in detail. Patrick, *The Mayaguez Operation*, p. 13, states that extraction operations began at 1800 but does not say who ordered them.

CHAPTER 7

1. Hendricks, "The Battalion Operations Officer," p. 105.
2. Nail Tapes.
3. Clausewitz, *On War*, book 1, "On the Nature of War," chap. 1, sect. 21, "Not Only Its Objective but Also Its Subjective Nature Makes War a Gamble," pp. 85–86. See Beyerchen, "Clausewitz," pp. 73–75, for a lucid and insightful discussion on this point.
4. 40th ARRS Flying Daily Log; information to the author.
5. Sheffield interview; Mason interview (Mason was copilot of Jolly Green 44). Some sources imply that the original destination was *Coral Sea*, but the absence of maintenance personnel or replacement aircrew members aboard argues against this.
6. Norman-Newland Time Line; U Tapao Status Board.
7. Davis interview.
8. See McNemar interview for the dispositions of the perimeter; Davis interview for Echo's withdrawal.
9. *Assault on Koh Tang*, p. 32, has Knife 51 going in at 1850, apparently on the basis of elapsed times on the Nail Tapes. The Norman-Newland Time Line has Jolly Green 43, which followed Knife 51, on the LZ between 1847 and 1850, and I have adjusted the time accordingly. Sunset was at 1822; civil twilight fell at 1844 and nautical twilight at 1910 (U.S. Naval Observatory, *Nautical Almanac for the Year 1975*, p. 99).
10. Hendricks, "The Battalion Operations Officer," p. 105.
11. Statement by Lt. Col. Austin, 19 May Subic Bay press conference; CINCPAC 191902Z message (USAFHRC), n. 183 above.
12. Johnson, Austin, and Quinlan, "Individual Heroism," p. 34; Hendricks, "The Battalion Operations Officer," p. 105.
13. *Assault on Koh Tang*, pp. 32–33.
14. Patrick, *The Mayaguez Operation*, table VI-5: "USAF Weapon Delivery Data," p. 84, has A-7s expending as late as 1900.
15. Nail Tapes.
16. Mason interview; information to the author, Robert Gradle; Norman-Newland Time Line. Analysis of the Nail Tapes indicates extreme tactical competence on the part of the gig's crew.
17. Nail Tapes.
18. *Assault on Koh Tang*,
19. Mason interview. Bounds had equipped himself with a special—and unauthorized—microphone that, unlike the standard boom microphone, shielded the receiver element from windblast. As a result, his interphone transmissions could be understood clearly when he was leaning outside the cabin to obtain a clear view (author's observation). (Bounds used the technique to good effect as the author's flight mechanic in Frequent Wind.)
20. Trune et al., *History of 56th SOW* (April—June 1975), p. 25.
21. Nail Tapes.

22. The AC-130 in question apparently arrived at about 1930 (*Assault on Koh Tang*, p. 35).

23. McNemar interview.

24. Davis interview; McNemar interview.

25. Des Brisay Chronology; Chief Master Sgt. Wayne L. Fisk account of final extraction, facsimile to author, 10 January 1991.

26. Davis interview; McNemar interview.

27. UHF/DF gives relative and magnetic bearing from the receiving aircraft to a transmitting station or aircraft automatically by means of a rotating loop antenna. A transmission of about ten seconds is required for a good bearing, and the receiving aircraft cannot transmit while the feature is activated.

28. For the final extraction, see *Assault on Koh Tang*, pp. 35–37; Nail Tapes; and Fisk facsimile to author. The account of the withdrawal in *Assault on Koh Tang* (abridged in Des Brisay, "Fourteen Hours," pp. 148–49) draws on a 56th SOW intelligence debrief of Knife 51's crew and Des Brisay's debrief of Captain Wilson. It agrees both with Des Brisay's working notes from the Nail Tapes (USAFHRC) and Fisk's account.

29. Fisk facsimile to author; McNemar interview.

30. Author's journal; Fisk facsimile to author; Davis interview; McNemar interview.

31. Norman-Newland Time Line; Buckley interview.

32. Wachs, *Working Draft*.

33. Orr Kelly, *Brave Men, Dark Waters: The Untold Story of the Navy SEALs* (Novato, Calif.: Presidio Press, 1992), pp. 177–79.

34. Rodgers interview.

CHAPTER 8

1. Clausewitz, *On War*, book 1, chap. 4, "On Danger in War," p. 115 (emphasis added).

2. 170115Z May 1975 message.

3. Armor probably prevented damage to Jolly Green 13's second-stage flight control servos and may have kept Jolly Green 42 from losing an engine (Battle Damage Reports, 40th ARRS). The author's examination of Jolly Green 13 indicated that .50-cal./12.7-mm rounds (14.5-mm cannot be categorically ruled out) easily penetrated the quarter-inch titanium armor plate at the close ranges encountered on the LZs. Conversely, the armor proved essentially impervious to .30-cal./7.62-mm rounds; indeed, in the author's previous experience, an AK-47 round at point-blank range barely scratched it. It is doubtful that any helicopter could have survived the fire that engulfed Knife 23 and 31 on the east beach, but the lack of explosion-retardant foam clearly increased the loss of life aboard Knife 31.

4. 56SOW 170738Z June 1975 message to CINCPACAF, repeating *Henry B. Wilson's* 070700Z June 1975 message to COMSEVENTHFLT.

5. Lamb, *Belief Systems*, p. 165.
6. ABCCC Voice Transcripts (FM).
7. Col. Neil L. Eddins interview, *CINCPAC/IG Inquiry* (Eddins commanded the 388th).
8. Patrick, *The* Mayaguez *Operation*, p. A-15. *Okinawa*, with three companies and a full complement of helicopters, was scheduled to arrive on the morning of the eighteenth.
9. Austin interview, 4 November 1975; Johnson to Gayler memo. Many of the Communist bunkers were of recent construction.
10. Rodgers interview.
11. Patrick, *The* Mayaguez *Operation*, p. 71. Plans were apparently made for ABCCC to relay communications from marines on the island to Johnson, but this was not done.
12. Austin interview (*CINCPAC/IG Inquiry*).
13. James M. Perry, "As Panama Outcome Is Praised, Details Emerge of Bungling during the 1983 Grenada Invasion," *The Wall Street Journal* 71, no. 63 (Monday, 15 January 1990): A1, A12. Vice Adm. Joseph Metcalf, who commanded the operation, is quoted (A-12) as saying that the map of Grenada that he used in the operation was dated 1895. The U.S. Defense Mapping Agency delivered complete, up-to-date charts of Grenada a week after combat had ended. The impressively short reaction time of the mapping agency was rendered irrelevant by budgetary restraints that precluded maintaining current charts of presumably noncritical areas.
14. Thomas A. Keaney and Eliot A. Cohen, *Gulf War Air Power Survey Summary Report* (Washington, D.C.: Office of Air Force History, 1993). The *Summary Report* is 276 pages long: the full survey encompasses five volumes containing the reports of seven task forces addressing various aspects of the conflict.
15. Adam B. Siegel, "An American Entebbe," *Naval Institute Proceedings* 118, no. 5 (May 1992): 96–100, is the basic source. For the helicopter aviators' perspective, see Capt. Robert A. Doss, USMC, "Out of Africa: Rescue from Mogadishu," in the same issue of *Proceedings*, pp. 103–105.
16. Siegel, "American Entebbe," p. 99.

APPENDIX A

1. The frequency bands given were typical for U.S. military aircraft radios at the time. Cf. T.O. 1H-53(H)B-1 (1 November 1973), 4–5 to 4–17.

APPENDIX B

1. William R. Fails, *Marines and Helicopters, 1962–1973*, pp. 12–13, 60. *H* was for helicopter, *R* for cargo, and *S* for Sikorsky; 2 indicated that it

was the second Sikorsky-built navy cargo helicopter. The army designation was H-37.

2. Nor is the problem unique to aerospace systems: the army's problems with the Bradley fighting vehicle are a case in point. The Sikorsky H-60 program shows that the problem can be overcome in helicopter procurement, but the H-60 is limited by the short-sighted and timid specification to which it was designed. Although exploiting technologies two generations in advance of the venerable UH-1 "Huey," the H-60 represents only a modest advance over the earlier machine in speed, payload, and range.

3. Fails, *Marines and Helicopters*, p. 13.

4. Ibid., p. 60.

5. Ibid., pp. 58–59, 62.

6. The CH-53E, the standard marine heavy-lift helicopter, has a seven-bladed main rotor and a larger tail rotor with the pylon tilted to provide additional lift. The MH-53J Pave Low III emerged from the ARRS night recovery system program to give combat rescue forces a low-altitude, night, and adverse-weather capability. It is fitted with terrain-avoidance radar and FLIR (forward-looking infrared), fully integrated into the avionics system. Originally fielded as the HH-53H, all Pave Lows were transferred to special operations with the disestablishment of ARRS in 1989. All air force H-53s have since been upgraded to J-model, Pave Low III standards.

7. Even as the air force H-53 program was getting underway, the air force relinquished to the army all combat helicopter missions except for rescue and special operations in return for army abandonment of fixed-wing ground-attack and cargo aircraft (Richard G. Davis, *The Thirty-One Initiatives* [Washington, D.C.: 1987], pp. 19–22).

8. The navy SH-3A/B was amphibious and had a boat-type hull with strut-mounted pontoons for lateral stability on the water. The air force CH-3C, on which the HH-3E was based, had sponsons instead of pontoons and was fitted with a rear cargo ramp.

9. Air Rescue Service issued a requirement for a helicopter aerial refueling capability in 1964. Preliminary flight tests with a dummy refueling probe on a CH-3C were conducted in December 1965, and the first in-flight fuel transfer from a CH-130P took place a year later (Tilford, *Search and Rescue in Southeast Asia*, pp. 82–83). The driving force behind this radical development, which many believed to be infeasible, was the H-3 Systems Project Office at Wright-Patterson AFB, Ohio, notably Maj. Harry P. Dunn, who pushed the concept earliest and hardest; James Eastman; and Richard Wright, who, along with Dunn, planned and flew the early flight tests.

10. Probably the best of these was the West German M3, which fired the same 7.62-mm round as the minigun, weighed about twenty-six pounds, and had a cyclic rate of 1,200–1,300 rounds per minute. The U.S. M60 infantry machine gun, later mounted on the HH-3E, was even lighter at twenty-three pounds but fired only 550–600 rounds per mi-

nute—in my judgment, marginally adequate. I became involved with helicopter armament issues as ARRS chief of tactics in 1978–79. The above is based in part on rescue's institutional memory of the original armament decision.

11. Tilford, *Search and Rescue in Southeast Asia*, pp. 90–93.
12. The array of technical orders for air force aircraft begins with the basic flight manual, in this case T.O. 1H-53(H)B-1, or the "dash one." The -2 is the organizational maintenance manual, the -3 is the structural repair manual, the -4 is the illustrated parts breakdown, the -5 contains the basic weight checklist and loading data, the -6 is the functional check flight manual, the -9 is the cargo-loading manual, and the -21 is the aircraft inventory master guide. This only scratches the surface.
13. Information to the author, Lt. Col. Vernon Sheffield, 9 January 1991.
14. As a result of the advent of fixed-wing aircraft with negative static and dynamic aerodynamic stability controlled with fly-by-wire systems, this generalization is no longer strictly correct. My reference here is to classical aerodynamic theory and mid-1970s technology.
15. Air force regulations required the use of oxygen above an altitude of ten thousand feet MSL (mean sea level); however, the requirement could be waived for brief exposure. In practical terms, eleven thousand feet was the service ceiling for the H-3 and H-53, and we rarely stayed above ten thousand feet for long.
16. T.O. 1H-53(H)B-1 (1 November 1973), 3–9, fig. 3–3.
17. The dash one followed the ring vortex theory, but in muddy wording that inspired little confidence (T.O. 1H-53[H]B-1 [1 November 1973], 6–1).
18. Including, for the record, the T-37, T-33, H-19, H-21, H-3, and C-131/T-29, plus assorted light aircraft.
19. Author's notes of ARRS/MAC H-53 briefing, 2 December 1977, Scott AFB, Illinois (henceforth ARRS/MAC Brief), a summary briefing of all air force H-53 accidents prepared and given by an ARRS/MAC standardization-evaluation team.
20. Review of the accident report and discussion with one of the pararescuemen in question, Eglin AFB, Florida, spring, 1974.
21. Author's journal. I read the accident investigation report as soon as it was released.
22. ARRS/MAC Brief.
23. Findings of the Collateral Board Investigation. I conducted the investigation.

Glossary

ARRS —Aerospace Rescue and Recovery Service. This was the USAF rescue command, formerly Air Rescue Service, subordinate to Military Airlift Command.

—Aerospace Rescue and Recovery Squadron.

BLT —Battalion Landing Team. It was the Marine Corps term for an infantry-based, battalion-strength team capable of conducting opposed air-mobile or amphibious operations with appropriate lift and firepower support.

CH —the air force designation for a cargo helicopter, applied to special operations helicopters.

CINCPAC —commander in chief, Pacific: in command of all U.S. forces in the Pacific. Headquartered at Pearl Harbor, Hawaii, CINCPAC is traditionally an admiral.

CINCPACFLT—navy abbreviation for commander in chief, Pacific Fleet: the operational commander of U.S. naval forces in the Pacific.

collective —a helicopter's primary control for power application and up-and-down movement in a hover. It is so called because it changes the pitch of the main rotor blades simultaneously, or collectively. The collective, more properly the collective pitch lever, is controlled by the pilot's left hand.

COMUSSAG/7AF —commander, Seventh Air Force [and] United States Support Activities Group (Thailand).

CS —a type of riot-control tear gas, dispensed from canisters by A-7s.

cyclic —the primary pitch-and-roll control on a helicopter, analogous to the control stick on a conventional aircraft. The cyclic pitch lever takes its name from the fact that it cyclically changes the pitch of each main rotor blade in the course of a single rotation. The cyclic pitch lever controls the helicopter in pitch and roll.

.50-cal./12.7-mm—a standard category of heavy machine gun widely used in an antiaircraft role by Communist forces in Southeast Asia in 1945–75. Soviet 12.7-mm machine guns were used along with captured American .50-cal. weapons.

GSF —ground security force. In the context of the Phnom Penh and Saigon evacuations, it was a body of marine infantry detailed to provide helicopter landing zone security. See LZ.

H —Department of Defense designation for helicopter. —air force designation for rescue, e.g. HC-130, the specialized rescue version of the C-130 turboprop transport.

HH —air force rescue helicopter designation, e.g. HH-53.

Iron Hand —the radio call sign assigned to specialized fighter- bombers equipped and trained to detect and attack radars associated with radar-controlled antiaircraft missile and gun systems.

Khmer Kraham —a contraction of *Yothear Khmer Kraham*, Khymer for the Communist Cambodian Army. In the context of this study, it was the Khymer Rouge Army.

LZ —helicopter landing zone.

MAC —Military Airlift Command: the combined command charged with control of all U.S. military airlift headquartered at Scott AFB, Illinois. It was the parent command of ARRS.

PACAF —Pacific Air Forces. Headquartered at Hickham AFB, Hawaii, PACAF had administrative control of air force tactical forces in the Pacific Theater.

RPG —rocket-propelled grenade.

7AF —Seventh Air Force. It was the command organization for USAF tactical forces in Southeast Asia, headquartered at Nakhon Phanom RTAFB following the American withdrawal from Vietnam.

SOS —Special Operations Squadron.

TAC —Tactical Air Command. The USAF command headquartered at Langley AFB, Virginia, it was charged with managing air force tactical air power assets—most importantly, tactical fighters.

TF —task force. Standard U.S. Navy terminology for a force assembled for a specific operational task.

13AF —Thirteenth Air Force. It was the parent organization of USAF tactical air forces in Asia, headquartered at Clark Air Base, the Philippines. The Thirteenth had administrative responsibility for USAF tactical air forces in Thailand while the Seventh exercised operational control.

USSAG —United States Support Activities Group (Thailand), the successor to MACV (Military Assistance Command Vietnam).

Bibliography

ARCHIVAL MATERIALS
(USAF Historical Research Center [USAFHRC], Maxwell AFB, Alabama):

CINCPAC Command History, 1975. Appendix 1, "Eagle Pull." Camp H. M. Smith, Hawaii: 1976. (SECRET, declassified 1985.)

CINCPAC Command History, 1975. Appendix 6, "The SS *Mayaguez* Incident." Camp H. M. Smith, Hawaii: 1976. (TOP SECRET, declassified 1985.)

CINCPAC/IG Inquiry into Availability of Intelligence during Mayaguez. Colonel Duane E. Vandenberg. Headquarters PACAF: 15 November 1975 (SECRET, declassified 1987.)

Des Brisay Chronology. "Chronological Listing of Events." A chronology of significant events and communications compiled from message traffic and tapes of voice transmissions, attached to notes collected by Captain Des Brisay.

History of the 56th Special Operations Wing (U), 1 January—31 March 1975. Vol. 2, *Unit Historical Reports.* 11 July 1975.

Kawanami, Kenneth K. *History of the 3rd Tactical Fighter Wing, April—June 1975.* Clark Air Base, Philippines: 30 June 1975. (SECRET, declassified 1990.)

Memo with enclosures. Brig. Gen. James H. Johnson, USA (PACAF/IG), to Adm. Noel Gayler. "SS *Mayaguez* Seizure," 17 November 1975. (SECRET, declassified 1987.)

Mol, Col. William D. "End of Tour Report." Commander, 432nd TFW, 13 March—31 December 1975 (USAFHRC).

Norman, lst Lt. Norman D. *History of the Fortieth Aerospace Rescue and Recovery Squadron, 1 January—30 June 1975.*

Reed, Col. Robert A. "End of Tour Report." 1 July 1974–30 June 1975.

Sprague, Col. Roger L. "End of Tour Report." 388th TFW (DCO). 13 June 1974–6 June 1975 (USAFHRC).

Trune, Capt. Geoffrey W.; Capt. Richard L. Brasher; and Sgt. David T. Turley. *History of the 56th Special Operations Wing, 1 April—30 June 1975.* Vol. 1, Narrative (29 September 1975).

Wachs, 1st Lt. Calvin. *21st SOS Unit History Working Draft.* 17 May 1975 (USAFHRC).

PRIMARY MATERIALS:

Author's notes. ARRS/MAC H-53 Accident Analysis Briefing. Scott AFB, Illinois, 2 December 1977.*

Battle Damage Reports. HH-53C 68–10364 [Jolly Green 11], 69–5793 [Jolly Green 12], 69–5794 [Jolly Green 13], 69–5795 [Jolly Green 41], 69–5785 [Jolly Green 42], and 69–5792 [Jolly Green 43]. Internal 40th ARRS quality-control maintenance documents detailing in tabular and schematic form each hit sustained by size, shape and location of hole, and damage inflicted.*

56th SOW 170738Z June 1975 message to CINCPACAF.*

Fisk, Chief Master Sgt. Wayne L., USAF. Account of final extraction (facsimile, 10 January 1991).*

40th ARRS Daily Flying Log, 13–18 May 1975. A photocopy of the squadron log for the days in question detailing flights by sortie, aircraft tail number, aircraft commander, type of mission, departure and destination stations, and hours of flying time logged.*

40th ARRS Draft Recommendations for Decoration for Heroism. The final working drafts of recommendations generated in response to the activities of 15 May, prepared for crews instead of individuals. These were based on interviews conducted by the author and a small team under his supervision and contain details not found elsewhere.*

Keith, Special Agent James Dixon. Narrative, 28 August 1994. A brief recollection of the events of 15 May 1975.*

Norman, 1st Lt. Norman D.; and 2d Lt. James E. Newland. Time line (a series of parallel time lines giving locations and activities of 40th ARRS helicopters on 15 May, to the minute in most cases).*

ORAL HISTORY INTERVIEWS:

Baughn, Brig. Gen. Richard M., USAF. Interview by Hugh N. Ahmann, 20–21 March 1979. USAF Oral History Interview #K239.0512–1119, USAFHRC.

Brown, Maj. Charles D., USAF. Interview with author, 28 May 1987.*

Buckley, Maj. Raynor L., USAF. Interview with author, 28 May 1987.*

Burns, Lt. Gen. John J., USAF. Interview by Hugh N. Ahmann, 5–8 June 1984, January 1986. USAF Oral History Interview #K239.0512–1587, USAFHRC.

Davis, Lt. Col. James H., USMC (Ret.). Interview with author, 14 September 1991.*

Kennerly, David Hume. ABC "Good Morning America," 30 April 1985.*
McNemar, Sgt. Maj. Lester A., USMC. Interview with author, 23 December 1991.*
Mason, Maj. Henry M., USAF. Interview with author, 28 May 1987.*
Ohlemeier, Maj. Terry D., USAF. Interview with author, 1, 2, and 3 June 1978.*
Pacini, Philip M. Interview with author, 29 May, 1 and 3 June 1987.*
Rodgers, J. Michael. Interview with author, 10–11 June 1987.*
Sheffield, Lt. Col. Vernon L., USAF. Interview with author, 1, 2, and 3 June 1987.*

OFFICIAL REPORTS AND TECHNICAL PUBLICATIONS:

Herrington, Maj. Stuart A., USA. *The Third Indochina War 1973–1975: A Personal Perspective.* Air Command and Staff College Report no. 1040–80. Maxwell AFB, Ala.: May 1980.
Patrick, Urey W. *The Mayaguez Operation.* Center for Naval Analyses Report CNS 1085. Arlington, Va.: April 1977. (SECRET, sanitized and declassified 11 April 1980.)
USAF Technical Order (T.O.) 1H-53(H)B-1. 1 November 1973.
US Naval Observatory. *The Nautical Almanac for the Year 1975.* Washington, D.C.: U.S. Government Printing Office, 1973.

SECONDARY MATERIALS:

Ballard, Jack S. *Development and Employment of Fixed-Wing Gunships, 1969–72.* Washington, D.C.: Office of Air Force History, 1982.
Batchelder, Col. Sydney A., Jr.; and Maj. D. A. Quinlan. "Operation Eagle Pull." *Marine Corps Gazette* (May 1976): 47–60.
Beyerchen, Alan. "Clausewitz, Nonlinearity, and the Unpredictability of War." *International Security* 17, no. 3 (Winter 1992–93): 59–90.
Bowers, Ray L. *Tactical Airlift.* Washington, D.C.: Office of Air Force History, 1983.
Butler, David. *The Fall of Saigon.* New York: Simon and Schuster, 1985.
Cao Van Vien, General. *The Final Collapse.* Washington, D.C.: Center for Military History, 1983.
Carey, Brig. Gen. Richard E.; and Maj. D. A. Quinlan. "Frequent Wind: Part One, Organization and Assembly." *Marine Corps Gazette* (February 1976): 16–24.
———. "Frequent Wind: Part Two, Planning." *Marine Corps Gazette* (March 1976): 35–45, 44.
———. "Frequent Wind: Part Three, Execution." *Marine Corps Gazette* (April 1976): 35–45.
———. "Frequent Wind," in *The Marines in Vietnam 1954–1973, an Anthology and Annotated Bibliography.* 2d ed. Washington, D.C.: 1985. Pp.

217–39. An abridged reprint of the three-part article in *Marine Corps Gazette* (February—April 1976).

Davidson, Lt. Gen. Phillip B., USAF (Ret.). *Vietnam at War: The History, 1946–1975*. Novato, Calif.: Presidio Press, 1988.

Des Brisay, Capt. Thomas D. "Fourteen Hours at Koh Tang," in *The Vietnamese Air Force, 1951–1975: An Analysis of Its Role in Combat, and Fourteen Hours at Koh Tang*. USAF Southeast Asia Monograph Series. Vol. 3. Washington, D.C.: 1977.

Drea, Edward J. *Nomonhan: Japanese-Soviet Tactical Combat, 1939*. Fort Leavenworth, Kans.: U.S. Army Combat Studies Institute, January 1981.

Dunham, Maj. George Ross; and Col. David A. Quinlan. *U.S. Marines in Vietnam: The Bitter End, 1973–1975*. Washington, D.C.: History and Museums Division, Headquarters, USMC, 1990.

Fails, Lt. Col. William R. *Marines and Helicopters, 1962–1973*. Washington, D.C.: History and Museums Division, Headquarters, USMC, 1978.

Guilmartin, John F., Jr. "Ideology and Conflict: The Wars of the Ottoman Empire, 1453–1606." *The Journal of Interdisciplinary History* 17, no. 4 (Spring 1988): 721–47.

Hyman, Harold M. *Quiet Past and Stormy Present? War Powers in American History*. Washington, D.C.: American Historical Association, 1986.

Johnson, J. M., Jr.; R. W. Austin; and D. A. Quinlan. "Individual Heroism Overcame Awkward Command Relationships, Confusion, and Bad Information off the Cambodian Coast." *Marine Corps Gazette* 61, no. 10 (October 1977).

Lamb, Christopher. *Belief Systems and Decision Making in the Mayaguez Crisis*. Gainesville: University of Florida Press, 1989.

Lane, John J., Jr. *Command and Control and Communications Structures in Southeast Asia*. Vol. 1, Monograph 1, *The Air War in Indochina*. Maxwell AFB, Ala.: Air Power Research Institute, 1981.

Mets, David R. *Land-based Air Power In Third World Crises*. Maxwell AFB, Ala.: Air Power Research Institute, 1986.

Morocco, John; and the editors of Boston Publishing. *Rain of Fire: Air War, 1969–1973*. Boston: Boston Publishing, 1985, p. 38.

Ravenstein, Charles A. *Air Force Combat Wings: Lineage and Honors Histories 1947–1977*. Washington, D.C.: Office of Air Force History, 1984.

Rowan, Roy. *The Four Days of Mayaguez*. New York: 1975.

Shils, Edward A.; and Morris Janowitz. "Cohesion and Disintegration in the Wehrmacht in World War II." *Public Opinion Quarterly* (Summer 1948): 280–315.

Spectrum 1, no. 3 (n.d., ca. 30 May 1975). A special issue of the official bimonthly publication of USS *Midway's* Public Affairs Office devoted to Frequent Wind.

Tilford, Earl H. *Search and Rescue in Southeast Asia, 1961–1975*. Washington, D.C.: Office of Air Force History, 1980.

Tillman, Barrett. *On Yankee Station: The Naval Air War over Vietnam*. Annapolis, Md.: Naval Institute Press, 1987.

Tobin, Lt. Col. Thomas G.; Lt. Col. Arthur E. Laehr; and Lt. Col. John F.

Hilgenberger, USAF. *Last Flight From Saigon,* ed. Lt. Col. David R. Mets. Vol. 4, Monograph 6, USAF Southeast Asia Monograph Series. Washington, D.C.: Office of Air Force History, 1978.

Tran Van Tra, Colonel General. *History of the Bulwark B2 Theatre.* Vol. 5, *Concluding the Thirty Years' War.* Ho Chi Minh City: 1982. Trans. Foreign Broadcast Information Service, Southeast Asia, Report no. 1247.

Watts, Barry D. *Foundations of U.S. Air Doctrine: The Problem of Friction in War.* Maxwell AFB, Ala.: Air University Press, 1984.

Williams, Maj. F. D. G., USA. *SLAM: The Influence of S. L. A. Marshall on the United States Army.* Fort Monroe, Va.: Office of the Command Historian, U.S. Army Training and Doctrine Command, 1990.

Wood, Walter J. "'Mayday' for the *Mayaguez:* The Company Commander." *U.S. Naval Institute Proceedings* 102, no. 11 (November 1976).

Zeybel, Henry. "Truck Count." *Air University Review* 34, no. 2 (January—February 1983): 36–45.

*In author's possession.

Index